barcode in back

Blood on the Carpet

Blood on the Carpet

ADAM CLAPHAM

*I hate to spread rumours but
what else can one do with them?*

AMANDA LEAR

QUARTET

First published in 2011 by
Quartet Books Limited
A member of the Namara Group
27 Goodge Street, London W1T 2LD

A catalogue record for this book
is available from the British Library

ISBN   978 0 7043 7209 2

Typeset by Antony Gray
Printed and bound in Great Britain by
T J International Ltd, Padstow, Cornwall

Contents

CHAPTER 1

A Young Person's Guide to the Television

I always console young people who are suicidal after failing exams with the advice, 'If at first you don't succeed, try something else. If God wanted you to pass,' I counsel, 'surely he would have lent you his flying colours. He must have other plans for you.' I had less excuse for failing than most because I had *connections*. I was aiming for the top – King's College, Cambridge. It was a pity I had allowed myself to be pushed into the science stream at school. The arts subjects were well taught in small classes by the best teachers to the academically bright. Science was cattle class for the don't-knows. In those days you couldn't attract good science teachers for love or money, especially to an arts-orientated school. Britain was tooling up for the post-war age and any potential teacher who knew a beaker from a Bunsen burner could command a princely salary in the New Jerusalem. That's where we, the don't-knows, were destined. We were to be the vanguard of Harold Wilson's white heat of technology. The really gifted schoolboy scientists managed to upgrade themselves to club class, or even first, but most of us jogged along uncomprehending in the back of the plane. If a little learning is a dangerous thing, we were lethal.

The tutor at King's who had marked my entrance exam was gloomy. 'Like so many from your school, you don't seem to have any under-standing of the *concept* of chemistry. I don't think you have any idea why anybody bothers to teach it, let alone why you should learn it.' True. And my solitary A level, in physics, was acquired only because my teacher had looked back through the previous ten years' exam papers and correctly computed the likely questions we would be asked. The King's tutor was a decent young man. 'Look, I know your grandfather was Vice Provost and our most distinguished historian. I know your father is a King's man. But things have changed. These days we really only give places to those with academic merit. I don't want to be rude, but you don't seem to have a lot of that.' The school I left without distinction comprised a thriving commune of talented weirdos, many the sons of artists, writers and musicians who sought a more progressive and informal environment for their offspring than most public schools then offered. The school may not have helped me through the King's entrance exam but it had taught me the most important lesson of all – how to find out what I wanted to know. It's nothing special now but then it was a revolutionary concept and my school its principal proponent. In those days the convention was to make you remember facts and figures parrot fashion. But I was taught to teach myself – and there was no better lesson for a television researcher, as I was not so much later to find out. Now of course there's Google to do all that sort of thing for you, so there's probably no need for school at all.

To be fair, there was one other vital lesson the school dinned into us, but one that we learnt from each other not the teachers. It was a far more useful maxim than the absurdly trite school motto, *Et nova et vetera*. It was, quite simply, that bullshit baffles brains. No doubt, the school would have translated it pretentiously for their glossy brochure as *Merda taurorum animas conturbit*. There were, of course, contemporaries of mine whose stars shone brightly in the real world, Sir John Eliot Gardiner, Simon Standage, Quinlan Terry, a Lord Chief Justice and a Crown Prince of Jordan. But, for most of my chums, it was the talent plausibly to charm the hind legs off a donkey, to convince those who should know better of the mythical merits of some dubious cause, that perhaps best justified the outlandish school fees that nearly bankrupted our parents.

Luckily for me, the school was very serious about its theatre, the headmaster even more so. Life behind the scenes suited me well. The stage manager could smoke and drink with impunity, stay up late and never go near the verdant playing fields. But it was hard work. If you can supervise a three-hour performance of *King Lear*, with its temperamental thespians, myriad scene changes, a wind machine to crack your cheeks and a load of mewling schoolboy extras, milling around in the wings awaiting their exits and entrances, you are well on the way to becoming a producer.

Had I been unlucky enough to have been born seven months earlier than I was, there would now have been a most unwelcome martial interlude. I would probably have spent my two years' compulsory National Service square-bashing at Catterick Camp in Yorkshire, but I could have been sent to fight the Communists in Malaya, the Mau Mau in Kenya or the Greeks in Cyprus. Instead I spent six months in Grenoble learning French, and then an agreeable spell in Birmingham delivering hogsheads for the local brewery. There I learnt the city's execrable Brummie accent in order to protect myself from the contempt of my drayman friends. If you wanted to be pompous about it, you could say that I had now graduated in the art of thriving. This turned out to be a handy qualification for my future career, one that was now slowly beginning to come into focus.

I had an admirable aunt who at that time was a professional stage manager at the prestigious Old Vic in London. She showed me around. I was horrified at the squalor of it all, the terrible hours and ridiculously low salaries. Surely television was a better bet. My father had quite other ideas. He was a budding captain of industry and he felt that my best bet was to bud along in that direction too. Another admirable aunt, another of his sisters, was more in sympathy with my naïve ambition to enter the world of show business and she was practical with it. She was head of accounts for a newspaper group and her boss had *connections* with the newly opened Anglia Television. It was part of the commercial network that had recently opened in competition with the only other TV channel, the BBC. I was summoned for an interview and, not surprisingly, I immediately landed a job. Not surprisingly because the management had been forced to strengthen its output of regional programmes and had launched a forty-five-minute daily magazine programme with a staff of four – five if you counted the studio director who was far too grand to do any work outside the studio control gallery. Goodbye *I Love Lucy*, dear viewers, and welcome instead to the gritty, rough edges of real life, the regional magazine programme. It was 1960 and I was hired for a trial period of six weeks, at ten pounds a week, on condition that I equipped myself with a car. My salary was exactly the average wage of an agricultural worker. The difference was that he didn't have to buy a tractor.

Anglia Television was housed in the old red-brick Corn Exchange, bang in the middle of Norwich, next to the main post office and opposite the Royal Hotel, which served excellent meals for the wealthier of the farming community on market days, while the bar dispensed strong drinks on a nightly basis to those of us who had just come off the air and needed also to come off a high – the exhilaration of a live broadcast. The old Corn Exchange had been divided into a big and a small studio with offices all around. The output of the station wasn't ambitious. Eight hours of local programmes a week was all that was required to secure the exclusive right to sell television advertising time throughout Norfolk, Suffolk, Bedfordshire, Cambridgeshire and parts of Lincolnshire and Essex. Enforcement was the responsibility of the Independent Television Authority whose consul in the Norwich outpost was a benign retired general. In those days he was the only member of the Independent Television Authority who could receive our local programmes. The signal from Anglia's transmitter at Mendlesham in Suffolk was too weak to reach London. So Anglia depended on the general's goodwill. He was handsomely buttered up.

Most of the network programmes were made or bought by the big companies like Associated Rediffusion in London, Granada in Manchester and ATV in the Midlands. They controlled everything and pumped a feed of their programmes to Norwich where local programmes were slotted in. Of course Anglia would far rather have made no programmes at all; the secret of commercial television's profitability is to collect *in* the advertising revenue not waste any of it on producing programmes. The snag was that the ITA kept an eagle eye on the promises that had been made by those who had bid for a 'licence to print money', as the Canadian newspaper magnate Roy Thomson had tactlessly put it, rather letting the cat out of the bag. Anglia's first year had not pleased the ITA with its tacky glamour shows and now was the time to repair the damage with a regional replica of the BBC's highly successful *Tonight* programme. Our job was to do for East Anglia what *Tonight* did for the whole country – friendly current affairs but with a local bias, plenty of rustic characters, a few laughs, a music spot and loveable presenters in the studio.

By the time *About Anglia* was in full swing there were five researchers, four setting up studio items and one out and about looking for film stories. There was a bright and aggressive Australian producer who looked after political stories and her fellow-producer, Dick Gilling, supervised the nightly content and its running order, chose the films that were to be made and was what we now call the commissioning editor. He was a pipe-smoking, slightly donnish figure who had come to television from screenwriting for real films. He would surprise us all with whoops of joy when he came across a newspaper or magazine photograph of a dolly bird with big boobs. None the less, he seemed very mature and wise. He was twenty-seven. On his office wall was a large noticeboard with lots of hooks screwed into it. On to those he would hang little strips of card, each representing a studio interview, a regular music spot, the weather forecast, a short film – whatever the components were for the programme on that day of the week. When an item went down Dick would shuffle the little cards, moving an interview scheduled for Tuesday that now could not happen until Friday, for example, and then putting his head on one side to consider what little card to move across to fill the gap that had now appeared in Tuesday's running order. As a last resort he had squirrelled away a couple of stand-by films.

For me as a rookie researcher it was the most extraordinary experience. After any edition of the programme, but especially after a humdinger, people in shops and pubs, in schools and factories – all over the newly created region – talked of nothing else. A goof-up on air; a piglet that thought it was a puppy; a man with concrete teeth that progressively disintegrated during his live interview; a particularly rude-looking sugar beet. These were gossip-worthy moments for our fast-growing audience, viewers who had never before been treated to the compliment of a television programme exclusively their own. Everyone loved *About Anglia*. And here was I, one of its principal providers. I would hear people in the street telling jokes that I had suggested for the previous night's script or regaling their friends with descriptions of the dotty people I had booked to appear on the programme. What a morale booster. To me this was real show business and it was fun.

First among equals of the *About Anglia* presenters was the formidable Dick Joice. Before the Anglia gravy train had steamed into view, Dick had been a modest tenant farmer for the 7th Marquess Townshend of

Raynham, Anglia's toff Chairman. Naturally a farming programme was one of the station's first offerings and Dick had landed the job as presenter. He was good. A roly-poly, ruddy-faced man with horn-rimmed glasses and a marked Norfolk accent, he could have been the barman across the road at the Royal Hotel. And that was his attraction. He had 'mine host' written all over him. The rather intellectual fellows from London whose job it had been to plan the new magazine pro-gramme envisaged someone with more gravitas and perhaps a little more learning than Dick as the show's host. In no time they were brusquely pushed aside and Dick installed himself in the front man's chair. He was a great success in an enormously popular show. The anaemic local BBC station was hopelessly outmatched and *About Anglia* ran for thirty years.

The other front-of-camera star was a tall, suave and handsome young man called Bob Wellings. He had caught the acting bug at Cambridge and this was his big professional break. He became and remains one of my best friends. Way back then, at twenty-six, he seemed awfully old and wise. I was flattered to accompany him to a pub or a restaurant because, as Anglia's heart-throb, he was treated like royalty. Everything would stop, the best table would be prepared for him, autograph books would appear from the kitchen, girls swooned. This was the high life and I basked in the shadow of his celebrity. Bob went on to present *Nationwide*, a high-profile live daily show on BBC1, and he became something of a national treasure. In real life, he was diffident and self-effacing and sometimes a trifle long-winded, especially when he erred and strayed from the point of his anecdote (he's still like that). Yet on air he always amazed us. As soon as the floor manager cued him, he would launch forth briskly, succinctly and professionally without losing any of his considerable charm.

Dick Gilling was an inspired father figure for us researchers. He balanced the need to have a strong, earthy flavour to the programme with expectations of us that would stop us from turning into turnips ourselves. He strongly encouraged us to bring a little culture to the programme, to dilute the rural fare. We had Cambridge on the doorstep and Benjamin Britten just down the way in Aldeburgh; Angus Wilson lived just outside Bury St Edmunds and the King's Lynn Festival brought

Yehudi Menuhin and Michael Tippett within our grasp. Bob Wellings was superb at these interviews, urbane, relaxed and on top of his brief. There was a particularly memorable interview with Kingsley Amis, who managed to drink most of a bottle of Scotch with Bob and me in the hospitality room before we went on air. I never again saw him perform on television with quite such lucidity and animated enthusiasm.

One of the founders of Anglia Television was John Woolf, the head of Romulus Films, the company that had produced *The African Queen, Moulin Rouge, Three Men in a Boat* and *Room at the Top*. On the back of this track-record, Anglia had been given a substantial number of network drama slots. I had a bright idea and suggested that L. P. Hartley's superb novel *The Go-Between* should be adapted as one of these plays. It was set in Norfolk, at the heart of the Anglia region, and it was a cracking yarn. Dick Gilling encouraged me to try writing the screenplay myself. When it was done Dick sent it to the formidable Jenia Reissar at Romulus Films. She was a legendary casting director who had proposed Vivien Leigh for the role of Scarlett O'Hara in *Gone with the Wind*. She controlled access to John Woolf and made a good many of the important decisions herself. She promptly sent my screenplay back with a note saying that neither Romulus nor Anglia had any plans to produce *The Go-Between*, but thank you very much all the same. Blow me, a few years later I read in the papers that *The Go-Between* is going to be made as a feature film with a fabulous cast – Julie Christie, Alan Bates, Edward Fox, Margaret Leighton and Michael Redgrave – directed by Joe Losey, famous for *Accident* and *The Servant*. But not with my screenplay. I have since learnt, sitting on the other side of the fence, that one of the commonest causes of unhappiness for freelance writers and producers is the perception that film and television companies (and radio stations) read proposals, routinely reject them and then produce them anyway – without acknowledgement or payment to the person who sent in the idea in the first place. What we freelance petitioners sometimes forget, in our isolated paranoia, is that other people often have the same good idea: there is a finite number of them – and it may be a genuine coincidence that something we have suggested is subsequently produced. It didn't feel like that to me when *The Go-Between* was released to great acclaim.

It won the Grand Prix at the 1971 Cannes Film Festival and later featured on the British Film Institute's list of one hundred best films. I never did find out whether I was the father of the idea but I remain dead suspicious to this day. It was some consolation to see that I hadn't been replaced by any old hack. The screenwriter was Harold Pinter:

> Losey is perfectly served by his screenplay writer Harold Pinter, who has adapted L. P. Hartley's novel with scrupulous fidelity, yet adds to it his own uncanny skill at depicting people who use words to conceal themselves rather than reveal their meanings. In this guilty setting of privilege and deceit, Pinter is in his element.
>
> Alexander Walker, *Evening Standard*

My screenplay wasn't *that* good.

Anglia was the perfect apprenticeship not only in the techniques of television production but in the art of handling the kaleidoscope of top public figures I mixed with as part of my job. I had covered the Alde-burgh Festival for *About Anglia* and I developed a love for Benjamin Britten's music, going back to the festival on my own account to see *Peter Grimes, Billy Budd* and *The Turn of the Screw*. The following year I managed to wangle an invitation for Anglia to film at a garden party where we interviewed both Benjamin Britten and his partner, Peter Pears. I sat with the great composer while he tried to persuade me – *me!* – that both BBC Television and ITV should broadcast far more operas and concerts, instead of wasting time on interview programmes like the one we were then engaged on.

The Norfolk and Suffolk *haut chatterati* were astonished to find such coverage on 'commercial' television (said with a sneer). Although they left us in no doubt that ITV was beyond the pale, there seemed to be a mystic bond that protected the television interests of our hierarchy, the Marquess Townshend, Aubrey Buxton (who went on to establish *Survival*) and like-minded gentry on the main board. Three incidents illustrate the arcane intrigues in this cloistered world of the county establishment. The first was the shocking news that one of the studio directors had run over and killed a sailor who was hitch-hiking on a very dark and wet night. The director was a drunk. We all waited mutely, expecting him to be arrested at any moment and charged at least with manslaughter. We all knew the scandal would do terrible damage to Anglia's reputation. Nothing happened. Just recently, I learnt that the marquess himself had been involved in two serious motoring accidents as a young man.* In one of them a fellow army officer was killed. It was never established whether it was the marquess or the dead man who had been driving. The studio director returned to work. The subject of his accident was never mentioned.

The second far less dramatic example was almost trivial, but it touched a raw nerve with the toffs. It concerned an item that I had set up for the programme on what I was about to learn was a particularly sensitive subject. It was a debate between a master of foxhounds and an opponent of hunting. Those against blood sports have since managed to persuade Parliament to ban the hunting of foxes completely, of course. But at that time it was a minority view, especially in the shires – home to posh hunts like the Cottesmore. At nearby Sandringham, where Aubrey Buxton often dined with his pal Prince Philip, talk of a hunting ban was heresy. The foxhunting controversy was scheduled to be aired live in that night's programme. Everything was fine when rehearsals started. My participants were raring to go and their cars had been booked to bring them to the studio, so I set off to research some other story. When I watched the programme that night at home the item had been dropped. Later I learned that the hire cars had been quietly cancelled along with the participants and in their place was one of the stand-by films. It was an unprecedented move and, when I tried to find out who had called for the change, there was much shuffling of feet and rolling of eyes.

The third disconcerting incident was in a way the most disturbing. One night, the national *ITV News* immediately preceding *About Anglia* led on the story that Lord Mancroft, a Jewish director of Norwich Union, had been forced to stand down. It was soon revealed by the press that the Arab boycott office in Syria had threatened to close down the insurance company's lucrative operation in Bahrain unless it got rid of Mancroft. So savage was the worldwide criticism of Norwich Union

* Obituary, *Daily Telegraph*, 29 April 2010

that Sir Robert Bignold was later forced to stand down as Chairman (and – those were the days – was replaced by his cousin). This should have been a major local story for us but no mention of the scandal was ever made on *About Anglia*. Could the reason have been that Sir Robert Bignold was also a director of Anglia Television and Norwich Union was one of its largest advertisers? Or that the Chairman of Anglia, the Marquess Townshend, was also a director of the Norwich Union, later to be its Deputy Chairman? Perish the thought. At the time, I thought all this was Freemasonry at its most clandestine. Now I think it more likely that Anglia's *omerta* sprang from that strongest of all ties, the centuries-old blue-blood ties of the English landed gentry. The marquess was, after all, the grandest of Norfolk's non-royal grandees. His family had been powerful in Norfolk since the fifteenth century. The bond had survived centuries of storms far more troublesome than these.

Almost as potent as the toffs was the all-powerful trade union, the Association of Cinematograph Television and Allied Technicians, the ACTT. It could take ITV off the air – and it did, some years later, for ten whole weeks. When the order came from the ACTT to down tools, bang went the advertising revenue. Like newspapers, ITV was left with all the costs of running a business with zero income. The ACTT had established an infamous catch 22 to protect its existing members and hinder the promotion of new staff. The 'closed shop' meant you could not direct unless you were a member of the technicians union and you could not join the union unless you were already employed as a technician. So those of us who were part of the editorial team would never be allowed to direct films or direct in the studio although we did the lion's share of the work. The union-protected directors would swan into the control gallery after a liquid lunch at the Royal and spend the afternoon cursing the 'bloody researchers' because nothing could ever be ready by then. But in the after-glow of a good programme they sometimes graciously acknowledged our contribution.

Anglia was a cauldron of internal politics and intrigue. It was here that I learnt the techniques essential for preferment and survival in this horribly cut-throat business. The vast majority of the employees were local recruits in harmless roles, selling advertising, painting scenery, typing, make-up – all those ancillary functions that make a television station work. But the officer class, the toffs, were locked in a bitter ideological war with the much liked programme controller, a distinguished light-entertainment producer from the BBC called Stephen MacCormack. The bone of contention, not surprisingly, was the cost of programmes. MacCormack had a penchant for girlie shows, end-of-the-pier spectaculars, all glitter and cleavage. They were very expensive to produce since they involved moving the only outside-broadcast unit and dozens of technicians from Norwich to Clacton, Southend or Yarmouth, putting them up in hotels and paying overtime and mileage allowances. Worse, the professional entertainers employed agents who expected their clients to be properly paid.

One day, the perfect weapon to sabotage these popular shows presented itself. Peter Yolland was an experienced director who had come to Anglia with a long track-record of light-entertainment production. He was flamboyant, with showbiz written all over him, but a touch naïve. He proposed a massive seaside spectacular, a star-studded summer show on Yarmouth pier with expensive comedians, sequinned dancers, the lot. The catch was that he couldn't have access to the theatre until after the performance on the Saturday night and he had to be ready to admit the television audience for the Anglia show by six o'clock on Sunday evening. Eighteen hours to strike the stage set, build a new one for the television production, light the theatre, rig the cameras and rehearse the dancers, singers and musicians. The toffs sensed a sensational flop, which might help them win the argument. The show was given the green light. Dick Joice invited me to travel with him in his large Jaguar to witness the ensuing disaster.

The game plan was to sack Stephen MacCormack, citing the Yarmouth fiasco, and then to cancel all his forthcoming light-entertainment shows, thus saving piles of money and leaving slots to be filled by cheaper factual programmes which would also earn the necessary brownie points with the Independent Television Authority. The problem was that Stephen was on the main board of the company and nobody had the courage to demand his dismissal while he was in the same room. So an elaborate scheme was devised. Stephen was dispatched to Montreux as Anglia's representative for the first ever Rose d'Or award ceremony. While he was away, an extraordinary general meeting of the main board was held to oust him. When Stephen returned to Norwich he was informed of his fate and told that the company would be assembled in the studio at lunchtime to make a presentation to him and wish him farewell. At the appointed hour, the chief executive rapped for silence and made a short speech praising the departing programme controller and wishing him all success in his future career. Stephen MacCormack shocked the assembled company with his opening words. 'But I don't want to go. I am very happy here . . . ' It was an awful moment, the humiliation of a decent man we all admired. He was never to work in the business again and his mortification was compounded, years later, when he was invited by old friends to drinks at a BBC Club in London. He arrived straight from work dressed in the uniform of a private security firm. The chief executive who had been forced to axe MacCormack also fell from grace a few years later. He ended up as a minicab driver and one day was sent by his radio controller to deliver a videotape to Anglia's London office in Park Lane. The story has it that he cheerfully did so, stopping to chat for a while with his erstwhile underlings.

Augmented by the local news team, *About Anglia*'s tightly knit and highly motivated pack of researchers and two producers, all under thirty, produced five programmes of lively, live television a week – nearly half the required quota for all Anglia's local programmes. *About Anglia* was without a doubt one of the best local magazine programmes in Britain and, along with *Survival,* it made Anglia the most talked-about regional television station, helping East Anglia forge a cultural identity and even a degree of political cohesion. Its success reflected glory on the presenter, Dick Joice, who manoeuvred ruthlessly to gain control of the air time and budgets made available by the demise of Stephen MacCormack's entertainment department. It did not take Dick long to expand and strengthen his empire, to seize the day-to-day running of the station in an iron grip. Dick Joice was by no means the last of the presenters I was to meet who snorted power like a randy bull, but it was remarkable that this regional idyll of farmland, forests and fens should nurture such a formidable specimen. I had been warned.

CHAPTER 2

Fact and Fiction

It had never happened before and it will never happen again. The BBC announced a mass-recruitment drive. Advertisements appeared everywhere suggesting that the brightest young things should get in touch with the BBC. Something big was about to happen. BBC Television was about to launch its second channel, only the third network in the whole of the United Kingdom. What's more, the BBC proudly announced, BBC2 would soon be the first channel in Europe to broadcast in colour.

I sent in my application form and hoped for the best. Soon I was called for an interview, the last of the day. The members of the Appointments Board were tired and cross; they had been interviewing all day. I was starting behind in the race because I was not an Oxbridge graduate, unlike all my inquisitors. Worse, I knew three of the four by reputation to be the most formidable in the BBC firmament. Grace Wyndham-Goldie was the Assistant Head of the mighty television Current Affairs Department. Donald Baverstock, the recently appointed Controller of Programmes, had made his name as editor of *Tonight*, and Alasdair Milne, who had succeeded him, was playing a central role in executive producing the phenomenally successful *That Was The Week That Was* and protecting it from establishment flack and the poplar press. The fourth member of the panel was an Appointments Department grey man. I sensed that his opinion was irrelevant in the face of such fire-power. I was given a rough time. 'What did I think of *Tonight*'? That was an elephant trap, if ever there was one. Were I to praise it or criticise it I would be asked for further and better particulars and the truth was that we all repaired to the Royal Hotel bar as soon as *About Anglia* came off air so I had seldom watched their precious programme. I gave some obfuscating answer about being on air on the rival channel and thus unable to watch *Tonight*. Alasdair Milne immediately butted in, mostly

I suspect, to show off to his colleagues how on the ball he was, '*About Anglia* goes off air five minutes before *Tonight* starts,' he snapped, like the irascible terrier that he was. It was downhill after that. The bored board went for the kill, slowly pulling the wings of a wounded butterfly. Not my finest hour. In due course the rejection slip arrived, but I had concealed a crucial fact from the Appointments Board. I was already working full-time for the BBC. I had been advised to keep this quiet because there was a good chance I would have been disqualified from the fast-track stream for which the formidable panel had been inter-viewing. And, bless the BBC, it is so vast that its left hand seldom knows what its right hand is doing.

Six months earlier, after two and a half years at Anglia, I had landed a six-month contract as a scriptwriter for ABC Television, a division of the Associated British Picture Corporation. It was a stylish and opulent company, housed in a film-studio complex that it had acquired from Warner Brothers on the Thames overlooking Teddington Lock. ABC was a major supplier of drama to the ITV network and it had just started making *The Avengers*, with Honor Blackman and Patrick Macnee, soon to become the biggest TV stars in the country and – wow – they used to sit at the next table to me in the canteen. After Anglia this was a Hollywood-like heaven. I rented myself a riverside apartment close and thanked my lucky stars. The studios were buzzing with life. The for-midable Canadian producer, Sydney Newman, had been brought in to reinvigorate television drama, crucially with *Armchair Theatre*. His inspiration was the Royal Court Theatre in London, which had startled the complacent drawing-room-comedy world with John Osborne's *Look Back in Anger*. Newman engaged many of the Royal Court's writers to work for *Armchair Theatre*. Alun Owen wrote *No Trams to Lime Street*, Clive Exton, *Where I Live*, and Harold Pinter, *A Night Out*. To the bewilderment of many a cautious television executive, the audience figures for these shocking new plays were outstanding, averaging twelve million viewers a week – an incredible figure for serious drama, much helped, it has to be said, by *Sunday Night at the London Palladium*, which immediately preceded them. Between 1959 and 1960 *Armchair Theatre* achieved top place in the ratings for thirty-two out of thirty-seven weeks.

Just before I arrived at ABC's Teddington Studios, Sydney Newman had been poached by the BBC to run all its television drama. There was a superb new series to greet him. *Z Cars,* a gritty real-life police series, was taking the country by storm. It ran for sixteen years. Superbly written by John Hopkins, Troy Kennedy Martin, Alan Prior and Alan Plater, *Z Cars* exactly reflected the philosophy that Newman wanted to instil throughout his drama department – real life in the raw. Newman's first move was to replicate *Armchair Theatre* with *the Wednesday Play.* He commissioned Dennis Potter to write *Stand Up, Nigel Barton!* and Ken Loach to direct Jeremy Sandford's *Cathy Come Home.* In a recent British Film Institute poll, *Cathy Come Home* was voted the second greatest British television programme of the twentieth century (after *Fawlty Towers*). Newman originated another key milestone in popular entertainment, *Dr Who.* He was the single most important influence in establishing quality contemporary drama on British television. Back at the ABC studios his aura still powerfully stimulated and inspired the drama department.

Years later I made the move from factual to fiction production. Had I realised, in those distant days, that I was at the epicentre of a new wave of writers, directors and producers, perhaps I would have jumped ship and learnt to become a drama producer. If I had known the enchanting Sidney Newman as well as I did much later, he would surely have encouraged me to take the plunge. A contemporary of mine at ABC who did manage to make the move from fact to fiction was Ted Childs. He had started his career as a trainee director at ABC. The first time you were allowed at the controls was to direct the Ad-Mags, fifteen-minute soap operas in which the actors were required to plug toothpaste and deodorant, shampoo and instant coffee, while heroically trying to act out the soap opera's groaning plot. Everybody in the business was embarrassed as hell by Ad-Mags but the audience lapped them up. The best-known, Associated Rediffusion's *Jim's Inn,* ran for three hundred fifteen-minute episodes – all live. Its ratings often surpassed those of real programmes. Ted Childs remembers directing ABC's Ad-Mags:

They were cheap and nasty generic studio-based vehicles for

advertisers too poor or too mean to have proper filmed commercials made. ABC's flagship in this esoteric area was *What's In Store*. It involved an ageing actress called Doris Rogers mincing round a set which was a crude representation of part of an old-style department store, singing the praises of inferior floor polish and the like.

Dreadful they may have been but Ad-Mags were a wonderful training ground for young directors like Ted. He went on to direct many of ABC's high-profile factual programmes, later choosing to become a drama director. He was to climb to the very pinnacle of the industry as Chairman of BAFTA and Head of Drama at Central Television. It was he who brought us *Kavanagh QC*, *The Sweeney* and *Inspector Morse*.

In the office next door to mine overlooking Teddington Lock was a trendy new religious programme, *The Sunday Break*. Its name reflected what had gone before it in that slot: nothing. There had been a bizarre rule that from 6.15 p.m. to 7 p.m. ITV must close down so that people would go to church. In this brave new world, *The Sunday Break* filled the void. It shocked the traditionalists, the more so when Sydney Newman's predecessor as head of *Armchair Theatre* burst drunkenly into the studio control room and stabbed the young woman directing *The Sunday Break* – live, on air, blood all over the carpet. It was just a lovers' tiff, we were told, no loss of life, a kiss at the hospital bed, half a dozen stitches and all was forgiven. The tabloid press was in ecstasy. Here was a real-life drama whose plot was as gripping as *Armchair Theatre*'s being made in the studio next door.

My contract at ABC was to write and research a motoring programme – pretty tame stuff compared with the excitements just along the corridor. But there was an upside for this recently promoted twenty-three-year-old researcher. I had to travel to Manchester every week to record the programme at ABC's studios in Didsbury. At the airport the company limousine awaited with a respectful driver holding up a card saying 'ABC Television – The Scriptwriter'; it was definitely an improvement on being a 'bloody researcher', and it paid three times the salary. But now there was another scriptwriting post on offer, this time at the BBC in London, and I jumped at the chance. With BBC2 just around the corner, it was important to position myself for the wealth of new opportunities it would bring. If there were jobs for the boys, I wanted one of them.

My first BBC job was based at the very heart of operations in the Presentation Department at the Television Centre. All the programmes, trailers, promotions, weather forecasts and on-air announcements were routed through the master control room there. Presentation was also responsible for the duty office, the destination of all the telephone calls to the television service from the public. It was manned by long-suffering and incredibly tactful staff, sweet-talking and logging complaints, nearly all of them trivial. One regular was an old buffer who called himself Colonel Charles of Petersfield. I once volunteered to help out in the duty office and I was so annoyed by the inconsequence of his nightly bombastic attacks on my poor colleagues that I returned one of his irascible calls. He was completely taken aback and behaved like a lamb after that; but he still called every night. Years later, when I was far more senior, I tried to persuade the bosses to take less notice of the number of complaining letters and telephone calls. The press always made such a meal of them. Yet, typically there were usually no more than a hundred and fifty complaints for a programme watched by eight million viewers – statistically of no significance. In any case, as I kept pointing out, the telephone calls and letters came from viewers in no way representative of the audience. Most were from lonely and often eccentric people with nothing better to do.

My position turned out to be more ghostwriter than scriptwriter. It was to compile *Points of View*, a five-minute slot for readers' letters, broadcast in peak time just before the *Nine O'Clock News*. The presenter was the author and quizmaster Robert Robinson whose on-air manner oscillated from the benign, through acerbic to sarcastic. In real life he was like a formidably well-read teddy bear. He would rewrite my draft script in the twinkling of an eye so that it sparkled with wit and *bon mots*. What a teacher he was! The purpose of the programme was to fill a gap in the schedules. Most programmes lasted twenty-five or fifty minutes and the news had to be exactly on the hour. *Points of View* was also a convenient fig leaf to suggest the BBC cared what its viewers thought. The truth of the matter was that Robert Robinson made it a most entertaining interlude, with his witticisms directed at the viewers who had written in and the mandarins who paid his salary. One of my maverick colleagues, Jack Bond, would always tell people that we used to write some of the more bizarre viewers' letters ourselves. It is totally untrue. There were literally sacks of them to choose from, probably more than ten thousand letters a week. I will concede we might occasionally have *rewritten* some of the letters to make them legible on the screen or perhaps to shorten them a little but there was no need to make anything up. As Mark Twain observed, 'It's no wonder that truth is stranger than fiction. Fiction has to make sense.'

Jack Bond left the BBC, planning to become a real director making films for the cinema. A couple of years later he persuaded me to take a month's leave of absence to work as assistant director on his first feature film, *Separation*. Mark Twain would have been disappointed: as a work of fiction it made no sense at all. The production was so *nouvelle vague* that no one had the vaguest idea what it was about and I had a terrible problem even finding out which scenes Jack and his scriptwriter cum leading lady, Jane Arden, were in the mood to shoot the following day. It is mercifully all a blur, but I do remember Jack collapsing with laughter when I yelled through the megaphone, just as we were about to begin shooting in Fenwicks of Bond Street, 'Stop the cash registers, please.' I also had to act, to play a manic depressive in a psychiatric hospital with the brilliant character actor Terence de Marney. I must have been in character before we shot the scene. I felt both manic and depressive. The artist who should have played the patient never showed up or, more likely, we forgot to book him. I also led a bunch of stark-naked hearties in a pillow fight at the Richmond Swimming Baths – but none of us had any idea what it all meant. The filming caused dreadful trouble at the pool. The feathers from the pillows clogged up the filter system, paying customers were outraged at the nudity and the havoc and the manager was hell-bent on murdering the director. For the inevitable re-shoot, Jack donned a Groucho Marx-style disguise, hoping that he wouldn't be recognised. 'I know who you are,' yelled the baths manager instantly, yanking off Jack's camouflage moustache. 'You're Jack Bond. Get out!'

No one ever got paid on *Separation* which made the burly riggers and the surly scene shifters turn very nasty indeed. With a soundtrack by Procol Harum, the film ran for just a week at the almost empty Chelsea Essoldo in the King's Road and, briefly, at a trendy cinema in Greenwich Village, before sinking without trace. This is what the *New York Times* thought of it.

> Curiously, the very thing that at first seems to be the film's principal virtue – its intense subjectivity – eventually drowns it in a large body of glue which, in surreal critical terms, is known as the Sea of Pretension.

You get the drift. Just recently, the National Film Theatre decided to show the film again – for one night only. Jack invited me to come and see it, to meet all the surviving cast and crew, forty years on. I decide to give it a miss. I'm still not sure that I have recovered from the trauma of the *Separation* shoot. Looking on the bright side, it most certainly taught me what *not* to do when, years later, I was producing movies myself. Jack went on to produce a couple more weird films with Jane Arden and he worked successfully as a producer on *The South Bank Show* for Melvyn Bragg. I recently reminded him of a long-ago lunch, at a favourite BBC restaurant, when he had proposed to me that the BBC should commission him to film a real bank robbery. In order to avoid spending many years behind bars, he proposed that I should write a get-out-of-jail-free letter to the Commissioner of the Metropolitan Police on BBC writing paper and post it just before the raid took place. I was to explain that Jack and his team should not be prosecuted because they were filming a bank raid, not robbing a bank. A completely potty idea. I was about to tell him so when an enormous figure climbed on to the bench seat of the table behind ours in the restaurant and glowered over the partition, which separated us. It was Huw Wheldon, by then the formidable Managing Director of Television. He had overheard our bizarre conversation. 'Oh no, you don't!' he bellowed, just like they do at the pantomime. Even now Jack will be planning his next maverick moment. Although I am very fond of him, I still dread his telephone calls.

I had only been working in the Presentation Department for six weeks or so when President Kennedy was assassinated. The on-air reaction was a shambles. The duty presentation editor held a key which gave him access to an emergency kit with instructions on what to do in a national emergency, for instance if the Queen died or if the country came under nuclear attack. When he heard Kennedy had been shot the presentation editor initially followed the rule-book to a tee. He interrupted the live transmission of *Tonight* with an in-vision announcement, 'We regret to announce that President Kennedy is dead.' Instead of returning to *Tonight* he ordered that the BBC revolving globe, normally used between programmes, should be left on air. Then he sought guidance. This is where the trouble began. All the BBC big cheeses were attending the annual dinner and ball of the Guild of Television Producers and Directors at the Dorchester Hotel. Finally Kenneth Adam, the Director of Television, came on the line. It was agreed that the BBC should return to its normal Friday-night schedule, subject to further interruption with any news updates. After an unprecedented and panic-inducing nineteen minutes of the revolving globe, programmes did return to normal with *Here's Harry*, a sitcom starring the comedian Harry Worth. But the restored calm in the presentation control room was soon rent asunder by the arrival of the big bosses in full evening dress. They had decided to hot-foot it back from the Dorchester. Some of them were by no means sober enough for this delicate moment. The collective decision, certainly the wrong one, was to continue with the advertised schedule. Next up was an episode of the folksy Highlands serial *Dr Findlay's Casebook*. Well over two thousand phone calls of criticism poured in, followed by almost five hundred letters and telegrams – and that really was a significant number of complaints. However, by 11 p.m., four hours after the news of Kennedy's death, the BBC had its act together again and, with its usual professionalism, Ned Sherrin's *That Was The Week That Was* team presented an inspired live tribute of readings and songs, featuring the leaders of all three political parties. So powerful was the accolade that it was broadcast the next day on American network television – an unprecedented salute from across the Atlantic.

The launch of BBC2 was only months away and the *Points of View* team was asked to devise a daily programme for the new channel. The Television Service was almost doubling its output, so similarly ambitious attempts at empire building were frantically under way in every production department. The pilot we produced was a novel programme called *Line Up*. That was the name of the technical preparation cameras required before going on air. It was an in-joke but a good title because the concept was to preview that night's viewing. To prevent it looking like a blatant promotion for the new channel, *Line Up* would also preview programmes on BBC1 and ITV and include critical reviews by independent contributors. This frightened the horses on the sixth floor and, when I came to watch the first day of BBC2 – I had moved on again by then – *Line Up* had been relegated to the very end of the evening and renamed *Late Night Line Up*, which certainly spoilt the in-joke. Thanks to Joan Bakewell, Michael Dean and Denis Tuohy, and my colleagues behind the scenes, *Late Night Line Up* became the new channel's illustrious and much talked-about flagship. It ran for eight years.

My old boss at Anglia, Dick Gilling had, not surprisingly, managed to enter the BBC through the front door and he was now ensconced in a large and empty office block, along the railway line, on the wrong side of Shepherd's Bush Green, assisting the one-time Olympic runner and sports journalist Chris Brasher to devise a leisure programme for BBC2. Dick asked me to join him in the bleak and pretentiously named Kensington House. We both had misgivings about the programme's concept but it was a huge challenge, an ambitious weekly peak-time programme. Most important of all, there was no union to prevent Dick and me from becoming directors. The master plan for BBC2 was that each night of the week would cover a different area of interest. So Thursdays were for leisure, Tuesdays adult education, Saturdays sport, Sundays light entertainment and so on. It remains the daftest idea ever tried on a mainstream channel. What better way to alienate all of your viewers most of the time? All that was certain at that stage was our new programme's name, *Time Out*. It was to be alarmingly long at seventy-five minutes and live. What was needed was a disciplined full-time editor who could make some clear decisions about what *Time Out* was to cover and how. Someone with a gift for recruiting an able production team in double-quick time. There was no time to muck about because we only had a few weeks to get the show on air. Chris Brasher had quite the wrong profile. Absurdly, he had been allowed to negotiate a part-time contract as editor of *Time* Out so that he could continue his sports column in the *Observer*. He may have done a wonderful job pacing Roger Bannister to achieve the four-minute mile. He was a passable reporter on the *Tonight* programme, a good sports journalist and a perfectly nice guy. But he was quite the wrong man for this very difficult job.

BBC2 began with a bang and a whimper. The bang was the explosion at Battersea Power Station that prevented the channel going on air as planned. The whimper was the reaction of the audience, the few people who had the right sort of television set to watch the delayed first night. In the early weeks there were, of course, some wonderful programmes. You would expect that of any new channel. But the relentless promotion campaign for BBC2 inexplicably featured mother and baby kangaroos called 'Hullabaloo' and 'Custard'. Insulting? Tacky? Ill considered? It looked as if it hadn't been thought out at all. The measured view of the public and the management was that BBC2 was a dog's dinner or was it a pig's breakfast? I can't remember now.

CHAPTER 3

Quest for David Attenborough

Somehow *Time Out* struggled on air with a mish-mash of minority sports, a live relay from the Palio in Siena, a fashion item from a club in Soho and lots of hairy outdoor sports that were programme editor Chris Brasher's forte. The producer of the motoring section of the programme had irretrievably fallen out with Brasher and, in a petulant unilateral declaration of independence, had set up his own programme called *Wheelbase*. He was given no extra facilities and he was forced to go on air live in the *Time Out* studio without rehearsal, jumping into the *Time Out* director's seat in the control gallery while the *Time Out* end credits rolled. It was about as sensible as an airline pilot touching down on the tarmac and vacating his seat for another pilot to take off again without slowing the aircraft down.

I kept Brasher happy, setting up items on the Eiger and the Matterhorn and some incomprehensible new sport that he was mad about called orienteering, but only so that he would allow me to do my own thing. I was far too junior to have any influence on the shape of the programme as a whole. Indeed Brasher jealously guarded his role as programme editor – a pity because he was such a bad one. None the less, my first research assignment was a juicy one. The film was to be called *The Ski Explosion* and for it the producer, Bob Duncan, planned to follow a group of young people, destined for the ski slopes, as they travelled by train overnight to Austria. He would take the film crew on the train and I was to go ahead and set everything up in the new ski resort of Lech. That meant that I could jet out in comfort. The nearest airport to Lech was Innsbruck but the BBC travel office refused to let me fly there. They said it wasn't safe for winter flying and they booked me instead to Zurich and then on to Lech by first-class rail. I had never travelled first class on a train before and I have never since experienced the gluttony of a first-class lunch on Swiss Railways. God bless the BBC. It began with champagne then pâté de foie gras and half a bottle of Pouilly-Fumé. With the veal escalope, another half bottle, this time of a rather good Beaujolais-Villages. After that the most delectable cheeses, followed by blackcurrant sorbet and a drop of Armagnac with the coffee.

And then to work. Lech was a quite charming, small mountain village with one serious hotel, the Gasthoff Post. The BBC Travel Department had excelled again. I was given a room with a blazing log fire looking straight out on to the ski slopes. I went for a walk along the only street in the town, snug in my newly acquired thermal underwear, boots and heavy anorak. Lech was about to grow into a massive resort. There were new buildings going up everywhere. This exactly illustrated the title of our film, *The Ski Explosion*. The tourist office was expecting me and they loaded me up with every sort of brochure and, more importantly, free passes on the ski-lifts for the film crew. On my way back to the hotel I noticed a most unpleasant and pungent smell coming from the little stream that ran beside the road – sewage. Immediately I thought of the terrible typhoid outbreak in Zermatt only eighteen months earlier. There the problem had been that the resort had developed so fast that the drainage couldn't, and didn't, keep up with the town's expansion. It looked to me as if Lech had the same problem. Although it was a Saturday afternoon, I decided to telephone BBC News Information in London. It ran a wonderful service providing press cuttings on almost any subject under the sun. The first thing you did when you had a good idea for a programme was to send for the cuttings. That put paid to any rival production team pipping you to the post. News Information were very on the ball when I explained the situation and they promised to look up 'Zermatt' and 'typhoid'. There was, of course, no such thing as the Internet. Even fax machines hadn't been invented. The only way News Information could send me the facts quickly was to type out the relevant cuttings on to a telex machine – a cross between an old-fashioned typewriter and a primitive telephone. Whatever you typed was converted into holes in a punched tape. This was then fed down a telex line, holes were punched into a tape at the other end, and the telex apparatus typed it all out like a telegram. Only newspapers and big businesses normally owned such machines because they were very expensive to run and no more reliable than you would suppose them to be. By luck, there was a telex in the tourist office and I gave its number to the News Information people in London.

I then repaired for the evening to a rather jolly-looking bar to await overnight developments. It was about a hundred yards up a steep path immediately behind the hotel, merrily decorated with lanterns and fairy lights. Everything was covered with snow and steps had been cut in the ice so that you could climb easily from the hotel to the bar. They were serving a rather flamboyant drink there which I had never seen before, called the Atom Bomb. It seemed to be a concoction of brandy, vodka and spices, bubbling gently in a crucible over a small flame. When the histrionic barman came to serve you a drink, he would first set it on fire like a pudding at Christmas and then douse the flames with a liberal application of Moët & Chandon. After a few of these nuclear noggins it was time for bed. What I hadn't noticed when I had climbed up to the bar was that, as well as the path I had climbed up, there was a parallel ski piste – or it could have been a toboggan run – precipitately descending from the bar's entrance to the back of my hotel. Piste was the right word for it and for me. In my befuddled state it would seem that I chose the piste rather than the steps because the next thing I knew I was lying on my back, outside my hotel, completely covered in snow – shaken, not stirred.

The next morning the welcoming smile of my friends in the tourist office had turned to ice. The News Information people in London had done a wonderful job. They had telexed a thorough compilation of the cuttings relating to the Zermatt typhoid outbreak. The six-foot-long roll of telex paper, laying out the grizzly facts, was spread out on the office floor. No one could fail to understand what I was up to – checking to see if Lech, like Zermatt, was susceptible to typhoid. The tourist-office staff were aggrieved. Later, they brightened up a bit because my producer, Bob Duncan, and the crew had arrived overnight with his skiers and come to look for me in the tourist office. I explained my faux pas and asked for his help. That, it seemed to me, is what producers are for. He did a grand job, chatting up the girls, pacifying them. Then, like a conjuror, he produced an enormous box of Cadbury's chocolates with an exaggerated flourish and presented it to the lady manager. 'Don't worry,' he said. 'Trust me, I'm in charge.' And then, with a wink towards me, he added, 'He's only the bloody researcher.'

During the next few months I managed to swing many more trips to the Continent. I had discovered a wonderful ruse, a loophole in the cumbersome BBC machine. There turned out to be a European Broadcasting Union agreement that allowed any of its member countries to request a film crew from another member and reciprocate in facilities rather than cash. So you could request Norddeutscher Rundfunk, for example, to provide a film crew in Germany. In due course, NDR would ask the BBC for a crew to shoot in Britain in return. The fortuitous glitch was that there was no system in the BBC of charging the individual programme for the facilities the BBC would later have to reciprocate. Ergo it would not cost *Time Out* a bean. It was not difficult to persuade Brasher that it was cheaper to send me to make a film in an EBU country than it was to have me film with a BBC crew in the middle of the Television Centre car park.

He liked the first proposal I submitted. There was a daft old aristocrat in Bournemouth called Arthur Frederick Daubney Olaf de Moleyns, 7th Baron Ventry, whose hobby was flying airships. He spent his life tracking them down and persuading their owners to let him take the controls. He had found one that plied its trade by displaying advertising slogans as it flew over the Baltic beaches and holiday resorts. It was vast and needed twenty men to dock it and release it at the windswept aerodrome near Lübeck where we first encountered it. I couldn't help thinking of the disaster that befell the German airship the *Hindenburg* in New York in 1937. As we boarded the gondola beneath the gigantic sausage-shaped leviathan my mind was filled with infernal flames and screams of pain. We chugged along for an hour or so perhaps a thousand feet above the beach at Travemunde. Suddenly the pilot turned off the engines. In those days, before hot-air balloons became commonplace, there were not many who had sampled the eerie experience of weightless travel. We were completely still in a cloudless sky, looking down on a great sweep of ocean. There, gleaming white and set in cobalt, was the ferry headed for Malmö and another returning from Helsinki. In the shallower waters you could make out the pleasure boats and, far away in the distance, you could hear the sounds of children playing on the beach hundreds of feet below. It was magic, just magic.

Lord Ventry was thrilled not only because he was allowed to fly the airship for a while but, being a bit of a show-off, he was rather looking forward to starring on television. It would have been cruel to tell him how few viewers would see him on the new BBC channel. (One cynic quipped that it would be cheaper to send everyone a video of the day's programmes than to broadcast them.) We had shot all the film we needed on that one glorious summer Sunday but, to be on the safe side, we had asked for the use of the airship for a second day. When we arrived at the airfield we found, to our surprise, a different pilot waiting for us. It transpired that this was the captain. He had taken the weekend off and it had been his deputy who had flown us the day before. As we reached cruising altitude the cameraman and his sound recordist started making preparations to film Lord Ventry. My job was to hold the 'sun-gun', a powerful battery light that illuminated the whole gondola. As soon as I switched it on there was a terrifying shout, almost a scream, from the captain. 'Turn it off, turn it off now! Turn that light off!' I obeyed at once. I couldn't help thinking of all those caricature Luftwaffe pilots who were so horrid to Kenneth More in *Reach for the Sky*. There was an animated conversation in German between the captain and my cameraman, the only one of the five of us who spoke both our languages fluently. When we had all calmed down and the situation had been explained to me, an icy shiver ran down my spine. The airship, it turned out, was kept aloft by six thousand five hundred cubic metres of hydrogen, not the inert gas helium that we had supposed. Hydrogen is as flammable as you can get and the captain's concern was that a spark from the battery light would create an instant inferno. We finished our work obediently and thanked God when we were safely on the ground. If I had been the Pope I would have kissed it.

Almost by chance, then, I had become a film director. The much more frightening and difficult live multi-camera studio direction was still to come but how much easier it had been to make a film than at Anglia where you always had to explain laboriously but tactfully to a union-approved director what was required. A good film editor patiently pointed out all the mistakes I had made and soon I was flitting around the European Broadcasting Union countries, borrowing free film crews and having a ball. While the ACTT union had a firm hold on ITV, the BBC determined to keep it at bay and encouraged an in-house staff union that was much more in tune with the realities of life. Chris Brasher had taken full advantage of this flexibility and hired Charles Lagus, a gifted and unflappable one-man-band cameraman, who had travelled to the remotest parts the world with David Attenborough making natural-history films for *Zoo Quest*. Charles claimed that they would decide together where they both most wanted to go and then David would go to the Natural History Museum and find a rationale for the expedition. David had left the BBC by now and Charles was rather at a loose end until Brasher's offer came along. He came equipped with a camper van that carried all the camera equipment, basic lights, sound recording equipment, baked beans and plenty of duty-free whisky.

The first time we worked together was on a project ominously supported with enthusiasm by Chris Brasher. The proposal was to make a blockbuster on the world of the treasure hunter. I set off with Charles Lagus in his camper van for France where I had discovered a White Russian who had located the wreck of the Spanish galleon *Nuestra Señora de la Concepción*. The ship had sunk after hitting a coral reef north of Hispaniola (now Haiti and the Dominican Republic) on its way from Mexico to Spain in 1641. She carried between one million and four million silver pesos weighing as much as 140 tons – and jewellery, pearls, emeralds and gold. The wreck had been discovered in 1687 and 68,511 pounds of silver had been salvaged, but that was only about a quarter of the treasure on board. Now my White Russian was fitting out a small ship in the Normandy port of Fécamp hoping to recover the rest.*

* Alexandra Korganoff failed in his quest, but in 1978 an American treasure hunter salvaged six thousand silver coins and other artefacts worth $13 million from the wreck of the *Nuestra Señora de la Concepción*.

Charles and I had plenty of time to chat in his camper van; downing Scotch from sunset to bedtime, he enchanted me with stories of his adventures with David Attenborough. Although I had never met him, I came to like the sound of Charles's mischievous bright-eyed and bushy-tailed companion. Meanwhile, the deadline for the treasure special drew near and Brasher had allotted it two whole editions of *Time Out*, two hours of air time. It was to be a mammoth pull-together of specially shot material, library film, interviews in the studio with treasure hunters from around the world, dramatic reconstructions, gold bars from the Bank of England, even a clip from the Charles Laughton swashbuckler, *Captain Kidd*. I compiled a 'best-buy' list of the most likely places around the world for our viewers to find treasure, which, to my surprise, came up trumps for at least one of our tiny audience. My colleague in this ambitious venture was *Time Out*'s highly experienced studio director Tom Conway. The studio would have to look fabulous and Tom and I agreed that we needed an extrovert and enthused presenter, probably someone who was well known as an explorer. Shiver my timbers if he didn't immediately suggest David Attenborough. I shot the idea down at once. 'Too boyish,' I remonstrated. In fact he was quite a bit older than he appeared. He looked twenty-five but he was in fact thirty-eight. He had recently resigned from the BBC to study social anthropology at the London School of Economics, so his programme *Zoo Quest* wasn't on air and I couldn't demonstrate my prejudice; but my instinct told me we needed a presenter with more gravitas. Tom was a good deal more experienced than me so I quickly backed off and we compromised. 'Why don't we get him in for lunch?' I asked. Talk about asking the mountain to come to Mohammed!

David duly arrived and the three of us walked down the corridor towards reception, aiming for a favourite lunchtime haunt, the local Bertorelli's. By chance my overall boss, the disagreeable Aubrey Singer, Head of Features and Science Programmes, was leaving his office at the same time. He greeted David, so Tom and I walked on ahead. Not much later David caught us up. 'Cunt,' he said, 'that man's a cunt.' He didn't look as if he even knew the word, let alone ever used it. We sat down to lunch and I was amazed to find this young fellow from *Zoo*

Quest was bang up-to-date on BBC politics, scathing of the knaves and dismissive of the fools. It was a long lunch and we gossiped about everything. I told him that I thought the BBC was an awful ass sometimes. My example was close to home. It had just been decreed by the Head of BBC2 that *Time Out* didn't deserve another series and yet its editor, Chris Brasher, had been asked to propose the programme to replace it. 'That's madness,' I exclaimed. 'It's so obvious that Brasher's the problem. Is this the BBC policy – if at first you don't succeed, carry on regardless?' We parted company after offering David the job of presenting the treasure special. He seemed keen to accept but it meant interrupting his social anthropology course and he asked for time to think it over. A few days later there was a message for me in the office. David much regretted that he couldn't accept our offer, much as he would have liked to. If we watched the *BBC News* that evening we would see why. There had been a palace revolution on the sixth floor and David was now Controller of BBC2. Neither he nor I ever mentioned the lunch.

We soon learnt what had happened. Huw Wheldon the flamboyant presenter of *Monitor,* and by this time Head of Documentaries, had led a delegation of department heads to Kenneth Adam, the Director of Television, and told him they all refused to work for Donald Baverstock, the Head of BBC1, any longer. Baverstock was rude, dismissive of any but current-affairs and news programmes and bad tempered, in short impossible. Huw had won the Military Cross for bravery on D-Day and it stood him in good stead now. Baverstock was not used to being crossed and he fought back fiercely. But the enemy held all the aces. He was offered three choices. He could switch to be Head of BBC2, upgraded to controller status, he could go on a fact-finding tour of the BBC's overseas offices or he could run the Paris office. I happened to be on my way to Paris the day this announcement was made and I couldn't resist showing the morning newspaper to the incumbent head of the Paris office. My word he was cross.

Baverstock turned down all three options and flounced out of the BBC for ever. (He had been one of the tormentors at my ill-fated Appointments Board interview so I confess I allowed myself a moment's

Schadenfreude.) But the excitements were not yet over. Alasdair Milne, another of my three tormentors, decided to resign in sympathy with his chum Baverstock. Arrogance was the glue that sealed their friendship. The tabloids reported Milne's disdainful proclamation in a probably made-up but plausible quote, 'If the BBC's not big enough for Baverstock, it's not big enough for me.' Later Milne was to be brought back into the bosom of the BBC, caused me no end of trouble, rose to the top as Director General, and then got fired; such are the snakes and ladders of outrageous fortune. With Baverstock gone, the way was clear for some radical rejigging. What should have happened, of course, was that, the BBC2 boss, Michael Peacock, the principal architect of its disastrous launch and continued inability to attract viewers, should have been given his marching orders too. Instead he was promoted to BBC1 to replace Baverstock. If at first you don't succeed . . .

There were plenty of reasons why BBC2 had begun so badly under Peacock, not least a severe shortage of money which persisted until the advent of colour television in 1967 with its much enhanced licence fee. But Peacock was the real problem. He burned with the same arrogance as Baverstock and Milne – not surprising since conceit was the brand identity of all those bright young things in Current Affairs. He was the brightest of high-flyers, express-tracked too fast, Icarus personified. He had been editor of *Panorama* by the age of twenty-five, Head of Television News by thirty and he was still only thirty-three when they gave him BBC2. On the bright side he couldn't do so much damage to the well-established BBC1 as long as he remembered to keep his department heads happy. In fact he did well but, within a couple of years, he foolishly resigned to go and help David Frost start London Weekend Television. That was another game that swiftly ended in tears.

Now that David Attenborough was Controller of BBC2 morale rocketed skywards. There was big change in the air. Not many weeks passed before rumours were circulating about the replacement for *Time Out* and a diminished role for Chris Brasher. Could it be that Attenborough had remembered our lunchtime discussion?

CHAPTER 4

Desmond's Weepies

Chris Brasher was full of bounce. He showed me the proposal he had prepared for the new programme. He was a good journalist and the paper he had prepared was impressive. It made out the case for single-subject in-depth journalism as had been pioneered in the *Sunday Times* 'Insight' column. The twist in the tail was that he had persuaded Desmond Wilcox, a star reporter on ITV's *This Week*, to join the team with his film-director friend Bill Morton. The pair of them had made some films that were extraordinary because they dealt so frankly with dramas from everyday life – the *Armchair Theatre* of real life. One involved filming outside a roadside pub on New Year's Eve and grabbing interviews with the drunk, even legless, partygoers and asking them on camera whether they thought they were fit to drive. It was a shocker and it made a major contribution to the tightening up of the drink-driving laws. Another classic of the Desmond/Bill team was *The Negro Next Door*, a harrowing examination of race relations – interviews with a black family and a confrontation, mediated by Desmond, with the antagonistic white neighbours. Those of us who had a feeling for this sort of 'human' television were fervent admirers and we kept asking, as each new Wilcox/Bill film came up, 'Why has no one ever thought of doing that subject before?' and, 'How did they find those people and how did they persuade those people to do that?' Chris Brasher confided in me that he and Desmond were to be the two senior reporters on the new series and that they would share its editorship. 'Ho, ho,' I thought. I knew Desmond by repute. Shared editorship, my foot.

As we now knew to be the pattern, nothing was ready as the deadline for the new show approached. Its working title was *Man Alive*. Nobody really thought it the right one but it survived the series' sixteen-year run. The production team was nothing like fully recruited and very few film reports commissioned when Chris Brasher panicked and set off for America with Michael Latham, the senior producer, to shoot the first film for the new series. They shot a corker of a film about Dr Michael DeBakey, one of the first-ever heart-transplant surgeons. Desmond and Bill were still working out their contracts at ITV and my treasure-hunting partner Tom Conway and I were left to mind the shop. It was not long before the *Radio Times* started pestering us for advance information about the new series. We were at least able to give them the provisional title. But they needed more than that and there really wasn't any more, so I sat down and wrote the most anodyne *Radio Times* billing ever: '*Man Alive*, a programme about people and the situations which shape their lives'. It's hard to believe but it remained the generic weekly billing of the series for years.

While Chris Brasher was filming in Texas, I made several visits to Associated Rediffusion's offices to take my marching orders from the new bosses. I was given a horrid assignment. Desmond and Bill wanted to kick off the new series with a documentary about paedophiles, as they are now known, or child molesters as we called them then. What's more, anonymity was not acceptable. I had to find criminals who could be persuaded (presumably against their better judgement) to appear face to camera. One of my recently recruited colleagues had resigned from the BBC rather than research the film; that was how I found myself in this most unenviable position. Desmond was to be the reporter and he and his partner sensed the need for added fire power. It came in the shape of an ex-*Daily Express* foot-in-door man called Gordon Thomas, who went on to become a suave best-selling author and tax exile. He presented himself to me as a caricature sleazy journalist, whispering out of the side of his mouth, looking over his shoulder to see if we were being followed. I suspect he had read too much Raymond Chandler. Gordon had a contact high up in the Liverpool police, a senior detective who drove us around the seedier suburbs of Liverpool so that Gordon and I might talk to convicted paedophiles who had served their sentences – in the comfort of their own homes. The unmarked police car that had brought us was parked around the corner with Gordon's contact sitting patiently at the wheel. I still find it shocking that this detective (who went to the top of his profession) should offer such a service to journalists or that Gordon and I felt able to accept it. As you would expect, we were rebuffed, insulted and threatened by most of these pathetic figures, but we found a couple of them who agreed to appear face to camera.

Gordon also had contacts in child welfare and one day a letter arrived for him at the office which simply contained a name and an address. It turned out that the person named had recently moved in with a single mother of three young daughters. Gordon's contact obviously hoped that the publicity of our broadcast would send him packing. Mr Smith, as I shall call him, was living with his new girlfriend and her daughters in a tiny terrace house in a narrow back street in north London and he had sensibly insisted that we keep his whereabouts secret. The unhelpful cameraman insisted on placing a gigantic spotlight on the pavement outside the house to light the tiny front room. The curious neighbours gathered like flies. The interview went well and my producer now had the bit between his teeth. 'We need to see Mr Smith leering at children,' he said. 'But we have agreed we won't give any indication of where he lives,' I protested. 'Leave it to me.' With that the producer marched back into the house. 'Come on now, Mr Smith, let's be getting some fresh air into your lungs.' And with that the producer, the film crew and a bewildered Mr Smith set off for the playground in Regent's Park – and, lo and behold, we had the title sequence.

The most harrowing interview to shoot was with a mother in her council flat whose daughter had been murdered in a sex attack. I had read an interview with her in one of the tabloids and she had given the moving quote about her child's murderer: 'That man is breathing the air my daughter should be breathing now.' I assumed the quote had been made up by the journalist, so when she used it powerfully in her interview with Desmond, I wondered, was this what people meant when they talked of life imitating art? Had this mother read the made-up quote attributed to her in the newspaper and decided to use it in her television interview or had she really said it to the tabloid journalist in the first place? What shocked me most was watching rushes of the interview, back at the BBC, with Desmond and his partner. They were chortling in triumph as the bereaved mother's sadness turned first to sobbing and then to anger. Desmond had played her like an instrument and she sang like a bird.

If you work in this kind of journalism you are forced to examine the moral issues that confront you almost on a daily basis. I knew what the impact of an appearance on television was likely to be. Our interviewees had no idea. And this highly charged programme, *What Shall We Tell the Children?* bothered me more than any other has since. Our interviewees had all served their prison sentences, paid the price and were expected to reintegrate into society. By appearing on *Man Alive* I supposed they were sabotaging their own fragile chance of rehabilitation and laying themselves open to the wrath of the mob. I don't think I said this loudly or persuasively enough at the time. Yet the film we eventually broadcast was a model of common sense. There were interviews with psychiatrists like Dr Anthony Storr who helped keep the temperature down and it was at the very least enlightening, not to say intriguing, to watch paedophiles respond to rigorous questioning on television for the very first time. One of the participants I was most worried would suffer the outrage and probably violence of his neighbours phoned to thank me for giving him the opportunity to get the matter off his chest. 'Everyone's being so helpful now they understand me.' You could have knocked me down with a feather.

The plan had been to kick off the *Man Alive* series with *What Shall We Tell the Children?* What better route to a flying start? The answer, of course, was for it to be labelled too hot to handle and cancelled in a blaze of publicity – and that's what happened. So *Man Alive* made its debut with Chris Brasher's report, *The Heart Man,* the viewing figures much enhanced by all the alarums and excursions. Desmond argued fiercely and effectively for *What Shall We Tell the Children?* The new BBC2 Controller, David Attenborough, came up with an ingenious solution. He declared the film was a fine contribution to the channel but unsuitable for early-evening viewing. The answer, he said, was a later transmission slot. One was swiftly found. Of course, now even more people watched the disputed film. *Man Alive* was emerging as a brand. Desmond had worked on the *Daily Mirror* and his mastery of the media to promote his own interests was always formidable. Most senior BBC folk thought that sort of thing rather vulgar. Those were the days.

Now the battle lines were beginning to be drawn between the rival reporter-editors. The trouble had started while Chris Brasher was still in Houston with Dr DeBakey. He quite rightly surmised that Desmond was deliberately stirring up trouble for him at home. He sent a telex: IMPOSSIBLE CONCENTRATE REPORTING MAJOR STORY CONSTANT SNIPING AT REAR. It turned out to be an early symptom of much tumult and calumny, the fight for the crown. It didn't take long for the matter to be resolved. Desmond had very quickly learnt the BBC ropes and which string to pull. He had won over to his side the entrepreneurially gifted bully-boy Group Head, Aubrey Singer, who dripped with the putrid marinade of internal politics. Although it was Aubrey who had appointed Chris Brasher and championed him even after the debacle of *Time Out*, he now spotted a more likely winner in Desmond and vaulted on to *his* bandwagon. Brasher was toast. Some years later Aubrey was unaccountably to recall Chris Brasher to head one of the departments in his by then vast empire. Whatever his motive it cannot have been remorse because Aubrey knew only the destructive emotions – and indeed was destroyed himself, not many years later, after he had unaccountably been promoted to be the Managing Director of Television. The Director General invited him for a jovial weekend shooting and summarily fired him on the journey home. An even crueller defenestration awaited him, as we shall see. Brasher didn't last long on his second time round. A sinister warning had appeared in an anonymous newsletter circulating in his deeply unhappy department: he would be shot by a sniper while he chaired the departmental meeting. He wasn't but he was toast – again. With Aubrey's connivance, Desmond snapped up the headless department and merged it with his own, king of the castle.

The first two years of *Man Alive* were in some ways the most striking because there was nothing else quite like it on television. Colour had not yet arrived and the half-hour black-and-white films were fast-paced and self-assured to the point of cockiness. Viewers liked their tabloid editorial line. The old guard held the BBC's impartiality to be sacrosanct so it was refreshing to see films with attitude. The Director General, Hugh Greene, had made a speech saying that the BBC had no right to be impartial in such matters as poverty, crime and race hatred. We used that as a licence to editorialise like mad – on the side of the angels, we were convinced. We brooked no argument from defenders of the status quo. Hugh Greene had also persuaded the BBC governors and the government that the BBC need not attempt to achieve political balance within every single programme, that there need only be balance 'overall'. To mark this dispensation, David Attenborough commissioned James Cameron to present *One Pair of Eyes* for BBC2. Any crusty Conservative of that era would tell you that the BBC was run by left-wing radicals, what with *That Was The Week That Was, Man Alive* and Sidney Newman's *The Wednesday Play*. Indeed there *were* many high-profile anti-establishment programmes because the substantial new intake of young people reflected the world outside. Harold Wilson had succeeded Sir Alec Douglas-Home as Prime Minister and it was time for change, just as it had been two decades earlier, when Winston Churchill was kicked out in 1945, and was to be again, three decades later, with the election of Tony Blair.

Critics of the *Man Alive* series were multitudinous. They dubbed it derisively 'Desmond's Weepies'. There was a grain of truth in the slur. When it was time to view other producers' rough cuts Desmond would crouch expectantly over the viewing machine like a dog waiting for a juicy bone. When the on-screen sobbing started he would heave a satisfied sigh of relief and then often fall asleep. But these critics often chose to forget the extraordinarily wide range of topics the series covered. *Man Alive* made more than thirty films a year, so Desmond had to allow producers a good deal of freedom in the choice of subjects. One that opened up another new world for me was producer Michael Latham's *Man Alive* profile of David Lean, which we filmed while he was shooting *Dr Zhivago*. Because the book was banned in the Soviet Union and American film companies were most unwelcome there, MGM decided to shoot practically all of it Spain. Only the snow-covered exteriors were shot in Finland and Canada. I was to set it up and persuade the big stars to give interviews. Nowadays, those sort of documentaries are two a penny. Film distributors now treat television as a tool not a rival. MGM was ahead of the game and its publicity people went out of their way to make us welcome. When I reached Madrid Airport, there was no question of all that boring stuff like customs and immigration. An MGM executive and limousine met me at the foot of the aircraft steps. Since the film's rushes had to be shipped through the airport to Los Angeles every night, MGM had greased the necessary airport palms to ensure a permanent trouble-free transit.

Undeterred by the dissimilarity between Moscow and Madrid, the production team built a replica of Red Square in the unwholesome suburbs of Madrid. At first sight it was startlingly realistic. Only as you approached did you realised that the whole set was an astonishing optical illusion. When I walked across the square to the Kremlin, the top of the dome hardly came up to my shoulder. In the Madrid film studios that MGM had hired for the duration, Spanish extras, clad as Cossacks in heavy fur costumes, wilted miserably in the searing heat. The only high point of their dreadful day of boredom and discomfort was the free lunch. Two great trestle tables were set out, under the only shade on the lot, seating fifty or more on either side. One table offered magnificent Spanish paella, tapas and litre bottles of red wine. The other provided, for those who preferred American fare, steaks, hamburgers, coffee and Budweiser.

David Lean was notoriously difficult and reclusive and, as it turned out, in no great mood to change his spots just because a BBC crew was hanging around. Indeed, he saw us as a distraction and a pain in the arse. It soon transpired that he felt much the same about his actors and they, naturally, reciprocated with knobs on. I learnt later that when Lean had gone to the airport in Ceylon to welcome Alec Guinness for the shooting of *The Bridge on the River Kwai*, his first words to his star were, 'I didn't want you to play the lead in my film.' Omar Sharif, Julie Christie and Geraldine Chaplin were forthright and funny, mostly bitching about their director. Freddie Young, the legendary lighting cameraman who had also shot *Lawrence of Arabia* for Lean, was more resigned than bitter, reminiscing later, 'David was inclined to take the credit for everything. Oh, he'd pat me on the back, give me a hug, but he seldom divulged my contributions to the world.' But the world recognised his contributions. He won an Oscar on each of the three films he shot for David Lean. This *Man Alive* film was a hit with BBC2's slowly burgeoning audience largely because MGM's hype for *Dr Zhivago* was overpowering and everyone wanted a first glimpse of the movie that was to win five Oscars and become one of the great box-office hits of all time. However, reflexive films about showbiz didn't really warrant the investigative skills and sardonic tone that distinguished the *Man Alive* brand. Luckily *Late Night Line Up* and then Barry Norman's *Film Night* came along to attend to such matters, leaving us to get on with setting the world to rights.

We were lucky that Trevor Philpott, the seasoned *Tonight* and *Picture Post* reporter, joined the *Man Alive* team at about this time. He was used to working with no editorial assistance, no director and very fast. His contributions to the series were always entertaining and often very funny. He made a gripping programme about politics – no easy thing – by tackling the subject in an off-beat way. He called it *The Losers* and we found for him two politicians, one Conservative and one Labour, who were both standing for Yorkshire constituencies in the 1966 General Election and were both one hundred per cent certain to lose. A young chinless wonder, Eton and pinstripe, was standing in a tough, militant, mining constituency. And an overweight railway signalman and National Union of Railwaymen shop steward was standing in a constituency of landowners and Range Rovers, fox-hounds and horses, green wellies and headscarves. It's not hard to imagine how appealing this film was, compared to an evening of Robin Day in the election studio. Trevor went on churning them out. I also worked with him on a send-up of private detectives. We filmed one who was checking on malingerers for an insurance company. This entailed the private eye crawling, on his hands and knees, into the back of his clapped-out little van and spying through a hole he had made in the side. Not surprisingly, the net curtains of the quiet suburban south-London street where we were filming started to twitch – and, in a trice, a police patrol car screeched to a halt and the private detective was pulled out of his vehicle, bum first. I swear that if we hadn't claimed him, the police would have taken him away and locked him up.

I was not as yet a fully fledged *Man Alive* director, but the chance came when I proposed that we make a film about phobias. Desmond was keen but none of my seniors seemed madly enthusiastic to direct it. In the days before the Internet, it was practically impossible to find interviewees for such programmes. How could we hope to trace people who were anyway ashamed of their phobias, people frightened of heights, dogs, birds, people, inside, outside and, would you believe, rhubarb? We decided to put small ads in the national press. It hadn't been tried before and it was rather frowned on. I defended the policy stoutly since it opened up lots of intimate subjects to our cameras. Jeremy Isaacs, who ran the rival *This Week* and had been Desmond's boss, annoyingly used to answer our classified ads that we hoped nobody in the business would have spotted.

My phobics were a collection of most ordinary people who recounted extraordinary, irrational but terrifying fears that they had usually kept hidden from their nearest and dearest. The television camera has a unique power mendaciously to reassure that what it records is con-fidential – and those who have trusted it are thus the more devastatingly betrayed. A husband will tell the camera what he has never told his wife – even when she is sitting right beside him for the filmed interview. Sometimes, though, the intimacies of the television confessional seem to have beneficial effects. One tough young man in Corby would take hours to get to his workplace because he was petrified of the dogs he met on the way to the bus stop. He was just as scared of what his workmates would think if they found out about his fear. However, after the programme was broadcast he told us that now he was treated like a gallant hero. The reporter on my phobias film was Angela Huth, one of Desmond's new recruits, and subsequently a celebrated novelist. She was as inexperienced as I and we both got the giggles listening to our next phobic. He was a telephone engineer droning on, as if he were reading the telephone directory, about his terror of leaves and green plants. Her toe-curling leading question to him, 'Have you ever had any frights with rhubarb?' became a standing joke around the office. (The answer, incidentally, was, 'Yes,' which was, of course, why Angela asked the question in the first place.)

Anyone who has seen Alfred Hitchcock's 1963 film *The Birds* must have sympathised with the middle-aged phobic office worker who answered one of our advertisements. She suffered from what she described as a 'mortal fear' of birds – pigeons in particular. Her life was made hell for her by her need to commute through Waterloo Station every day. She agreed to allow us to film her going to work. It was my first fully-fledged directing assignment for *Man Alive* and I had to succeed. The filming was sensational. The poor woman could have been a trained actress as she darted around, shielding her face and her hair from the ubiquitous pigeons. The look of stark horror on her face, when a bird approached her, would have been deemed histrionic by any sophisticated film director. It would be wrong of me to deny the rumour that spread around the office like wildfire. Yes, I did buy some birdseed *pour encourager les oiseaux* but – and this is my feeble excuse – there would have been plenty of pigeons there anyway.

CHAPTER 5

A Tangled Web

I was the researcher chosen to set up *Man Alive*'s first major American tour, which was thrilling for me because I had never been to the United States. Summertime was a quiet time in the office for Desmond, the programme editor, and these trips became an annual event for Desmond, the reporter. He had worked in America as a correspondent for the *Daily Mirror* and his enthusiasm for the country was infectious. America was home to so many wonderful stories. No stiff upper lips, no anal retention here. Everyone, high and low, was refreshingly accessible and happy to talk to the BBC until the cows came home. If you needed an interview with a police chief or a congressman you simply phoned him up and fixed a time for filming later the same day.

The Pride and the Shame was a poignant and anger-making essay on the scandalous treatment of the Native American, its title derived from President Johnson's exhortation to 'remove the blush of shame that comes to our cheeks when we look at what we have done to the first Americans in this country'. Much had been written and filmed about the shameful treatment of Australia's aboriginals. There were stirrings of collective guilt, an awareness of a need to make amends. Not so in the USA. I did the research and recommended that we focus on the Cheyenne Sioux tribe in South Dakota. These once-proud native people were living in despair, below the poverty line, despised and neglected. Legally all Native Americans were under the federal protection of the Bureau of Indian Affairs. Its headquarters festered somnolently, just a few streets from Capitol Hill. The BIA administered eighty-seven thousand square miles of land, held in trust for two and three-quarter million native Americans, mostly belonging to the five hundred and sixty-four federally recognised tribes. Yet the BIA was the very worst sort of bloated and demoralised government bureaucracy, employing one member of staff for every seventeen Native Americans. An aura of failure and hopelessness pervaded the offices of BIA headquarters. This is where you ended up if you couldn't hack it. I could smell a story.

The nearest sizeable town to the Cheyenne Sioux tribe is Rapid City, South Dakota. The local man for the Bureau of Indian Affairs was buoyant and useless. He directed me to a new housing estate along Interstate Highway 44. There were homes for perhaps fifty families – not much to meet the needs of the seventy thousand or so Sioux living in the state, but a showpiece and an upbeat billboard to fortify the complacency of passing motorists. Hanging around the sleazy late-night bars on the outskirts of town, drunken Native Americans staggered and brawled in Hieronymus Bosch tableaux, entirely ignored by the white citizens of Rapid City. In my hotel room the next morning the radio told me of a tragic suicide from the night before. The dead Native American had killed himself because he could no longer feed his wife and children. He had lost heart at the hopelessness of it all. His death was not just a pitiful cry for help, it seemed to me that it was a tragic metaphor – the Native American deprived of his birthright and his livelihood, usurped and despised in the new America. The suicide seemed to me the crux of the story and I set off to the local radio station to see if they had made a recording of the morning news bulletin that we could use in our documentary. They had and they gladly made me a copy. Back in the hotel bar that evening I was approached by the sort of redneck that it is best not to tangle with. Massive, swaggering, foul breath and drunk. Was he copying Clint Eastwood or was it the other way around? 'Hear you're from BBC England and want to put that dead Indian on your TV program.' Then he told me why I should show no sympathy to the Native American. It was not a pretty speech.

You could have heard much the same and worse in the American South. I did. President Johnson's Voting Rights Act had just become law, giving millions of black Americans the chance to vote for the very first time. In my Memphis motel I encountered a group of young Washington officials who had been sent to Mississippi, just across the border, to ensure that elections were conducted fairly. They had been forced to cross into Tennessee, to Memphis, to find a place to sleep. Every hotel in

Mississippi had refused them rooms. Sending them on their way, the redneck hotel owners and their customers in the bar had cursed them. I am not easily shocked but I still shudder at the dreadfulness of those threats and obscenities. The young federal observers had stumbled upon the nightmare world that Alan Parker was to visualize in *Mississippi Burning* two decades later.

Thirty-five miles down a dirt road to nowhere I found the perfect Indian township to illustrate the Native American's stark predicament. Incongruously, it was called Cherry Creek, a shanty slum, mired in unemployment and poverty. There were only two wells supplying drinking water and no provision for sewage. It was almost unbearably hot while we were there in summer but the temperature fell way below freezing for months during the winter. Yet many of these dignified descendants of a warrior people were homeless and sheltered at night in abandoned cars. The most shocking aspect of the Cherry Creek community was the presence of half a dozen rival Christian missionary churches of different denominations. Each Sioux family was expected to give ten per cent of its income to the church. Our astonishment became disbelief when we learnt that nearly everyone was surviving on government welfare cheques; and our disbelief turned into anger when we found that the free rice came in bags labelled, 'A gift from the people of the United States of America', in English on one side of the bag, in Vietnamese on the other. Not a lot has changed in the four decades since we made our film. The Cheyenne Sioux recently announced that they had the highest suicide rate in the world among ten- to twenty-four-year-old males.

Before we left for America, David Attenborough, the BBC2 Controller, had dropped a bombshell. *Man Alive* was to be one of the first BBC2 programmes to be made entirely in colour starting in the autumn of 1967. The running time of the series was to increase from thirty to fifty minutes and the number of weekly programmes to an astonishing fifty-one. Nowadays it is unthinkable that any such series should run for the whole year. Adding even more power to Desmond's elbow, David commissioned an on-going series of ten-minute films called *Times Remembered*, beguiling nostalgia featuring sprightly elderly people and their enchanting reminiscences. Its main purpose was to provide a common junction with the *Nine O'Clock News* on BBC1 but it also became a perfect training ground for young directors and a place to try out new reporters. Jonathan Dimbleby was one of them. *Man Alive* had hit the jackpot with this substantial increase in air time and the resources to fill it. However, it came with a catch. Attenborough wanted us to change the series' format so that we had a means of offering possible resolutions to the stark and controversial dilemmas we presented each week. It was all very well to point the finger, he said, but we should try to offer remedies too. Some eight years later those strutting media peacocks, Peter Jay and John Birt, unveiled their Original Thought. Many programmes, they said, promoted a 'bias against understanding' because they neglected the significance of the 'mission to explain'. No competent producer, least of all David Attenborough, needed such pretentious hokum to reach a common-sense solution to the *Man Alive* predicament. From now on, he proposed, the more controversial film reports should be followed by a studio discussion.

This was to be the epoch when *Man Alive* really took off. It was exactly the right series for the times. In 1968 the Vietnam War was at its height and student protest at its most riotous. Outside the United States Embassy in London, Tariq Ali and Vanessa Redgrave led a massive protest against the war. In Washington, a quarter of a million people demonstrated while General Westmoreland was requesting a similar number of extra soldiers to reinforce his troops already fighting in Vietnam. Martin Luther King and Robert Kennedy were assassinated within a couple of months of one another. Richard Nixon was elected President and the secret and illegal bombing of Cambodia began. *Man Alive* mounted two major programmes, jointly entitled *Protest in the Ranks,* examining resistance to the war and compulsory enlistment – the draft. Another two-part essay, *The Mood in America,* aimed to explain why the war was proving so divisive. In Europe there was turmoil too, a revolution against the status quo – the Prague Spring, student riots in France and Germany. This was the era of anarchy, the Baader-Meinhoff Group and the Red Brigade, the Beatles and the Rolling Stones, marijuana and free love. *Man Alive* was among the first to scramble on to the roller coaster, one of the first programmes on television to discuss the unspeakable, to show in glorious colour – and in close up – what our parents had deemed strictly taboo.

Lively studio discussions were prompted by films with provocative titles like *Would You Let Your Daughter Marry One? People in Chains, My Parents Don't Understand Me, Living with Death, Not on Speaking Terms.* The researchers did a wonderful job finding real people to match the mythical interviewees Desmond colourfully conjured from his imagination when he memorably briefed each team at the start of every production. I made my share of the studio programmes, including a debate about capital punishment, *Bring Back the Rope?* There hadn't been a hanging for four years and capital punishment for murder was about to be abolished. Naturally we invited the official hangman to take part and, much to our surprise, he agreed. Harry Allen had attended eighty-two executions and was chief executioner at twenty-nine of them. He was still on the government payroll and very anxious to get back to work. He arrived dressed as if for *Sunday Night at the London Palladium,* in a glittering red smoking jacket with a bright green bow tie. This was one of those debates where we woolly liberals quietly made sure that the right side won. It wasn't hard to do with a hangman looking like that and a bunch of the most grisly old-fashioned Tories yapping away like a bunch of dogs shut in kennels while the family cat sits outside and taunts them.

I also produced a two-part feature *Who'll Be Mother?*, which debated the rights and wrongs of delegating the care of your children. The first programme was about nannies and the second focused on boarding preparatory schools. By now we had learnt that a studio discussion was far more lively if the film report which preceded it was a touch on the polemical side. My researcher revengefully proposed we shoot the boarding-school film at the Gloucestershire preparatory school where he had been miserably incarcerated. We focused on three brothers. The first, an eight-year-old, was a new boy and as miserable as sin; the middle brother, aged ten, was stoic but admitted how much rather he would be at home with mum; and the eldest, aged thirteen and a prefect, was already an arrogant budding right-wing Tory. The film was devastating, the headmaster in the studio at a loss for words as he tried to defend the system. He later valiantly told a mutual acquaintance that he defended the BBC's right to make such a biased film because 'that is what living in a free country is all about', but I secretly knew that its flagrant partiality was a bridge too far. I resolved not to go to the same extreme again, or at least not quite so blatantly.

I tried my hand at studio direction but I was temperamentally un-suited to it. You needed the dexterity and reactions of a fighter pilot. I don't have them. Usually there is plenty of rehearsal time so that you can familiarise yourself with the daunting wonders of a television studio and the millions of pounds' worth of technical equipment that you barely recognise, let alone know how to use. A studioful of highly experienced technicians watches you silently, gauging your competence, because their reputations are also on the line if you cock it all up on the night. You start the rehearsal by taking everyone through the running order as it is scripted. 'Cue presenter on camera one.' The presenter waffles on for a while and then introduces the guests who have yet to arrive. Sometimes a researcher or two will sit in for them but usually all you see is a camera nodding to indicate that it is pointing at the right empty chair. There is nothing else to rehearse until the participants arrive except the closing title sequence. That's soon done because in rehearsal you can shoot it when you are ready. When it's the real thing you have to be all set to swing into the routine at the drop of a hat.

After the supper break, when you have been far too nervous to eat, this is it. The studio control room is buzzing with activity as the sound, lighting and technical engineers confer for one last time. You sit at a long desk in front of a vast bank of television monitors with the technical supervisor on your right. It's his job to help you keep your show on air if there are technical snags – just like a flight engineer in the cockpit of an aeroplane. On your left sits the vision mixer whose job is to select the different vision sources, live cameras, film and video inserts. Your PA is on her left, armed with at least two stopwatches. She has to count you down and get you on and off air on time. She has to cue in the film and video inserts, and ensure that the floor manager is informed of the timings and any changes that need to be made while you are on air. You are totally dependent on her for a glitch-free production. The floor manager welcomes the participants as they are shepherded into the studio from the hospitality room. They are given a quick sound and lighting check while the presenter deliberately steers them away from serious discussion until the programme is under way. Although this is a recording there will be no stops to interrupt the studio debate unless you very publicly screw up.

'One minute,' calls your PA. Then the floor manager, 'Settle down studio.' The red light starts flashing, the countdown begins, from forty-five seconds to thirty, from thirty to fifteen, ten seconds to three seconds and then a complete eerie silence as the clock ticks mutely down to zero. If it's live, there is a further panic-inducing feature. Presentation control is on the speaker, warning you by how many minutes the previous programme is over- or under-running. Through this cacophony, you are peripherally aware of the off-air monitor where the end titles of the previous programme are rolling, then the BBC2 symbol turning slowly on the screen. A tiny cue dot warns that we are about to go on air as a disembodied voice announces, 'This is BBC 2 and it's time for this week's *Man Alive* . . . ' Cue opening titles. Cue presenter. Now there is nothing on the script to help you except the ominous three words, 'Cameras as directed,' and you are on your own. The cameras are all mounted on heavy wheeled pedestals and it is entirely possible to trap all of them in one of their cables, like a fly in a spider's web. Then none of them can move at all. In my time at Anglia a calamity-prone director achieved this live on air. She ordered the television equivalent of 'Bail out!' and aborted the broadcast, going off air and handing over to the master control room with the plaintiff cry, at the top of her gin-soaked voice, 'Take me, Master!' God, you are relieved when it's all over!

I also got a chance to direct my first outside broadcast. This is some-thing to be recommended to all megalomaniacs. You are in charge of several enormous vans, blazoned with the BBC logo, containing every toy you could possible want to play with – cameras, track and dollies, booms, generators, masts to send the signal back to the Television Centre with a recording van as back-up. The director's control room is warm and luxurious. Everyone else is out in the wet and the cold. When I first started in the business, at Anglia as a 'bloody researcher', by a mistake I led just such a travelling-circus convoy up a cul-de-sac. Now, at last, I could avenge the brickbats that assaulted me then. Lights, camera, action! The *Man Alive* programme I was producing was called *Pity the Poor Farmer*. It was a savage indictment of the working conditions and wages of agricultural workers. We wickedly staged the town-hall-style debate in the Dorset courtroom from which a judge had deported the Tolpuddle Martyrs to Australia over a century earlier. Their crime had been to start an agricultural workers' trade union after their wages were *reduced* for the second year running. Although well represented in the debate, members of the Nation Union of Farmers were apoplectic. Somehow they and their smooth public-relations men managed to gain access to David Attenborough and unwisely, as he later told me, he agreed to try and placate them with a good lunch at the Television Centre. That just made them worse – more persistent in their complaints. David told me later that he had never been subjected to such sustained vitriol. This was surely not what he intended when he had prompted the new *Man Alive* to reflect a reasoned forum for rational debate. Always charming, he was difficult to read, but I think he was really quite cross with me.

Our job on *Man Alive*, as we saw it, was to present the uncomfortable truth. So, by definition, the public-relations man's job was to obstruct us. We became masters of guile and rather too pleased with ourselves. My first major PR defeat was at the hands of the army. Newspaper reports suggested that British servicemen and their families in Germany were living in appalling conditions. At the time, the British Army on the Rhine (BAOR) was vast, a Cold War monstrosity. When I arrived at its Rheindalen headquarters I was slightly disturbed that so many of the officers seemed distinctly eccentric. While there was small chance of Soviet tanks imminently rolling across the horizon, that is what these fellows were supposed to be there to prevent; it looked as if they had all been trained for *Dad's Army*. After endless briefings, the crackpot public-relations major told me that the officer I must see was Colonel Hamilton-Bailey. I was warned that he was very odd. 'He was in and out of Colditz like a dose of salts.' In fact the colonel turned out to be a suave and laid-back officer who was charm itself. He would have been more at home in a Hampshire country house than he was in this grim township, on standby for World War III. I told him my mission, to investigate the poor housing conditions of other ranks. I tried to soften the blow by suggesting that Whitehall parsimony might be to blame. The colonel reflected, as he lit his pipe. 'I know what,' he said. 'I'll call in my batman.' And with that he bellowed at the closed door, 'Sergeant!' Almost simultaneously the batman arrived at his colonel's desk, with a crash and a bang, as he stamped to attention and saluted. The colonel raised an eyebrow. 'Sergeant, you and your family live in army quarters here. What do you think of them?' Without a moment's hesitation the batman replied, 'I have a very good house, sir. My family and I are very happy indeed, sir.' With that he was dismissed with much about-turning and further stamping of feet. 'Well, you heard what he had to say,' said the colonel. 'I am sure you realise that if he had said anything else he would have been court-martialled. Is there anything else I can help you with?'

I was later able to reverse my misfortune. In the United States I pitted myself against a master of media manipulation and I won. When Desmond was ready for his next summer tour of America, we decided to make a documentary on the phenomenon of the legendary 'little old ladies in tennis shoes'. They are mostly middle-class, middle-aged white women who are obsessed with tracing their lineage back to the *Mayflower* and they all belong to at least one of America's myriad 'patriotic' societies. Their unspoken agenda is racism and anti-Semitism. These little old ladies were sinister because their numbers gave them enormous electoral power. While researching the film I made the mistake of lunching with a rather deaf little old biddy – who actually wore tennis shoes – at a swanky country club of her choosing in California. She spent the meal very loudly trying to convince me that Jesus was not a Jew. It was quite apparent from their reactions that many of the country club's members were.

The most important of all these 'patriotic' societies was and is the Daughters of the American Revolution, whose grandiose headquarters in Washington DC almost dwarf the nearby White House. Here I met the high-powered, aggressive head of public relations and explained what we wanted. I asked for introductions to some of the DAR state chapters. 'Wait a minute,' barked Mr Public Relations, 'I've come across your type from England before. How do I know your aren't one of those affable nice guys they send out from London who'll go back home and do a hatchet job on us?' You didn't often get asked questions like that in America. There was no tradition of edgy and critical documentaries. It was not the American way to carp at the American dream. Whatever my answer was it obviously didn't convince Mr Public Relations. Quite the reverse. Soon I found that he had circulated all fifty state chapters of the DAR warning them that some Commie from the BBC might approach them. He warned them, in the strongest possible terms, not to assist me in any way. Fortunately, the little old ladies in the states we had chosen were raring to go for this 'affable nice guy from London'. After all, didn't the Pilgrim Fathers come from there? 'Those fools in Washington know nothing,' they admonished, confidently but so mistakenly. The film we made can only be described as grotesque, so awful were the women we portrayed. We didn't distort. We didn't have to. They handed us their caricature on a plate. Partly to annoy Mr Public Relations and, also, because it was exactly the right title, we called our film *Daughters of America*. He was so angry, apoplectic with rage, that I think he would have killed me if I had dared join him on his end of the telephone.

In the heart of the old confederacy at Richmond, Virginia, I discovered a real *Gone with the Wind* character, someone I was convinced could be persuaded to spill the beans. Our Scarlett O'Hara was a bubbly, extrovert woman in her early thirties, unmarried, overweight and living at home in a strict churchgoing family. Because her good times were few and far between, she had a propensity for an over-indulgence in Jack Daniel's. After sharing far too much of it with me, she did indeed let the cat out of the bag. 'It's all snobbish rubbish, little nobodies trying to look big – that's why they join the DAR. Do you think I believe in all this patriotic crap? I spend my life living a lie. One of these days I shall shout it from the rooftops and they can do their damnedest to li'le ol' me. The whole thing needs to be blown sky high.' Scarlett expelled a whooshing noise, presumably to represent the disintegration of the DAR, and collapsed unsteadily, deep into the sofa. How I wished the cameras had been with me.

A few weeks later I returned with Desmond and the film crew. Scarlett sent her parents out for the evening so that she could enjoy a night with the boys from the BBC. The discreet cameraman slipped away from the party and prepared a private interview set-up in Scarlett's bedroom upstairs. When it was ready Desmond and I invited her to come upstairs. There was a flicker of hope in her eyes. Desmond and I had foresworn Jack Daniel's for the evening. She had not. Desmond made a rather good Rhet Butler. With the camera running, he coaxed from our Scarlett the gold dust that she had given me earlier. I telephoned her to thank her the next day. She remembered exactly what she had told us. 'Tell Desmond I hate him,' she said, with a rueful sigh. 'Oh well, someone had to say what I said last night. It's just a pity that it had to me li'le ol' me.' Then she suddenly brightened up. She seemed to remember Rhett Butler's very last words to Scarlet O'Hara, spoken by Clarke Gable in the film, 'Frankly, my dear, I don't give damn!' In a perfect world she should have added the immortal last line of the book, 'After all, tomorrow is another day.'

CHAPTER 6

Trouble in Paradise

I had wearied of the United States after two long hot summers working there. Now I had the chance to film in more exotic climes. It seems extraordinary to have to admit it, but it had not really dawned on me that you could leave home in midwinter, jump on a plane and leave the horrors of damp, dark and cold Britain behind. St Paul may have seen the light on the road to Damascus, but the penny didn't really drop for me until I touched down on the island of Mauritius, way south of the Equator, in the middle of March. I had left London on a freezing and miserable night and British Airways had spirited me to what could only be the Garden of Eden.

It was dawn and first I noticed the smells: cooking with coconut oil, incense, burning cow dung and frangipani at the temples, sweet, sweet fruit smells – mango, plantains, papaya. Then, as the sun climbed high into the sky, that unique and extraordinary dazzlingly bright green of the paddy fields: a painter would be ridiculed if he were to depict them as brilliant as that. And birds I had never heard before calling out the start of a new day – mynah birds and kites, bulbul and parrots. Pale shaded mountains, rivers and sea. Everywhere sugar cane festooning and cocooning the island. In the winter gloom of London it is hard to spot God's underlying game plan. On this, the island of the long-defunct dodo, you suddenly know what He was up to and, humbly, award Him full marks.

We were a crew of six from London and our researcher had gone on ahead to get everything ready. Our mission was to make a documentary about a retired British army colonel with an unusual way of supplementing his army pension. He went around the world organising Independence celebrations for those little red bits on the map that had missed out on the big bang when India had made the break in 1947.

53

Colonel Eric Hefford was on to his eighth Independence by the time we caught up with him in Mauritius in 1968; most of the others had been pretty small affairs – Botswana, Malawi and Guyana, those sorts of places. But it wasn't the splendour of the Independence celebrations we were after, more a gentle dig at the need for a British colonel to wind up the British Empire and make the whole thing go like clockwork.

We were met at the airport by Jamie, our researcher, who had found the most wonderful beach hotel for us with individual cottages laid out on a lagoon. At night the moon and the stars bathed the open-air restaurant and swimming pool with gold and silver light. A small group of musicians serenaded us with gentle melodies we had never heard before and love songs that I was soon enough to learn came from deep in the soul of Bollywood's most poignant singer, Lata Mangeshkar. The French and the British have both left lasting cultural footprints on this magical island but the majority population, descendants of Indian bonded labourers brought in to harvest the sugar cane, ensured that Bollywood was never out of mind.

This luxury hotel was pretty unique way back then. In the Caribbean there were many spots to equal its magnificence, but Mauritius, like Ceylon, the Seychelles, the Maldives and even India itself, was slow to learn the trick of parting the carelessly rich foreigners from their surfeit of dollars. This hotel was expensive, probably more than the BBC would agree to pay, so the seven of us held a council of war. I was in charge but comparatively untutored in the great BBC expenses game; I was happy to defer to wiser and more experienced folk. Jamie was from an extremely wealthy family and he rather turned up his nose at our sordid debate. Anyway it was he who had found this pricey hotel that was presenting the fiscal problem. The on-camera reporter thought of himself as a commanding officer so he had plenty to say. But it was John, the sound recordist, who was the most travelled and the most practical. We voted unanimously for his plan.

The BBC expenses rules said that everyone working away from base was allowed to claim a set travel and duty subsistence allowance (T&D) to cover the hotel room, all meals and laundry. When you were working in Britain there was no dispute: the trade unions had ensured that there was more than enough to cover your out-of-pocket expenses. When you went abroad the T&D allowance was fixed by some mystical liaison with the Foreign Office, which claimed to know the cost of living almost everywhere in the world. But there was a loophole that John commended to us. If you were in a remote place where no T&D allowance had been set (or perforce staying in 'a hotel of extravagant price'), you were allowed to claim 'actuality'. Instead of a set daily allowance you were allowed to claim the actual cost. The snag – a quite deliberate deterrent – was that you then had to keep receipts for everything and fill in the most gigantic expenses claim form – a nightmare if, like us, you were away from London for weeks.

John's plan was put into action. He went to the reception desk and negotiated the supply of a book of blank bills, the use of the office typewriter and the loan of the hotel's rubber stamp saying, 'paid with thanks'. He then sat down and typed out bills, one for each of us, from the moment we arrived in Mauritius to the day, three weeks later, when our flights were already booked to leave the island. The room rate on each of the bills John typed was marginally higher than the price we were actually paying and the laundry prices were entirely hypothetical. John stamped all the bills 'paid with thanks', returned the stamp, the book of unused bills and the typewriter to the recep-tionist and gave him a bribe equivalent to about a fiver. 'There we are, chaps,' said John, handing us each our receipted bill – and we had only arrived from London that morning – 'no more worries about expenses on this trip!'

It was not so very dishonest since we probably didn't make a dime but the ruse did save us time that we didn't have on paperwork that no BBC accountant could evaluate – especially the bits in Creole. But it was naughty. None of us would have liked to explain our conduct if we were found out. It was therefore a frightful shock to find out that our scam was suddenly in danger of being blown wide open. We were paying a courtesy call on the Director General of the Mauritius Broadcasting Corporation when he produced a perplexing telegram that he had just received:

FINISHED SOUTH AFRICA CONFERENCE EARLY STOP HOPE VISIT
MAURITIUS BROADCASTING CORPORATION NEXT WEEK EN ROUTE LONDON
STOP LOOK FORWARD MEETING STOP PLEASE ARRANGE ACCOMODATION –
ADAM DIRECTOR TELEVISION BBC.

He asked me if I could explain its meaning. I was probably the only
Adam the Mauritian DG knew, certainly the only one who was likely to
put 'Director Television BBC' after his name. The telegram struck fear
into my heart. I knew at once that it came from Kenneth Adam, the
BBC Director of Television, my ultimate boss. An extraordinary general
meeting was convened by the seven of us. If Kenneth Adam were
booked into the same hotel, our dodge might well be rumbled. We
wanted to prevent that at all costs. The problem was that there were
very few luxury hotels on the island and we were in the best one.
The Mauritian Director General came to our rescue. He knew of a
new, plush hotel that had just been completed for the imminent
Independence celebrations. He welcomed Kenneth at the airport and
told our boss how lucky he was to be its first guest. As usual, the BBC left
hand had no idea what the right hand was doing. The Director of
Television had no more notion that one of his crews was on the island
than we had that he was coming to call. However, we didn't relax until
he was twenty-five thousand feet above us, jetting home to London.

The island of Mauritius is bang in the middle of nowhere, six hundred
miles east of Madagascar and a thousand miles south of India. Half the
population is Hindu, a third Christian and the rest mostly Muslim.
There's African and European blood added to the mix. This polyglot
community was in party mood. Princess Alexandra was coming from
London to preside over the Independence celebrations. There were to
be brass-band march-pasts, firework displays, thrills from the police
motorcycle team, historical enactments by schoolchildren and, most
important of all, the ceremony of lowering the Union Jack and raising
the flag of the new republic. It was a massive jigsaw for Colonel Hefford
and he set about his task with energy and determination.

Yet it was not surprising that organisational progress was achieved
only at a snail's pace. Mauritius was not a very urgent place. 'It'll be all

right on the night' was the island's philosophy. That was not good enough for the military mind which was trained to assume that nothing would run smoothly unless it had been practised to perfection. A lifetime in the British army had taught Colonel Hefford that what hadn't yet gone wrong soon would. The trouble started in the capital, Port Louis. Fighting broke out between the Hindus and the Muslims – nothing very serious, but shops were looted and a few homes set on fire. Far too hastily Princess Alexandra was stood down and the King's Shropshire Light Infantry flown in from Singapore. In no time the British army was marching briskly down the high street behind the regimental band, which was blowing full blast; out in front, trotted the regimental mascot, a rather bemused goat. Peace was instantly restored. I had thought I had been born at least a generation too late to witness gunboat diplomacy. Not a bit of it.

The great day arrived. The British Colonial Secretary, Anthony Greenwood, stood in for Princess Alexandra. Thousands of children, beautifully turned out in white, formed themselves into their well-drilled depiction of the outline of Mauritius, just as they were supposed to. The police motorcycle display team suffered a minor mishap when two of the riders crashed into each other and had to be carted off on stretchers. However the Mauritius flag was hoisted without a hitch, the outgoing British Governor and the Colonial Secretary shook hands with the new Prime Minister and the delighted crowd rose to its feet to sing the national anthem for the very first time. The Republic of Mauritius was born. Thanks to Colonel Hefford, in starched white dress uniform with medals, it was a triumphant day for a new country.

Having brought peace so swiftly, the King's Shropshire Light Infantry had nothing much to do. Rather unsportingly they busied themselves spraying weedkiller on to the vast marijuana crop in the mountains that had passed unnoticed for years until the British army helicopters came along. Their boss, the personable Colonel Ballenden, was staying at our luxury hotel and had nothing to do at all. The troubles were not nearly serious enough to merit the attention a full colonel. He had come along for the ride. Singapore, he hinted, can be a bit of a drag, especially when there is nobody left to order about. His role was to keep out of the way of the men supposed to be doing the fighting. So, after dinner at the hotel, he would sit with me and the BBC team, looking out over the moonlit Indian Ocean, knocking back BBC-funded whisky, telling us hilarious but never politically contentious tales.

What none of us knew at the time was that the British government had secretly planned a very ambitious and morally dubious scheme for Mauritius. Had we discovered it then and exposed it, how different the history of the Indian Ocean might have been. But it was such a closely guarded secret that only a very few civil servants and their ministers were in the know. Colonial Secretary Anthony Greenwood, who had just benevolently overseen the birth of a new nation, was right in the thick of the skulduggery.

By an accident of history, following the Napoleonic Wars in 1814 Britain not only took possession of Mauritius from the French, it also acquired the Chagos Archipelago, a thousand islands set in a quarter of a million square miles of the Indian Ocean. Not a lot happened there – only three of the Chagos Islands were inhabited – and the only paid work was cultivating coconut plantations for absentee landlords. The islands are about as remote as you can get, halfway between Dar es Salaam in Africa and Jakarta in Indonesia, fifteen hundred miles north-east of Mauritius, and five hundred miles due south of the Maldives. If you were a B52 bomber, you would be licking your lips. Within your sights are Egypt, Libya, the Sudan, the Saudi Peninsular, Turkey, Iraq and Iran, Russia, China, Pakistan, Afghanistan, India, Burma, Thailand, Malaysia, Laos, Cambodia and Vietnam. At the height of the Cold War, when the Soviet navy was expanding as rapidly as the British were withdrawing east of Suez, the Americans became increasingly concerned at the West's military impotence in the region, its powerlessness to protect vital oil interests in the Persian Gulf. They wanted to construct a state-of-the-art military base on the Chagos Islands. Their problem was that they didn't own them.

Because the British had continued the French practice of administering the Chagos Islands as part of the colony of Mauritius, it had always been assumed the islands would remain a part of the new republic. But that was not what the Americans wanted at all. They wanted Britain to hive off the islands and lease them the biggest and best one, Diego Garcia, as an airbase. So, three years before we arrived in Mauritius for the Independence celebrations, Britain quietly bought the Chagos Islands from Mauritius for three million pounds and named its possession the 'British Indian Ocean Territory', or 'BIOT' for short. The fast dwindling British Empire had just created a new colony with fewer political rights than in many of the outposts of Empire that were still being dismantled. The foreign-policy imperative behind this retrogressive step? What the eye doesn't see, the heart doesn't grieve over.

Now BIOT was at liberty to lease Diego Garcia to the Americans. Since BIOT had no infrastructure of its own, it was left to the mandarins in Whitehall to fix it all up. As a way of saying thank you, the Americans agreed a discount of fourteen million dollars on the Polaris nuclear missiles that they were selling to a desperately cash-strapped Britain. Neither the US Congress nor the British Parliament was told about this handy little inducement that might better be described as a bribe. The Americans' next step was to insist that all the islanders be kicked out of Diego Garcia and, while we British were about it, would we please evict all the inhabitants of the other islands too? Ever obliging, Her Majesty's Government enacted an Immigration Ordinance to satisfy its demanding tenants. 'Immigration Ordinance' sounds a whole lot better than 'illegal eviction' of the islanders from their place of birth, but that's what it proved to be. Official papers, now in the public domain, expose the duplicity of the top civil servants whose job it was to implement this shameful British policy. A BBC analysis of previously secret files reveals the casual racism and devastating cynicism that infused the adminis-tration of government in the mid-1960s:

> British politicians, diplomats and civil servants began a campaign – in their own words – 'to maintain the pretence there were no permanent inhabitants' on the islands. This was vital, because proper residents would have to be recognised as people 'whose democratic rights have to be safeguarded'. Sir Paul Gore-Booth, senior official at the Foreign Office, wrote to a diplomat in 1966: 'We must surely be very tough about this. The object of the exercise is to get some rocks which will

remain ours . . . There will be no indigenous population except seagulls.' The diplomat, Dennis Greenhill, replied: 'Unfortunately along with the birds go some few Tarzans or Man Fridays whose origins are obscure and who are hopefully being wished on to Mauritius.'

Homeless, penniless and unemployed, the Chagos Islanders sank into despair in the slums of Mauritius. The British government paid six hundred and fifty thousand pounds to the Mauritius government for their welfare but nothing to the islanders themselves. Later modest compensation was offered on condition that they gave up their claim to a right to return home. Many refused to do so.

From 1971 Diego Garcia grew into a gigantic and vital component of US military strategy. It was from this base that B-52s bombed Iraq during Operation Desert Storm. In the hunt for Osama bin Laden and for the 2003 Iraq invasion, the base was of pivotal importance; for the American and NATO troops fighting in Afghanistan, it still is today. There is little doubt that nuclear warheads are now kept there. 'Even if the entire Eastern Hemisphere has drop-kicked us,' John Pike, the American founder of Global Security, boasts, 'the US plans to be able to run the planet from Guam and Diego Garcia by 2015.'

As the decades went by, the islanders who had lived long enough became even more determined to seek redress, and more effective at communicating the injustice the British government had inflicted on them. They were lucky that the lawyer they chose to represent them was skilful, patient and persistent. In 2000, after more than thirty years of legal battles, a British court ruled that there had been no legal justification for the removal of the Chagos people from their islands. The court quashed the Immigration Ordinance of thirty years earlier and gave British citizenship to all the islanders. Obstinate till the last, the British government retaliated. In 2004, it passed an order in council countermanding the court ruling, citing a feasibility study it had commissioned claiming that it would be prohibitively expensive to safeguard the islanders from flooding and earthquakes. Hogwash – the islands are physically very similar to the tourist paradises of the Seychelles and

Mauritius their nearest neighbours in the Indian Ocean, and all were spared serious damage in the catastrophic 2004 tsunami. Protecting the islanders was its paramount duty, claimed the British government, to gasps of astonishment and ribald laughter.

An Order in Council is the ultimate British establishment trump card. If ministers and officials have failed to have their way because Parliament and the courts have held them in check, there's always the Queen and her Privy Council of grey beards on standby to rescind a court's decision – to put everything back the way civil servants wanted them in the first place. An Order in Council takes but a trice – over a glass of sherry at Buckingham Palace, Windsor Castle, Sandringham, Balmoral or even Ascot – wherever it pleases Her Majesty. Not many of the islanders and their descendants have had the stamina or longevity to defeat the finely woven weft of British red tape and the decades of legal shenanigans.

Then, in 2006, to the delight and astonishment of the campaigners, the High Court declared the Order in Council illegal. It overruled the Privy Council, restoring its judgment in favour of the islanders. 'The suggestion that a minister can, through the means of an Order in Council, exile a whole population from a British Overseas Territory and claim that he is doing so for the "peace, order and good government" of the territory is to us repugnant.' That's about as forthright as judges ever get. You would think the government would have given up by this time and allowed the Chagos Islanders their pyrrhic victory. Like hell. In October 2008, the Law Lords (now the Supreme Court) overturned the islanders' victory and ruled that none of them could ever return to the islands. Their verdict was a close-run thing: two of the five judges dissented from it. As their last resort the islanders are now preparing their case for the European Court of Human Rights in Strasbourg

To circumvent a possible defeat there, the British government has now come up with a wheeze that is pure *Yes, Minister*. As one of the last acts of the Labour government, Foreign Secretary David Miliband designated the whole British Indian Ocean Territory a Marine Protected Area. We can be sure that, even while details are being finalised, some-where in the small print will be a clause to deny the islanders the right to return lest they harm the precious plankton. I doubt that the Foreign

Office officials lingered long on the paradox of it all: at the very centre of this intended environmental paradise lies the obscenity of Diego Garcia, the top-secret military base bristling with nuclear submarines, nuclear-tipped missiles and probably an arsenal of nuclear weapons. Britain and the United States are now negotiating to exclude Diego Garcia from the Africa Nuclear Weapons Free Zone that all but one of the African countries have signed.

With hindsight, it is easy to see that the British government had always been prepared to fight this legal marathon to the bitter end and beyond, determined to manipulate its foregone conclusion. It knew all along that the Americans would *never* allow the Chagos Islanders to go home – and when did we last say 'boo' to them?

CHAPTER 7

In Bed with Braden

Suddenly, there was to be no more travelling for a while. Desmond asked me to take over *Braden's Week* after its first season. For the next two years my job was to produce this prestigious Saturday-night BBC1 show in front of a live audience. First, I had to get to know the daunting presenter, Bernard Braden.

Bernie, as everyone called him, came to London from Canada in 1949 with his wife Barbara and their three children to try his luck in show business. Son of a nonconformist minister, he was born and brought up in the one-horse town of Kelowna, British Columbia, on the shores of Lake Okanagan. He joined the infant radio station CJOR in Vancouver and quickly made his name as an all-round performer – actor, presenter and singer. The bright lights of Toronto beckoned and there he met Barbara Kelly, aged sixteen. Most unsuitably she had been cast in a mystery play as the Virgin Mary and they married the following year. Together they scored a hit, starring in the serial *John and Judy* on the CBC radio network.

In London, Bernie fell on his feet at once. He was cast as Harold Mitchell in Tennessee Williams's play *A Streetcar Named Desire*, with Vivien Leigh playing the lead and her husband Laurence Olivier directing. Soon the Bradens became stars of BBC Radio. *Breakfast with Braden* and *Bedtime with Braden* made them both household names, high-profile public figures. In June 1950, they featured on the front cover of the *Radio Times*, and in 1951 the BBC gave them their own television show. Barbara added another string to her bow as a much-loved panellist on the top-rated panel game *What's My Line*, with Eamonn Andrews. It ran for twelve years.

Soon after Granada Television went on air in 1956, Bernie was invited to host a chat show for them, *Chelsea at Nine*. His biggest success on

ITV came in 1962 when ATV created *On the Braden Beat.* It was a Saturday-night prime-time magazine show, a mix of showbiz chat, consumer scams and whimsy, with a little music thrown in. Peter Cook and Tim Brooke-Taylor were frequent guests and Jake Thackray a regular singer. The show ran for five years and won a BAFTA award in 1964.

In 1968, Bernie called on Paul Fox, the Controller of BBC1, and offered to transfer his show to the BBC. It was an attractive proposition for Fox, the ideal show to round off his Saturday-night schedule and guaranteed a massive audience by *Match of the Day* which would precede it. Fox decided against asking the Light Entertainment Department to host it. Its head, Tom Sloan, was unsympathetic to hybrid shows like Braden's – part entertainment, part chat. Sloan was a glamour and glitter man. *The Black and White Minstrel Show* and *The Billy Cotton Band Show* were more his cup of tea. The great days of BBC television light entertainment came with shows initiated by Sloan's successor, Bill Cotton Jnr (*Monty Python, Morecambe and Wise* and *The Two Ronnies*).

The Current Affairs Department was another possible home for Braden's show, but Fox sensed, from his time as its head, that the department lacked the showbiz *élan* he required for a popular Saturday-night show. Desmond Wilcox had impressed Fox with his editorial flair and his talent for developing new series for both BBC2 and BBC1. These included several critically applauded *Tuesday Documentary* films that Fox himself had commissioned and a well-regarded factual series for BBC1, *That Monday Morning Feeling.* Within the *Man Alive* series itself Fox spotted glimpses of satire and general mischief that persuaded him that Desmond's team was the best to produce what was now going to be called *Braden's Week.*

Bernie brought with him a seasoned writer/producer called John Lloyd, whom Fox knew to be first rate. Before he left the BBC to freelance he had been deputy editor of the legendary *Tonight* programme, after Donald Baverstock and Alasdair Milne had moved on. He was a pocket-sized Welsh terrier, soft-spoken and shabbily dressed. He drank halves of bitter, smoked incessantly and mumbled his witticisms inaudibly – but he could transform researchers' notes into a polished script with a lucidity, wit and speed that was astonishing to watch. He proposed a radical change to the format that Bernie had brought with him from ITV. Instead of just Bernie talking to camera, Lloyd proposed that two of the researchers should join him on the set, so that there could be interplay between the three of them. The two researchers would report their stories to Bernie in a question-and-answer format. Like most such conventions it was phoney. Lloyd had written the whole script and then divided up the dialogue between the three performers to give it pace. The researchers were only two from a large team behind the scenes and were unlikely to have researched all the stories they presented. That's why, in such programmes, the lawyers preferred our reporters to say 'we' instead of 'I'. John Lloyd's format gave variety and pace to *Braden's Week* which stood it in good stead for a hundred Saturdays over four years and was later to be adopted by *That's Life* and much of the rest of the industry.

The clear favourite for one of these two on-screen-researcher roles was John Pitman, a twenty-eight-year-old seasoned journalist from the *Brighton Evening Argus*. He had learnt his television tradecraft as a researcher on *Man Alive* and he attracted many admirers in the BBC canteen with his witty and scandalous gossip. The second choice was more surprising. Esther Rantzen had studied at Somerville College, Oxford and graduated in English. She had acted with the Oxford University Dramatic Society, joined BBC Radio and soon landed herself a researcher's job on a very elegant and well-produced television series, *Your Witness*. The legal campaigner and author Ludovic Kennedy presented it and Tony Smith, its producer, went on to head the British Film Institute and then Magdalen College, Oxford. Also working on the programme as a researcher was Desmond Wilcox's wife Patsy. She and Esther became great friends and Desmond would sometimes go to the studios to watch the recording and join in the hospitality session afterwards. Desmond took a shine to Esther and offered her an equivalent position on *Man Alive*. She was not good at it. In those days, she was uneasy with ordinary people and uncomfortable tramping the menacing stairs of council blocks alone, where the lifts never worked or, if they did, they stank of urine. But she too had a great gift to amuse in the canteen and she and Desmond had become inseparable. Certainly, Desmond pressed strongly for Esther to be given the second vacancy for an on-screen researcher. But both Bernie and John Lloyd were realists and neither tried to block his plan. In any case, they both believed that she had potential and might be rather good.

When *Braden's Week* went on air it was an immediate success. John and Esther established a great rapport with Bernie and with each other. The series was far more journalistic and less showbiz-orientated than *On the Braden Beat* had been – and Bernie would have liked. But, its real-life stories of council cock-ups and consumer rip-offs played well with the audience and the press began to take notice. Another change from the ITV show was a regular slot for Harold Williamson, who had made a name for himself interviewing primary-school children on radio. Now he gladly agreed to do the same for *Braden's Week*. Another addition to the original show were revue-style spots, to separate the mores somber items, in which Chris Munds played the foil to delicious Hilary Pritchard – blonde, big boobs, long legs and a very sexy voice. The pair of them enacted gags so corny that they became a cult with our viewers. Our singer, Jake Thackray, was a most unusual personality who had also been a regular on the ITV show. He was a diffident and craggy Yorkshireman with dark good looks, the son of a policeman and educated at a Jesuit boarding school. He had taught in France and become a disciple of France's much loved satirical singer, Georges Brassens. Jake claimed to hate being a 'performing dick', but each week, accompanying himself on a rather battered guitar, he sang wonderfully rude songs for the new show.

After completing the first run of the series, John Lloyd decided that he didn't want to produce the show any more although he was happy to go on writing it – thank goodness, because I was now put in charge. The show had grown so much in scope that it was a punishing assignment. Because *Braden's Week* broadcast late on Saturday nights, it was recorded earlier in the evening, largely for the convenience of the invited studio audience. By the time all the clearing up had been completed and the artists and audience packed off home, it was usually so late that the team would stay on in the hospitality room at the Television Centre to watch the transmission. Then there would be the inevitable post mortem until long after the chimes of midnight. On Monday morning we all had to be back in the office preparing for the next week's programme. That was the relentless pattern for six months of consecutive Saturdays, with just one week off to make way for the *Eurovision Song Contest.*

Bernie was not easy to handle. He was old enough to be father to most of us and a big star before any of us had reached our teens. Like most people, he had as many bad ideas as good ones, but he required the most tactful persuasion and endless patience when he dug his heels in. Sometimes he would announce that he had invited some unheard-of lady singer to appear on the show. In fairness he was under constant pressure from song pluggers. Worse, his wide circle of showbiz friends kept goading him, reminding him that *Braden's Week* was his show. Once I relented. I felt that I had said no once too often. A frightful Canadian matron warbled while the studio audience fidgeted and the production team squirmed. At home everyone must have switched off. I never made that mistake again. The upside of Bernie's showbiz life was that he occasionally delivered stars who would otherwise never have agreed to appear on the show. Peter Sellers did a wonderfully witty and barbed piece for us about racial discrimination in the workplace. Armed with job advertisements from the evening paper, he phoned up pretending to be an Indian looking for a job – slightly moderating his 'Goodness Gracious Me' accent. When he was told that the vacancy had been filled, he would call again as a posh Englishman and, on several occasions, he was invited for an interview. The finale was, of course, over the top. He called back as an Indian to complain that his English friend had been called for an interview while he had been told there were no jobs available. He burst into hysterical tears and left the woman taking his call all of a-fluster. The serious point was not missed by the employers Sellers spoke to. They were furious – and we had broken a BBC rule by not declaring that Peter Sellers was calling on behalf of the BBC. This was a time when pressure groups promoting racial equality were on the move. Our item was grist to the mill.

My brief was to toughen up the investigative reporting and build the audience. We made three immediately visible changes to the first year's format. The plan was to populate the rather empty studio set and speed up the pace of delivery. First we invited Bernie's old friend, one-time senior radio announcer Ronald Fletcher, to read out the silly stories and misprints from the week's papers. He had played a similar deadpan role for Bernie on his radio shows. We also brought our most tenacious researcher to join John and Esther on camera. I had found Sean O'Reilly at the Oldham Press Agency when I was a *Man Alive* producer. The agency made a good living selling news and feature stories from the Manchester area to the national newspapers. Sometimes the narrative had to be buffed up a bit to make it saleable and Sean, with his strong Lancashire accent, was an endless source of comical stories about the method and madness of it all. He made life at the news agency sound like a present-day *Scoop.* With his long hair he looked about twelve years old and he was cheeky with it, bringing a hint of Northern anarchy to an otherwise rather Home Counties show. The grit in the oyster.

For the same reason we brought in singers Alex Glasgow from Tyneside and Iris Williams, the black contralto, from Cardiff to share the music spot with Jake Thackray. He was finding the weekly grind too onerous. Iris started life in a children's home and won a scholarship to the Royal Welsh College of Music and Drama. After *Braden's Week,* and her success in the charts, she was given her own television show and went on to international stardom singing in five concerts with Bob Hope. Alex Glasgow had written the songs and music for the superb BBC *Wednesday Play* by Alan Plater *Close the Coal House Door* . He had also composed and sung the theme song for another memorable TV play, *When the Boat Comes In.* His trite, revolutionary, hard-left politics were the less convincing because he spent the rehearsal period trying to ram them down the throat of anyone who would listen. In fairness, he could see the funny side:

> O, my daddy is a left-wing intellectual,
> Believes in full equality for men,
> But you should have heard the fuss
> When I failed the 11-plus,
> He packed me off to Eton there and then.

And that Eton education proved effectual
And my daddy is so very proud of me;
I've at last achieved some fame,
I've become a household name
As a right-wing homosexual on TV.

His ringing tenor voice, combined with his fine guitar accompaniment, gave a savage power to his lyrics. The first song he performed for us, 'The Mary Baker City Mix' was a sarcastic assault on civic planning – the wanton destruction of whole communities to make way for tower blocks:

Take your Mary Baker City Mix and mix yourself a city to a plan:
Take the super giant pack and make a few identi-cities while you can.
And while you sterilise and standardise and cauterise the
                                        ancient city's ills,
You'll find the architects and planners have all saved themselves
                                        a cottage in the hills.

It exactly set the tone I wanted: opinionated, pertinent, persuasive and palatable. A leading article disguised as a song.

We then cooked up a second weekly music slot. I think it was John Pitman's idea and he certainly did most of the donkey work. Each week we would invite a pop-star of yesteryear to come in and sing the hit which had made them famous. There is no doubt that there was a sadistic tinge to this plan but the exposure was irresistible to has-beens and their agents. Our musical director, Syd Dale, was superb at orchestrating the songs for his small backing group and coaxing the best out of the singers, many of whom had not performed in public for years. My favourite was Jessie Matthews. She became a major star in the 1930s because of the lead role she played in a Rodgers and Hart stage musical, later made into the hugely popular movie *Evergreen.* She then sank into obscurity, only to rise again as Mrs Dale in BBC Radio's long-running soap *Mrs Dale's Diary.* Jessie agreed to come on *Braden's Week* to perform the song from the film that had made her famous three decades earlier. The redoubtable sixty-three-year-old gamely entered into the spirit of things, vamping as camp as they come:

Over my shoulder goes one care!
Over my shoulder go two cares!
Why should I cry? It's blue above,
I'm free at last and I'm in love . . .

The heart of *Braden's Week* was its exposés. Some of the best ones came from our viewers but we also sought them out for ourselves – rip-offs and scams that were both good yarns and salutary lessons. In the fifty or so editions of the show under my stewardship, there were a couple of dozen serious complaints that called for the help of the BBC lawyers. It was fortunate that the BBC had libel and defamation insurance with the Prudential. Later it cancelled the premium to save money; then it was humiliatingly forced to cave in on several high-profile legal actions where it was in the right but couldn't afford the fight to prove it. Because *Braden's Week* was so high-profile, to do nothing was really not an option if you were exposed or ridiculed on the programme. The chances were that your friends and colleagues had seen the item – and maybe, even, had a good laugh at your expense. So, if your complaint had been rejected by me and then my bosses, *amour propre* dictated filing a writ against the BBC and telling everyone that you had done so.

It was not only our serious items that attracted litigation. John Pitman found a classic *Braden's Week* yarn in a West Midlands newspaper. An advertisement for car tyres incongruously featured a young lady with enormous boobs. He noticed that the down-market editions of the newspaper revealed practically everything but the posher ones had masked out most of the décolletage. Much laughter greeted our crudely animated caption card, jerkily raising and lowering the cleavage as John related the story. We were promptly sued for libel by the boyfriend of the girl with the big boobs. To our surprise the BBC lawyers took the matter seriously and early in the week following the broadcast John and I found ourselves crouched over a viewing machine with the girl, her astrakhan-coated, aggressive boyfriend and two barristers, one for them and one for us. Their barrister started it. He tried to suppress his giggles and pulled out a large spotted handkerchief. Then *our* learned friend started too. By the end of the item they both had tears running down their cheeks. They were practically rolling in the aisle. We never heard any more from the West Midlands couple. I hope the irate boyfriend and his lady were given a discount on the astronomical fees their distinguished QC was reputed to command.

The problem with litigation was the amount of my production time that it took drafting reports for the BBC lawyers and then hot-footing it across London to the High Court to brief opulently compensated and be-wigged barristers. Often they had only minutes to master their briefs before opposing a writ of restraint put forward by another expensive barrister on behalf of a client who supposed that *Braden's Week* was about to defame him. These hearings were nearly always timed by the plaintiffs for late Friday afternoon, in an attempt (as we saw it) to sabotage the next day's programme. Fortunately, the judges got wise to this tactic and became increasingly reluctant to issue writs of restraint at all.

One exposé that brought us a lot of press coverage originated with my own production assistant, Anne, niece of Val Doonican. She had heard from a friend that a factory in north London was relabelling a vast consignment of corned beef for one of the major supermarket chains. The tins were so rusty that many of them were leaking and it had become necessary to issue the labelling staff with face masks. The story checked out. We bought tins of the corned beef off the shelves of the supermarket chain all over Britain and sent them for analysis. A large number were found to be unfit for human consumption. The writ of restraint didn't get very far because our evidence was impeccable. On the Saturday morning of the broadcast, I received a telephone call at home from one of the supermarket's bosses. He was quite conciliatory, accepting that we had caught his company with its trousers down. Just one request, he pleaded. Could we please refrain from naming his supermarket chain? I must understand that food retailing was a very competitive business and that to lose a couple of market-share points would be disastrous. Worth a try, I thought. To do so, I pointed out, would wrongly implicate all the other supermarket chains. Our purpose was to discourage sloppy hygiene not prevent the sale of corned beef. Somehow, though, I have never fancied the stuff since.

The next big story we tackled had connections far too close to home for comfort. We started receiving a very large number of complaints about a travel firm called Clarksons Holidays which specialised in cheap package holidays to Spain. The story was familiar and later became the stuff of comedy sketches. Holidaymakers would arrive to find the hotel they had booked wasn't yet built or the plumbing hadn't been done – or some such variant – which indicated that the package-holiday company in Britain was, at the very least, cutting corners. The viewers who had complained had received unbelievably aggressive replies threatening legal action. We broadcast a short item on this new twist to the maxim that the customer is always right. It prompted an avalanche of letters from other viewers all claiming similar experiences. We set about a major investigation.

In the office immediately above ours was the *Holiday* programme. Its purpose, of course, was to report on a wide range of holidays with travel tips and consumer advice thrown in. It was an unashamedly escapist series, winning a substantial audience in the cold winter months – lots of bikinis and Caribbean surf – much of the content more aspirational than practical for all but the wealthiest of viewers. One of *Holiday*'s great attractions was that it was relatively cheap to produce because the travel companies paid a large proportion of the production crew's travel and accommodation. The danger to the programme's editorial integrity is obvious. In those days, to buy peak-time advertising on the ITV network cost around £550 a second, or £165,000 for just ten screenings of a thirty-second commercial – nearly two million pounds in today's money. On BBC1 the same effect could be achieved for free. Indeed potential customers were much more likely to trust the BBC's Cliff Michelmore or Frank Bough than they were to believe a commercial run incessantly on ITV. Naturally, all the travel companies vied for a slot on *Holiday* and the producer was fêted, flattered and flown first class until he didn't know whether he was coming or going – and that's putting it very charitably. He came to see me in a rage. What the hell did we think we were doing attacking Clarksons? Holidays were his business.

We were to lay off. *Holiday*, he told me angrily, had recently featured Clarksons and it made the BBC look ridiculous if another programme was contradicting his. Of course, his outburst made us all the more determined to expose Clarksons. We were invigorated by his attitude and the arrogance of the company's refusal to consider redress for the little people who had saved hard for their holidays.

What we should have guessed was that Clarksons was financially over-extended and that its tactics were designed to avoid paying back money it didn't have. It was carrying over a million passengers a year and industry sources put its loss at £4 per passenger. The last thing Clarksons needed was bad publicity on *Braden's Week*. This time there was no writ. A much more upsetting tactic was employed. On the Saturday we were planning to broadcast I received a telephone call in the control gallery at Television Centre where we were rehearsing. Could I come down to reception? It was the Chief Executive of Clarksons. 'I implore you not to broadcast your exposé. It will finish off the company and it will finish me off too.' We did broadcast but the company managed to stagger on for a couple more years until the three-day week and the OPEC oil boycott finally polished it off in the middle of the holiday season. Forty thousand people were left stranded overseas. Legislation was eventually introduced to ensure that victims like those who had complained about Clarksons* were in future to be eligible for compensation from the travel industry. What I didn't know at the time was that the sister of the Clarksons' Chief Executive worked for the BBC in the same building as I did. For years afterwards I was subjected to her understandably reproachful looks in the corridors and in the canteen. The producer of the *Holiday* programme and I remained on distinctly distant terms too.

The third year of *Braden's Week*, my second, was its first in colour. BBC2 had launched in colour three years earlier in 1967 but it had been a massive job to convert all the studios and ancillary equipment for the

---

* Clarksons Holidays was taken over by Court Line in 1972 for £1 and a 'subsidy' of £3.4 million from its parent company to cover the projected loss. Court Line went bankrupt on 15 August 1974. Clarksons went into voluntary liquidation the next day.

much bigger BBC1. Bernie and I had an on-going battle about the new studio set which was a simple rostrum with four desks, beautifully lit, set against a black cyclorama. The presenters, in all their finery, looked wonderful on the studio monitors but Bernie kept on complaining, 'You can't perform humour against black.' What I didn't properly take into account was that the look of the show was very bleak in black and white – and that was how most of our viewers still had to watch it. He was right but I was obstinate – a bit slow to give in – after the disaster with his matronly Canadian singer.

Colour gave a new confidence to *Braden's Week*. Even the vox-pops filmed in a street market came to life in a surprisingly festive way. Frankie Howerd came in to plug the feature-film version of his television series, *Up Pompeii!*, singing the theme song in full Roman-centurion costume against a rather corny-looking hardboard Colosseum from the Props Department. He was a nightmare – tantrums and slanging matches with the studio director. There was hardly time to rehearse the rest of the show, so determined was he to ensure that his spot was perfect. I wondered whether this was why Frankie had been out of work for so long before *Up Pompeii!* Or perhaps he had learnt the hard way that, in show business, a lifetime's good manners and consideration for other artists does you no good at all.

As the third series reached the end of its run, I complacently took the view that it had reached its cruising altitude. It seemed to be that there wasn't an awful lot more to do. Bernie never changed but John Pitman and Esther had emerged as stars. Esther loved it. She played to the studio audience, ad-libbed new jokes that no one had heard in rehearsal. The press had cottoned on to her and she was big in the tabloids and the Sunday supplements. John really detested all the public acclaim, at least that's what he said. He certainly seemed as embarrassed by it as Sean O'Reilly, who could never again hold his head up high with his tough and cynical news-agency colleagues. Sean, they sneered, had sold out. Maybe John secretly loved the acclaim but had taken heed of its fearsome perils and chosen to keep his vanity firmly in the closet.

And then Bernie bowled a googly, just when the team was at its most exhausted, yearning for the summer break. He told me that he had received an offer from the advertising agency for Stork margarine to appear in a high-profile series of TV commercials. He said he couldn't refuse the colossal sums they were offering him – and he wouldn't. Now it is true that Bernie lived very expensively. Barbara and he had a reputation for superlative parties at his house in Regent's Park; and Bernie was instantly recognisable about town, driving between night-clubs, cabarets and fashionable West End restaurants in his red Lincoln Continental convertible. On the other hand, *Braden's Week* paid him what seemed to me fabulous fees. I knew that we were on a collision course. The BBC view was that he was presenting a consumer pro-gramme and therefore it was totally unacceptable for him to appear in a commercial. I tried to persuade Bernie that the reason Stork margarine was offering such a gargantuan sum was *because* he was the host of a peak-time BBC consumer programme. I tried to coax him to think of the Stork offer like a pension, to be cashed in when eventually *Braden's Week* was taken off the air. The show was highly regarded by BBC1 Controller, Paul Fox, so that day of reckoning could be many years away if only Bernie said no to the commercial now. His view was that the BBC only paid him for half the year; he was a freelance, and any such restriction placed on him by the BBC would be an unfair curtailment of his need to earn a living. Stalemate. Desmond was always a good deal more persuasive than I but neither of us could make any headway at all. By then the whole team knew of the problem. They were angry with Bernie. Their own jobs were in jeopardy because there was no way the BBC would back down. Everyone knew that Paul Fox would sacrifice the programme rather than the principle – without a second thought. It was an eyeball-to-eyeball confrontation. Suddenly Bernie blinked first and the crisis was over. There would be no Stork margarine commercial. The summer break arrived and all was set for a fourth series in the autumn. Only Desmond knew that I had other plans for myself.

CHAPTER 8

Birth of a Nation

Enchanted by my first experience of the tropics in Mauritius three years earlier, I had spent a couple of holidays in India and Ceylon and made friends with many documentary-makers, newspaper journalists and radio producers. There was no television then, apart from an experimental channel in Delhi. I became intrigued by the colossal potential of broadcasting to propel the subcontinent into the twenty-first century. One Saturday evening, during the *Braden's Week* supper break at the Television Centre, I was idly looking at job vacancies on the noticeboard. I wasn't looking for a job, just filling in time until the studio audience arrived and we could get on with recording that night's show. An advertisement caught my eye offering travel and study bursaries to broadcasters of Commonwealth countries. Normally, I discovered, bursaries were awarded to young radio producers in Africa and the Indian subcontinent who came to London for training with the BBC. However, the trust administrator tipped me the wink that I stood a good chance if I submitted a high-quality proposal because the trust felt there weren't enough British candidates taking advantage of the awards to visit developing countries; most wanted to visit Australia – probably with a view to starting a new life there after they had completed their bursaries – a cut-price way of job hunting.

I wrote a proposal saying that I was particularly interested in an Indian experiment to transmit educational programmes directly into some of the poorest parts of the country by satellite. I added that I would also like to look at developments in educational broadcasting in Pakistan, Nepal and Ceylon. I was awarded a bursary – six months to travel the subcontinent, all expenses paid and, as it turned out, still on the BBC payroll. Yet this seemed the craziest career move ever. Here was I, producer of one of the BBC's highest profile programmes, opting out of it all. As it was later to turn out it was rather a good move but I was surprised at the time how laid back Desmond was about letting me go. On the other hand, I was in his good books because I had worked pretty hard for him over the previous seven years.

Within weeks of my arrival, India and Pakistan were involved in an all-out war. West Pakistan had been savagely repressing the more numerous people of East Pakistan. Millions of refugees were pouring over the border into West Bengal, one of India's poorest states. Sheikh Mujibur Rahman, East Pakistan's charismatic political leader, had won the all-Pakistan elections by a landslide. He should, of course, have been declared prime minister. Instead, he was immediately thrown into gaol. Prime Minister Indira Gandhi made a whistle-stop tour of world capitals, drumming up support for India's planned intervention to return the refugees to their homeland. Less public was the agenda to establish an independent democratic country to replace East Pakistan.

Mrs Gandhi's cause was much strengthened by the first major pop-music event to stir the international conscience, the Concert for Bangladesh. It was the brainwave of the Indian sitar player, Ravi Shankar, a Bengali himself, and his friend George Harrison of the Beatles. The Fab Four had gone their separate ways by then and Paul McCartney declined to take part because he was still smarting over the bust-up. John Lennon at first agreed to perform but when the others told him they didn't want Yoko Ono on stage, he sulked off too. Ravi Shankar, George Harrison and the ever-cheerful Ringo Starr were joined at Madison Square Garden by two megastars, Bob Dylan and Eric Clapton. Forty thousand New Yorkers came to witness and participate in this extraordinarily moving performance, broadcast live throughout the world.

Everyone knew that war between India and Pakistan was inevitable. Either side could have started the war; both were spoiling for a fight. The Pakistan air force attacked first, bombing five airfields. India's vast land, sea and air forces responded with all-out war. Massive assaults were mounted against West Pakistan and, in the east, Indian troops assailed the besieged Pakistan army. It was surrounded, outnumbered and cut off from escape by air or by sea. The war was all over in twelve days. The general commanding the army in East Pakistan was humiliatingly forced to sign the surrender document at a public ceremony witnessed by the world's media and a jubilant crowd of liberated civilians, tens of thousands strong. For twenty-eight months, the Indians held ninety-three thousand Pakistani soldiers as prisoners of war, bargaining chips in the peace talks. The dishonour has never been forgotten.

When the war started I was in one of the more remote parts of Nepal, helping an Indian film director with his documentary. Extraordinarily, there was an English-language newspaper available – CROWN PRINCE EATS FIRST RICE proclaimed the headline.* On the back page, beneath the gardening news, there was a tiny sub-heading: 'India declares war on Pakistan'. Time, I thought, to get a move on. No one knew then how long the war would last or how devastating it would be – but one thing was for sure: seats on aeroplanes would become increasingly hard to come by. I hurriedly hitched a lift on a small plane back to Kathmandu Airport where stranded American tourists hysterically screamed and shouted, 'You better believe it! You gotta get us out of here. We wanna go home!' I found out that an Indian Airlines plane would be passing through from Calcutta to evacuate its staff to Delhi. Quietly, so as not to start an American stampede, I inveigled myself aboard. 'Important BBC chap, have to be in Delhi to report the courage of India's valiant military forces to the outside world.' We flew beneath enemy radar, low through the towering Himalayan valleys. It was perfect weather – a spectacular, if hair-raising flight. Delhi Airport bristled with anti-aircraft guns – not a passenger plane in sight. It turned out that they had all been flown south to Madras for safekeeping. Foreign airlines had prudently set off for home.

Although I was technically off-duty as a producer, I was drawn to the action at All India Radio, buttressed with sandbags under its transmitter right in the centre of the capital. In the previous war with Pakistan, this station had been bombed. Now I had a lot of friends working there. The

---

* The baby was Crown Prince Dipendra. Thirty years later, after dinner in the royal palace in Kathmandu, he gunned down members of the royal family including his parents, King Birendra and Queen Aiswarya, before turning the gun on himself. On the death of his father, he succeeded to the throne but remained in a coma throughout his three-day reign.

news and current affairs staff were enthusiastically pushing the Indian line. So did the newspapers. I collected the front pages of the *Times of India* for the twelve days of the war, and a couple of months later, assembled the front pages of Karachi's leading newspaper *Dawn* – and laid them side by side. Each of the newspapers claimed that its side was winning – on every one of the twelve days of the war. Indian successes were suppressed by *Dawn*. Breakthroughs by the Pakistanis were ignored by the *Times of India*. Diametrically opposed interpretations of basic facts were offered on the editorial pages. So news of the surrender of East Pakistan was, not surprisingly, a terrible shock in West Pakistan – now the only Pakistan. Had I ever failed as a television producer and ended up teaching media studies – a nightmare that many of my colleagues shared with me – what better background for a lecture on political propaganda.

A special programme covering the war was broadcast each night on the new television station that then only served Delhi and the surrounding countryside. It was ideal for the middle-class political junkies of the capital but rather perplexing for a farming audience more accustomed to instructional programmes on how to dig a tube well. The centrepiece of the evening's viewing was an English-language programme called *Panorama*, just like the BBC's flagship current-affairs programme. Melville de Mello was the perfectly typecast anchor, an Indian Walter Cronkite to the tee. As the rousing military music rounded off the programme, de Mello concluded dramatically with the stirring exhortation, 'Chin up, chaps.' I am afraid I laughed. Then I turned round and saw the sea of shocked patriotic faces staring at me. 'Sorry,' I mumbled. 'Very sorry.'

Back in Bombay a blackout of every single one of the millions of windows was being strictly enforced. There were aggressive vigilantes out and about. Cars had their headlights masked just as they were in Britain during the Second World War. It all seemed a bit daft, since Pakistan International Airways had been flying into Bombay for years, using instrument landing. Did the Pakistan air force really not know how to find the city without a clear view of the necklace of streetlights that decorate Marine Drive? There were terrible casualties when the two armies confronted each other on the borders of East and West Pakistan but, in the comfort and comparative safety of south Bombay, the whole event seemed distinctly *Dad's Army*. All that was missing were the goggle-eyed gas marks that used to terrify me as a child. Old codgers and boy cadets nervously clutching ancient Lee-Enfield rifles were expected to repel an enemy equipped with American M16 fighter bombers, not an hour's flying time away.

Most unusually in time of war, the senior officers, on each side of the conflict, knew one other. They had trained and raised many a toast together in the officers' mess at Sandhurst, Portsmouth and Cranwell. In Calcutta, I bumped into a BBC radio engineer who had been sent from London to facilitate the news correspondent's radio dispatches. He had been listening in, on the old British army radio frequency, to the military action as India invaded Pakistan. Too many people were talking at once. Suddenly the BBC engineer heard the commander of the Pakistan forces address his counterpart on the Indian side, in impeccable Sandhurst English. 'My dear fellow, I would be most obliged if you would switch to another frequency.' 'By all means, old chap,' responded his opposite number. 'Roger over and out.' When the Indian navy captured a Pakistani battleship off the Indian coast, the two naval commanders were filmed embracing each other on the bridge like long-lost brothers, which, in a sense, they were.

My eccentric Scottish friend, James, had lived in India all his working life and spoke a smattering of several of its languages. He was most mysterious about his past but I gleaned that he had planted tea in Assam and mischievously denounced the American Peace Corps in Ceylon as spies, causing them to be thrown out of the island. He had some most undesirable friends. Among them was Richard, a vain young Australian who was later sacked as a newsreader by Hong Kong Television after drunkenly predicting the first-ever snowstorm, live on air. The three of us decided, I can't remember quite why, to visit the newly liberated country of Bangladesh.

Richard had Communist Party connections in the Bombay under-world, much disapproved of by the politically very conservative James. Somehow Richard persuaded his political chums to give him a visa for the new country. So it was only James and I who had to brave the Bangladesh Deputy High Commission in Calcutta *en route* for Dacca. The place was packed with journalists from all over the world, clamouring for visas. Many were British, using racially insulting language that would have got them locked up back home. A harassed Deputy High Commissioner, just appointed by the new country of Bangladesh, tried to calm them. But he had no staff: the government of Pakistan had always given the best jobs to West Pakistanis and they had all fled. His Excellency was at his wits' end and really grateful when I offered to be his typist. But there was a major snag. The only rubber stamp available for the visas said 'Government of Pakistan' and that, of course, could not be used. So the Deputy High Commissioner decided that he would have to write all the visas out in longhand. It was getting late. James and I were becoming irritated with the hacks as they continued to be a disgrace. It may not have been the decent thing to do but we did it. I offered the Deputy High Commissioner our two passports first and he laboriously wrote our visas into them. As soon as he had finished, we thanked him and disappeared. 'Serves the bastards right,' we thought. My only sympathy was for the harassed and decent diplomat we left in their loutish care.

Dum Dum Airport wasn't built for tourists and it hardly acknow-ledges their requirements even today. Ours was to be the first civilian plane into Dacca Airport. The bomb craters there had been more or less patched up. We sat, waiting for take-off to the new country, wondering what the hold-up was. Suddenly a van screamed across the tarmac. Trouble, we thought, big trouble. Two Australian diplomatic heavies jumped out of the vehicle and hurriedly loaded the aircraft hold with booze for their High Commission in Dacca. Sod the starving millions waiting for their help in a notionally teetotal Muslim country.

Because the Pakistan army had surrendered so speedily, Dacca itself had been largely spared and there were one or two half-decent hotels. Mine must have been one of the best because who should enter the lift on the sixth floor but Lieutenant General Jagjit Singh Aurora, General Officer Commanding the Indian forces. This was the man who had led the army to victory and taken the surrender of the Pakistani army only a few days before. I was nearest the lift buttons, in awe. 'Press the titty, old chap,' ordered the general.

Dacca was awash with fortune-seekers. Perhaps the least attractive was John Stonehouse, Postmaster General in the recently defeated Labour government. Officially he was there to host a sumptuous War on Want lunch – as it turned out, for a load of foreign bigwigs who may have wanted lunch but certainly didn't need it. But his prime concern, I learnt, was to sabotage the chances of one of Britain's top-security printing firms, De La Rue, from landing the contract to print banknotes and stamps for the new country. Evidently he had some interest in a rival security printer. He was lobbying to have De La Rue blacklisted and denied entry to the country. This seemed to be the beginnings of a juicy scandal so I passed the story to my BBC colleagues back in London. Nothing came of it at the time, but not much later, Stonehouse did a disappearing trick. He left his towel and flip-flops on a beach, hoping everyone would think he had gone for a swim and drowned. He was on the run for years and ended up, rather satisfactorily, in gaol.

By now James, Richard and I had managed to obtain rooms at the exclusive Dacca Club on the racecourse. It was important to us because Sheikh Mujibur Rahman was due to fly in the next day to greet his people there. On the eve of this momentous event, to which all of Bangladesh seemed to be making its way, we were invited to dinner at the club by one of its senior members, Fakhruddin Ahmed.* Our table was close to the bar which was noisy and getting noisier. The cause was a massive Indian army officer in filthy battle fatigues. He hadn't shaved for days and he stank to high heaven. He was clearly one of the Indian Special Forces team who had been training the freedom fighters and he was very drunk. He approached our host, whipped out an enormous revolver and held it to the side of his head. 'Mr Fakhruddin Ahmed,' he slurred, 'you are getting too fat dining with foreigners.' Nannies, when I was small, were supposed to prepare you for most eventualities of life,

---

* Dr Fakhruddin Ahmed served for twenty years at the World Bank and was appointed Governor of the Bangladesh Bank in 2001. He was Chief Adviser of Bangladesh (head of the interim caretaker government) from 2007–9.

but not this. If you are eating dinner and suddenly your host's brains are splattered all over your plate, what do you do? Carry on as if nothing has happened and hope that you are not the next one to go? Leap to your feet indignantly shouting, 'Stop that, I tell you?' Someone silently appeared from the shadows and quietly persuaded the drunken soldier away. James, Richard and I exchanged glances. 'Lor, love a duck!' is what nanny would have said.

Dawn the next day and the racecourse appeared already to be full beyond overflowing. A hundred thousand people, a million, it was impossible to judge. And such patience – the leader of the nation was not expected for hours. The three of us from Bombay faced an urgent problem. There was a beautiful VIP and press enclosure but we had no passes and no right to them either. And if push came to shove we knew we were no match for an excited crowd of impassioned Bangladeshis. The only solution was to forge our own passes and hope for the best. Fortunately I had some BBC stationery and a portable typewriter with me. I typed out some bureaucratic gobbledegook on three slips of paper, one for each of us, and signed them loftily, 'Huw Wheldon, Managing Director BBC Television', as indeed he was at the time. With an English coin and some carbon paper, I made three passport photos look as if they had been officially embossed. However, what made my passes look really authentic were the brass eyes and red-tagged lapel strings I extracted from the cartons of the three White Horse whisky bottles we had purchased at the duty-free shop at Dum Dum Airport.

From the bar in the Dacca Club we heard the plane circling low overhead, bearing the triumphant leader home. James, Richard and I set out for the press enclosure, proudly wearing our homemade passes. Security officers saluted and admitted us. Like everyone else in the new nation, we were in festive mood. How quickly in the subcontinent is sorrow set aside and *joie de vivre* restored. None of the three of us foreigners was quite sober as we waited with the multitude, but Richard was in boisterous mood. The crowd chatted quietly, a low buzz of excitement spreading as the plane started its final descent into the airport, just a few miles away. Suddenly Richard raised his right arm in a victory salute and bellowed '*Joi Bangla*' (Long Live Bangladesh).

The crowd let out a gigantic roar in response: '*Joi Bangla! Joi Bangla! Joi Bangla!*'

Richard, an actor *manqué* if ever there was one, delighted in the effect. James and I were furious with him. Supposing the crowd discovered we were not ambassadors of great nations but impostors having a good time? I don't like big crowds and I particularly didn't want this massive one not to like me. 'Just shut up, Richard, for God's sake,' James and I snarled. Fortunately attention moved to the motorcade as it approached from the airport. And there he was, garlanded, standing in an open car – the founding father of the new nation, the first Prime Minister of Bangladesh, Sheikh Mujibur Rahman. Complete and utter silence fell. Even the birds were silent. A gigantic and overwhelming mass of humanity gathered to hear its adored leader – and listened without a sound. He began to speak. He had no microphone and he did not need one. When he was done, his audience melted silently and contentedly away. Bangladesh was born.

The next day we set off as tourists for Chittagong and Cox's Bazaar. James knew the area from his days as a tea planter. We would stay in the Circle Officer's bungalow, he said. Somehow he fixed it and soon we were settling into the sort of comfort the British had always provided for themselves if not always for everybody else. The next morning my scrambled egg was interrupted by the sounds of automatic rifle fire. I was alone in the dining room. Through the window I could see a convoy of expensive cars and motorcycles racing towards me, Kalashnikovs blazing into the sky. The young men came bursting into the dining room. They paid little attention to me. They were obviously Mukti Bahini, the Bengali freedom fighters who had battled so fiercely alongside the Indian army. To my inexperienced eye they looked bloody dangerous.

At that moment James made his entrance. He summed up the situation and thundered at the intruders that immortal line from Goldilocks and the Three Bears, 'Who's been eating *my* porridge?' The guerrillas backed against the wall deferentially, even nervously, too young to recognise the technique of British bluff. James had served in the Indian army and was a master of it. 'Very sorry, uncle,' said their leader. 'We'll take our food after you.' They had come to reward their own valour with help-yourself free government breakfasts – the start of a three-day picnic celebrating their new nation. The vehicles required for this expedition seemed to have been acquired from diplomatic sources but we did not enquire. We bade them a cheerful farewell, not knowing then that they would come to our rescue so fortuitously within the next couple of days.

It was James who had the bright idea. 'Let's go to Burma!' By now we had reached the town of Teknaf on a peninsular, literally at the end of the road. We were on the southernmost tip of Bangladesh. To the west of us was the Bay of Bengal, to the east the two-mile-wide Naaf River. Beyond it was Burma, enticing, mysterious, the road to Mandalay. I really wanted to visit the country, as did Richard and James. But there were several snags. First we had no Burmese visas. Pleased as I was with my earlier efforts at forgery, I knew I could not hoodwink jumpy border guards with a homemade entry permit. Secondly, we knew that those who do have a genuine visa may only enter the country through its capital, Rangoon. 'Let's go and talk to the smugglers,' suggested James. With some difficulty we located their spokesman who was equivocal. 'Come back tomorrow morning and we'll give you an answer.' I was not convinced. There was a third difficulty for me. James and Richard were free spirits but I was a BBC producer. Might this jape not lead to an international incident that would embarrass the British government and damage the BBC? And what if they seized our boatmen, locked them up and threw away the key?

The smuggler was beaming. Overnight feelers had been put out in Burma. We could go. Not wishing to seem a coward, I cravenly concurred. As if this sort of thing happened every day, our boat was ready, complete with two-man crew. It was half miniature Arab dhow and half dug-out tree trunk. It was propelled by a gigantic sail – there was no engine. We set off across the river at a cracking pace, accelerating towards Burma with the help of a strong westerly wind. As we neared what turned out to be our destination, a village on the riverbank, we could see a man smartly dressed in a white sarong and shirt waiting for us on the jetty. He helped us tie up the boat and clamber ashore. He spoke remarkably good English. 'I am the customs officer. You must come to Immigration.' Immigration was a little wooden hut about twenty yards away. In it sat a solitary officer, also smartly dressed, with good English. (Where on earth did they learn their English and why?) There was no paperwork cluttering the immigration officer's desk. Since it was illegal to immigrate here, or indeed to emigrate, his workload was manifestly no more than the smallest interruption to his real life.

'Sir, we have come to visit your country of which we have heard so many good things,' we simpered, handing him our passports. There was quite a long pause while he studied them. 'You may not enter Burma. Permission is refused. One, you may only enter Burma at Rangoon. Two, this Maungdaw province is a militarily secure area. Three, you have no entry permits in your passports. However, since you are here you may stay for lunch.' With a sigh of relief from all of us I tentatively asked one favour. 'Sir, could you at least stamp our passports, otherwise no one will believe we have been here?' 'You haven't,' he replied conclusively. The customs officer beckoned us to follow him. He led us to a little restaurant near by, probably the only one in the village. It was deserted except for one table that was beautifully laid – obviously for the three of us. Thanks to the smugglers, the Burmese knew we were coming and, blessed sweet people, they had prepared a feast for us – with rice wine and beer.

Since we were not really in Burma it seemed a pity to have to leave. However, we knew we must not overstay our welcome, so we embarked for our return river-crossing to Bangladesh. The west wind was even stronger now and our boatmen's efforts against it were in vain. After half an hour of frantic paddling, we were still within spitting distance of the riverbank – still on the Burma side. Our boatmen were tiring fast. Suddenly, as if from nowhere, we heard the roar of a motorboat and heading towards us we saw the Mukti Bahini boys, still armed to the teeth. 'Can we help you, uncles?' It was a powerful coastguard boat they had acquired. In a quarter of an hour we were towed back and set ashore among the delighted smugglers of Teknaf. As the freedom fighters accelerated off across the river, they waved us goodbye. Richard raised his right arm and shouted loudly enough to drown the engine noise, '*Joi Bangla!*' James and I just looked at each other and shrugged.

CHAPTER 9

Man Alive and Kicking

Back in London after six months in the Indian subcontinent I was dismayed to find *Braden's Week* was now in crisis again, terminally as it turned out. At the end of the series that I would have produced had I not gone to India, the Stork margarine commercial returned to haunt the programme's future. The matter had been festering in Bernie's mind all the time that I had been away. He needed the money and he was now more determined than ever to demonstrate his right to take on freelance work. It would probably not have made much difference but I still regret that I had not been around to try and stop him. Bernie had been told what would happen and it did. Paul Fox cancelled *Braden's Week* and that was that. It turned out to be the end of a distinguished career for Bernie. The fifty-six-year-old much-loved veteran broadcaster never worked in the mainstream again. What a stupid, stupid decision he had made. He was almost broke when he died twenty years later.

In my last few weeks in India it had become apparent that momentous changes were afoot in the *Man Alive* unit. The gist of the messages had been that Aubrey Singer, the empire-building Group Head, was now empire consolidating and had decided belatedly to dispense with the services of Chris Brasher and amalgamate his department with the *Man Alive* unit under Desmond Wilcox. That made the new General Features Department a substantial force, with a wide portfolio of programmes on both channels. Desmond's partner from ITV days, Bill Morton, was leaving the unit to produce a new programme for the Music and Arts Department. Bill had never really made a mark as a programme-maker on *Man Alive* but he had been a superb moderator of Desmond's excesses. Desmond could get very excitable and send off explosive and imprudent memos to his bosses. He would dictate them flamboyantly, to an admiring audience of colleagues who had popped into his office to avail themselves of the hospitality cabinet. Bill would later talk Desmond down from his high, and the memos that were actually sent, while still vibrant and colourful, made their points just as well without invective, showing off or insulting the recipients. This was an important role I was about to take on.

Cynics say you needed two qualities to get to the top in the BBC. Good at memos and good at meetings. Being good at your job was an optional extra. But Desmond was very good at being a department head, charismatic, inspirational and passionately loyal in defending his producers' programmes at the meeting that mattered most, Programme Review. This was a weekly gathering of the heads of all the production departments to discuss the previous week's programmes. Many used the occasion to conduct vendettas against their counterparts in other departments. The Head of Drama, for example, might attack the production of *Match of the Day*. The following week the Head of Sport would lay into *The Wednesday Play*. Although the minutes of the meetings were supposed to be confidential, heads of departments couldn't resist revealing choice nuggets to their subordinates, especially when they had worsted a detested enemy. Programme Review was a well-patronised spectator sport. Because Desmond was obsessed by television, and he watched far more of other departments' output than they watched of his. His colourful criticisms of their programmes nearly always hit the mark and soon he had a loyal following both inside and outside the meeting. The sixth floor decided that it was time to recruit Desmond into the echelons of senior management.

This left a vacancy for the highly prestigious job, the editorship of *Man Alive*. Desmond made it quite clear that he wanted me for the job but it was not entirely within his gift. I had to appear before an Appointments Board on which he sat along with David Attenborough and his immediate boss, Aubrey Singer. I blotted my copybook when David asked me how I would control costs and I replied, too flippantly perhaps, that I intended to delegate such matters to the programme's accountant who had them in a thorough grasp and understood them far better than I. One of the other candidates gave a much better performance so David wondered whether he should be appointed and not me. He was persuaded otherwise by Desmond who claimed that my rival was big trouble. He was proved right. The disappointed candidate left the BBC and rose to great heights with his new employer but caused such turmoil that he was unceremoniously fired.

Many of the obvious candidates for the job had been reluctant to put themselves forward because David Attenborough had failed to address the actor-manager problem. Desmond was a brilliant, off-screen film reporter but, for some inexplicable reason, self-conscious and awkward as a studio presenter. He asked the right questions and followed them up skilfully but he was simply not in the first league. The dilemma was quite stark. If you were producing a studio *Man Alive* programme and you needed a better performance out of your presenter – or wanted to replace him – how on earth were you going to achieve either when the presenter was your boss and very touchy about personal criticism? Being the least vain man imaginable, Attenborough could not conceive that a sane colleague would allow such a conflict of interests to arise. Indeed, as soon as he became bored with management himself, he resigned from the BBC and took his chances as a freelance. So *Man Alive*'s senior directors had retreated into their own little worlds during the latter years of Desmond's editorship. They made very distinguished individual fifty-minute films but they had little interest in the series as a whole. Partly it was that they felt understandable pride in their own films with a 'directed by' credit on the end. But the real difficulty was the perennial problem of Desmond's dual role. As soon as I became the series editor, they implored me to return *Man Alive* to its original all-film format. But this was simply not an option. It would probably have cost no more in real money but the eccentric way of accounting then in force subsidised studio production. Besides, we just didn't have enough top-notch film directors to fill the huge quota of programmes that the *Man Alive* series was commissioned to make each year. Our studio debates filled the gap.* In any case, there was no way that Desmond, the head of a powerful new department, was going to relinquish his role as the presenter of *Man Alive*.

---

* Many years later, *Man Alive* was replaced by the all-film series *Forty Minutes*, staffed partly by freelance directors.

The studio programmes made a lot more work for me. I had to go across to the Television Centre and sit in the studio control room through most of the camera rehearsal to keep Desmond happy and under control. The *Man Alive* films fortunately took up much less of my time. I had inherited such a seasoned bunch of film-makers that, once we had agreed a subject and a way of treating it, I could leave them to get on with it and only became involved again when their rough cuts were ready for me to view. There was one notable exception, a film that caused me endless trouble. We had decided to make a documentary about gold smuggling, a cracking good yarn. Surprisingly, one of the major smuggling operations started in the sleepy market town of Royston, Hertfordshire. There, a long-established company of precious-metal dealers, Johnson Mathey, unobtrusively manufactured gold ingots for the Bank of England, foreign governments and other well-heeled customers who needed portable wealth, no questions asked. Vast numbers of ingots and gold tola bars were quite legally exported to the Middle East. Smugglers then transported them by dhow to India where one-kilogram ingots (now worth about £28,000) and ten-tola wafers (£3,500) were regarded as an essential part of the economy. Banks in India were then few and far between and the local currency was controlled by unconscionably stringent regulations. In any case, gold is far less likely to attract the notice of the taxman than a paper trail of bank statements and cheques. What's more, gold has always been the currency of marriage dowries and the means by which women are able to survive the inevitable rainy day. Importing gold was illegal so smuggling prospered as a multi-million-dollar business.

I had been introduced to the Gold Controller of India and he gave us a wonderful interview, real *James Bond* stuff, about high-speed boat chases and radio transmitters attached to fishing buoys marking hoards of illicit gold. My crew set off for Royston and enthusiastically filmed liquid gold being poured into moulds to make ingots. They then followed a consignment of gold down the A10 and filmed it being loaded on to a regular weekly cargo plane at Heathrow. In Dubai they shot a wonderful sequence as tons of gold were transferred from the plane to sinister-looking security vans destined for shadowy figures in the back rooms of the gold market. One of our researchers had already tracked down smugglers who would allow us to film their operation, transporting the gold by night across the Arabian Sea to rendezvous with their Indian counterparts off the coast of Gujarat. Then, out of the blue, the Indian Prime Minister, Indira Gandhi, proclaimed a State of Emergency. She was in deep political trouble and vainly hoped that the distraction of bringing an end to the world's largest democracy would save her skin. Her political rivals were thrown into prison along with most of the Indian Goldfingers and other assorted crooks and hoodlums. Overnight the smuggling of gold ground to a standstill. My crew sat by their hotel swimming pool in Dubai clocking up huge expenses, while I gnashed my teeth in London at the money that was being wasted. There was nothing for it but to call the crew back and write the whole project off. Then I had to find some serious economies to pay for the aborted venture. To this day, I have never even seen a ten-tola bar.

By a great stroke of luck, Tim Slessor came knocking on my door looking for a job. I had met him in South Dakota when we were making our documentary on the plight of the Native American. He had come to visit our cameraman with whom he had worked when he himself was a producer at the BBC. At the time he was teaching in the American Midwest. I had liked him at once. He was a straight-talking, outdoor type, crazy about sailing – and he had a passionate interest in the world of the American cowboy. He left the BBC to join Michael Peacock when the Controller of BBC1 defected to the newly franchised ITV station, London Weekend. It all went horribly wrong very quickly. Peacock was forced out and almost all of the highly talented staff he had plundered from the BBC resigned in sympathy and were then out of work. That was why Tim was now in my office asking for a job. I gladly gave him one. He was what Sir Humphrey Appleby of *Yes, Minister* would call 'sound'. Indeed he possessed the quality that senior civil servants most hanker after, 'bottom'. Tim was older than me and I came to depend on his common-sense, get-things-done approach. If there were any unexpected slots to fill, a hole in the schedule, Tim would buckle down and make the necessary programme, on budget and in the time available. By rolling up his sleeves himself, he set an example which encouraged the reporters, researchers and production assistants in the belief that studio programmes need not be second best and provided real opportunities for them to shine. He was of unimaginable help with Desmond in the studio. Finding Tim difficult to push around, Desmond sulkily nicknamed him 'Leather Balls', deciding that it was less demanding to do what Tim asked him to do than to pull rank or resist him head on.

Despite the misgivings of many of *Man Alive*'s senior staff, the best of the studio debates had a real immediacy that could not easily be captured on film. They created a sense of occasion and attracted critical and political attention that our ITV competitors, *This Week* and *World in Action*, would have died for. An indication that the sixth floor saw the merits of our studio debates was provided when BBC1 ordered a series of them, with Desmond presenting, under the generic title *The Question of* . . . The first one we made, *The Question of Confidence* stirred up a frightful hornet's nest. Its purpose was to explore the rift between the mainstream establishment and the post-sixties generation of protestors who regarded those in any kind of authority with utter contempt. The bunch of protestors our researcher and studio producer had chosen mostly came from the militant Claimants Union. Before we started recording the programme they entered into a noisy dispute with Desmond and me demanding to control the way the debate was conducted and telling us who should be allowed to speak, for how long and when. At one stage I thought we might have to call security and abandon the programme altogether. When we did eventually manage to calm things down and start the recording, the protestors predictably hogged the debate, hardly allowing their opponents the chance to speak. One of them, Shirley Williams, was so furious at the way she had been interrupted and mistreated that she left the studio muttering dire but unspecific threats. The programme had been recorded on a Sunday evening for broadcast very late that night. Desmond and I discussed whether or not we should savagely edit it. I argued that we shouldn't since it illustrated the very breakdown in communication that had caused us to mount the programme in the first place. My view prevailed, despite the surprise involvement of Aubrey Singer, who had bestirred himself to come to the studio on a Sunday evening only in order to ingratiate himself with the senior politicians gathered there. Goodness, was he going to regret that decision.

Shirley Williams had made plans to dine that evening with her friend Bridget Plowden, who happened to be Vice Chairman of the BBC. She arrived there spitting blood. They watched the programme together. There were not many other viewers since the programme didn't begin until 11.30 p.m., certainly none so passionate in their hatred of it. By extraordinarily bad luck a meeting of the BBC Board of Governors was scheduled for the next morning. Lady Plowden waxed ballistic. The new Chairman, Michael Swann, decided that the whole Board should view the programme. Alasdair Milne, the Director of Programmes, was instructed to conduct an inquiry, in which he established that Aubrey had been present on that fateful Sunday night and party to the decision not to edit out at least the worst of the barracking. In the cool light of day, I conceded to Desmond that I had been wrong to argue against editing, but Aubrey, by far the most senior person present, had, happily, to take a large part of the blame. The Governors' decision, released to the press, was, 'There shall be another programme.' Enforcing such an edict proved to be difficult since those of us who had been involved in producing the first one, egged on by our indignant colleagues, were most reluctant to make what we called 'an apology programme', especially when one of the Vice Chairman's friends was the source of the complaint. It rather made the point for the Claimants Union that the establishment only looked after its own. Eventually we agreed to make an entirely different programme called *The Question of Communication*. Honour was satisfied but, since hardly anyone had seen the first programme and the second bore little relationship to it, the machinations behind the scenes remained a damaging family tiff that a more experienced and less magisterial Chairman would discreetly have circumvented.

Man Alive caused a thorough nuisance of itself to both the Heath and Wilson governments by mounting programmes that questioned key policies, particularly planning, education, race and health. These were the subjects that made for impassioned studio debates – and they fired up a whole generation of students to be bloody-minded and stick up for their rights. It's rather tiresome now that there is no motorway box, the desperately needed inner-circle road planned for London. Foreign tourists must be perplexed at the way parts of the Great North Road through London are no more substantial than they were at the time of Dick Turpin. Thanks to programmes like *Man Alive*, one of Europe's most ambitious airports, at Maplin Sands on the Thames Estuary, was never built. Tower blocks were rased to the ground while waiting lists for council housing grew. *Man Alive* inspired the budding radical teachers and college lecturers who went on to indoctrinate a whole, bolshie generation. In mitigation, it must be said that we did promote a better understanding of citizens' rights, especially human rights, and frequently tackled the iniquities of racial and sexual discrimination.

By chance we soon managed to upset the new BBC Chairman Michael Swann again. One of our regular programmes focused on the way planning inspectors would commendably throw out proposals to destroy what was left of the countryside, only to be overruled by the government. Left-of-centre environmental protestors always accused big business of funding political parties to ensure no obstacle stood in the way of their dastardly plans. Whatever the truth, there was no doubt that government inspectors often managed successfully to frustrate ill-considered new schemes, only to see their reports thrown into the rubbish bin. We chose as one of our examples the government proposals to modernise Edinburgh Airport. These involved realigning the runway so that aircraft would take off and land over densely populated parts of the city. The topic particularly suited our brief because the independent inspector had already rejected the plan. Now the Conservative government planned to go ahead anyway. What we didn't know, when we embarked on the project, was that it contained a delicious and irresistible mischief-making quotient. The Chairman, Michael Swann, had previously been the Vice Chancellor of Edinburgh University and he still lived there – under the proposed new flight path. Further, it turned out that the Conservative Secretary of State for Scotland, Gordon Campbell, who was responsible for the controversial Edinburgh Airport decision, was one of Sir Michael's best friends. Better still, the feisty leader of the opposition to the scheme was *another* of Sir Michael's best friends and his doctor. The new Chairman, poor fellow, was lobbied mercilessly by his GP – on at least one occasion being forced to hear the arguments against the realignment of the runway while he shivered on his own doorstep in his dressing-gown and pyjamas.

The Secretary of State gave us a filmed interview, but his office asked for a written undertaking that we would not use it if he were no longer in office when the programme was broadcast. There was an election coming up and, quite reasonably, he didn't want to be seen defending a decision that was no longer his. When the *Man Alive* was broadcast the Conservative government had lost the election so Gordon Campbell was longer Secretary of State for Scotland. It was the incoming Labour government that announced what had been Campbell's plans for the new airport. Because those plans were attacked in the programme, Campbell wrote an angry letter to *The Times,* saying that he had given an interview to *Man Alive* defending his decision to allow the re-alignment of the runway at Edinburgh but that his contribution had not been used. We were all furious because it was he who had insisted that we leave out his interview if he were no longer in office when the programme went out.

I wrote a letter to the editor of *The Times* and properly – but unwisely as it turned out – routed it up the usual channels for the Director General's approval. If I had just sent it directly to *The Times*, my offence would have been treated as a very minor one; that's what I should have done. The Director General knew that his new Chairman was now between the devil of the Scottish Office and the deep blue sea of the peevish Edinburgh establishment. He refused to allow me to send my letter. I could hardly attack the Director General and the Chairman so I sent an excoriating letter to Gordon Campbell demanding that he write to *The Times* again, withdrawing his accusation. He, of course, immediately passed my letter over to his chum, Sir Michael Swann, who wrote a memorandum of textbook conciliation for the Director General to send on to me. He had earned high marks in his time as Vice Chancellor of Edinburgh University, by wielding emollience in place of water canon to cool the fiery radicals who ruled the roost there.* Later, on his first visit to our offices, Sir Michael made a special point of asking to meet me. He was ghoulish charm itself – like the consultant who has just told you your number is up. It seemed to me churlish to confront him when he was clearly proffering an olive branch, cunning fellow, so the record was never set straight, honour never satisfied. However, it was gratifying to learn later that among the reasons the electorate had decided to dispense with Gordon Campbell's services as their MP were his perceived mishandling of North Sea Oil, Scottish fishing rights and Edinburgh Airport.

My very last programme as editor of *Man Alive* was an investigative film about corruption in local government in Wales, boldly entitled *The Swansea Mafia*. It should have broadcast much earlier but the BBC lawyers hadn't been at all happy with it. The producer, Philip Geddes, and I thought they were being over-cautious. We knew the Fraud Squad was on the case and Philip's team had even compared notes with them. Eventually the lawyers reluctantly agreed we could broadcast a limp and limping version of the original feisty concept. We had watered down the commentary and our bold title, *The Swansea Mafia,* ended up, pathetically, as *Something in the Air?* – the diffident question mark to make doubly sure that we didn't upset anyone. There were two surprises after transmission. The first was an unequivocal denial by a local councillor that he had ever even spoken to *Man Alive.* Yet he was one of the most outspoken critics of corruption in the programme – there for all to see, dishing the dirt in big close up. Surreal. Next, a most unpleasant shock. A libel writ was served on us by Gerald Murphy, the Leader of Swansea Council, the main villain of our piece. By then he was

* Neil Tweedie reported in the *Daily Telegraph* (29.12.2008): '[Sir Michael] Swann told Harold Wilson in 1975 that, though the situation in the Corporation was "a picnic compared with Edinburgh University", he was concerned about "hippie" influences at the BBC . . . [H]e thought that too many young producers approached every programme they did from the starting point of an attitude about the subject which could be summed up as, "You are a shit." It was an attitude that he and others in the management of the BBC deplored, and they would be using their influence as opportunities offered to counter it.'

in prison, serving a sentence for corruption. The BBC agreed to settle with him out of court and pay him compensation. Sometimes, God and the BBC move in mysterious ways their wonders to perform.

CHAPTER 10

The Curse of Cromwell

There were other BBC2 series and their producers which needed my attention but none with the potential to be as politically controversial as *Man Alive*. For example, there was a documentary series to which each BBC region contributed one or more films, depending on how many directors it could spare and – which caused great aggravation – how many of their proposals had been selected by our coordinating producer in London. The series had a lousy title, *Look, Stranger*, which referred to W. H. Auden's poem. 'Look, stranger, at this island now'. If you didn't know the poem, how could you guess at the programme's content? It seemed to me to break the sensible BBC tenet that was drummed into us, 'Never overestimate the audience's knowledge nor underestimate its intelligence.' When *Look, Stranger* was put under my wing, by then in its third season, it was too late to do anything about the title.

Because of its provenance, the series was rather random in its subject matter, but that, in a way, was the point. Not surprisingly it threw up some interesting young film-makers, giving them their first exposure to a network audience. One new director at BBC Northern Ireland made a quite beautiful documentary about the Province, with an extraordinarily evocative soundtrack, largely comprised of Protestant and Roman Catholic folk songs, music that I had never heard. We agreed that he would make a fifty-minute *Man Alive*, developing and expanding his *Look, Stranger* film. Called *Sing Orange, Sing Green*, it was an essay that helped explain the roots of the Troubles in an extraordinarily moving way. It was applauded by the audience, the critics, Programme Review and the BBC Controller of Northern Ireland but I never commissioned another programme about Northern Ireland or the Troubles. The subject was never popular with the mainland audience and there was another reason: it was career shortening. In 1978, the Labour government's Northern Ireland Minister, Roy Mason, made explicit to the Controller of BBC Northern Ireland what ministers had previously preferred to leave as an unspoken threat: 'Bloody gentlemen of the BBC think they are above criticism. Airey Neave and Margaret Thatcher have come to see me [from the Opposition] and we're absolutely agreed that there should be no increase in your licence unless you put things right.' Mason also passed on his threat to BBC Current Affairs reporter Bernard Falk. 'Stay away from these [IRA] killers, Bernard,' he told him, 'remember the licence fee; get sharp, son.'

Airey Neave, Margaret Thatcher's close political confidant, was murdered by a car bomb at the Houses of Parliament just before the 1979 election that brought the Tories back to power. The Irish National Liberation Army claimed responsibility. A few weeks later, when the BBC screened an interview with an INLA spokesman, Mrs Thatcher angrily condemned the broadcast in the Commons. Less than six months later, Lord Mountbatten was assassinated by the IRA while he was on a fishing holiday with members of his family in the Republic. All this led the BBC to clamp down on interviews with terrorists. But the *Panorama* programme did not see this as a blanket ban on talking to Irish republicans. Its new editor, Roger Bolton, sent a young Jeremy Paxman to Northern Ireland with a film crew. Following a tip-off, they went to the border village of Carrickmore and filmed hooded gunmen holding up traffic in a protest against increased activity by British Security Forces in the border areas. The British press picked up on the story, accusing the BBC of colluding with the IRA. The Prime Minister, Mrs Thatcher, went 'scatty' at a Cabinet meeting, according to one account, and Home Secretary William Whitelaw advised the BBC Chairman, Sir Michael Swann, that the BBC would have to demonstrate that it was taking the breach seriously.

An internal inquiry ruled that the *Panorama* team should have been alert to the dangers, and that they should have informed the Controller of Northern Ireland. The editor of *Panorama*, Roger Bolton, was removed from the programme but, rather hurriedly, reinstated after colleagues vigorously protested on his behalf. Later, Bolton was to be responsible for the ITV documentary, *Death on the Rock*, an investigation into allegations that SAS marksmen had shot dead unarmed IRA suspects in Gibraltar. The film so enraged Mrs Thatcher and her government that it was widely rumoured to have contributed to Thames Television losing its licence to Carlton. The Head of Current Affairs at the time of the Carrickmore incident, John Gau, had been widely tipped to become Controller of BBC1 but the Chairman of the Board of Governors wouldn't hear of it. With promotion denied him, John left the BBC for the commercial sector.

Shortly after I left the BBC, my former department commissioned Paul Hamann's documentary *At the Edge of the Union* for the *Real Lives* series. It portrayed the daily lives of two politicians, both members of the Northern Ireland Assembly, Martin McGuinness of Sinn Fein and Gregory Campbell, a Unionist. Eddie Mirzoeff, the executive producer, regrets now that he didn't stick with the film's original title, *Elected Representatives,* to underline the legitimacy (but not necessarily approval) of the two participants. Mrs Thatcher's Home Secretary, Leon Brittan, alleged that the film would give terrorists 'the oxygen of publicity'. (He deliberately used Mrs Thatcher's graphic phrase.) While the Director General, Alasdair Milne, was on holiday, the Board of Governors viewed the film and banned it.* This caused a constitutional crisis, raising the question as to who ran the BBC, the management or the Board of Governors? *At the Edge of the Union* became a *cause célèbre* and a major international front-page story. All hell was let loose when staff, supported by their colleagues from ITN, noisily demonstrated against the Governors in a media circus outside Broadcasting House. 'We are the BBC,' declared the Chairman on behalf of the Board. 'I shall not be resigning whatever hits the fan.'† The Home Secretary back-pedalled like mad. When Milne got back to London, he skilfully managed to persuade the by now very shaken Governors to lift the ban – just as well really because the content of the programme was

---

* BBC Minutes of a Special Meeting of the Board of Governors to discuss *Real Lives: At the Edge of the Union*, 30 July 1985.
† BBC Minutes of a Special Meeting of the Board of Governors to discuss *Real Lives: At the Edge of the Union*, 6 August 1985.

quite unexceptionable. To save the Governors' face a negligible and cosmetic change was made, the addition of a fourteen-second shot of a bomb explosion, thus proving conclusively that political pressure rather than common sense had ruled the day.

Alasdair Milne was to pay heavily for his holiday. This public embarrassment that the Governors brought upon themselves was the most serious of several incidents that led to Milne's demise. They were exacerbated by his curt and clumsy management style, from which I was to suffer myself. It certainly didn't help his career that, a year or so after the *Real Lives* affair, Special Branch raided BBC Scotland unannounced, claiming that a television series being produced there was in serious breach of the Official Secrets Act; nor that the Board of Governors forced the Director General to settle an expensive libel action against an edition of *Panorama*, entitled *Maggie's Militant Tendency*, brought by a most unattractive bunch of right-wing MPs, including the now infamous Neil Hamilton. Events didn't help. Mrs Thatcher was furious about the *lèse majesté* she suffered on *Nationwide* over the decision to sink the Argentinian cruiser, the *General Belgrano*, in the Falklands War. An accumulation of cock-ups, poisoned with the deadly chalice of Northern Ireland politics, saw Alasdair Milne unceremoniously booted out of the BBC, the first-ever Director General to be sacked. The BBC Chairman, Marmaduke Hussey, called him to his office after a routine meeting of the Board. Alasdair describes the bombshell that awaited him:

> Hussey's lip trembled as he said: 'I am afraid this is going to be a very unpleasant interview. We want you to leave immediately. It's a unanimous decision of the Board.' I was stunned. What was he talking about? Perhaps I should have seen the plot thickening, but I hadn't . . . At home I was on my own. Sheila was out. As I prowled up and down the living room, the first impact was the humiliation of being discarded by such people without a word of explanation or discussion . . . Anguish was followed by despair.

There were also good editorial reasons why I steered clear of Northern Ireland. Over the years, before I became its editor, *Man Alive* produced several good programmes on the subject. However, the television audience in England, Wales and Scotland showed little interest in the Troubles, largely because the issues that divided Protestants and Catholics seemed so intractable and their spokesmen so unreasonable. Viewers outside Northern Ireland regarded Irish politics as 'a quarrel in a far away country between people of whom we know nothing', as Neville Chamberlain so memorably remarked, as he washed his hands of the Sudetenland. This was not a new problem. In his autobiography, Alasdair Milne remembers:

> Our colleagues in Belfast were more sensitive about the Stormont government than was common BBC practice with governments at Westminster. Indeed, Andrew Stewart, who was Controller there after the war, told me later that he had almost been treated as an unofficial member of the Northern Ireland Cabinet. There is a question to be answered one day as to how far the BBC – and Fleet Street, too, for that matter – was responsible for not informing the rest of the country of the conduct of political affairs in Northern Ireland in the fifties and sixties, At all events, the 'peace marches' of 1969, the introduction of the Army to secure the position of the Catholics and all that followed, were as much a shock to us in the BBC, I believe, as they were to the rest of the country.

The Troubles escalated spectacularly in the summer of 1969 when the Apprentice Boys of Derry, a Loyalist anti-Catholic organisation, staged their annual march through the town. Their clash with a civil-rights march was broken up by members of the B-Specials, the twelve-thousand-strong auxiliary to the Royal Ulster Constabulary. 'The bloodied heads and the vengeful use of batons horrified millions watching that evening's television bulletins,' writes Andrew Marr in *A History of Modern Britain*. More civil-rights marches followed and a brutal pitched battle was fought out in the centre of Belfast between Catholic residents, Loyalist extremists and the police. Hundreds of houses were burnt down. Harold Wilson and his Home Secretary, James Callaghan, agreed to send in the British army on condition the B-Specials were disbanded.

In the early 1970s, the BBC did make one immense effort to fulfil its responsibilities with a three-hour television special, *The Question of Ulster – An Enquiry into the Future.* It broadcast at the height of the Troubles, spookily just twenty-five days before Bloody Sunday, that infamous nadir in the conflict, when British soldiers killed fourteen unarmed civilians – and wounded as many more – at a political rally in Derry. Elaborate care was taken to ensure that all interested groups were invited to take part in the programme; that equal weight and time were given to contributors; that the rules of the debate were mutually agreed. It was a thankless endeavour. Christopher Jeans, one of the producers, remembers panic-struck orders from his bosses in London that were as swiftly countermanded when others of the contributors threatened to withdraw if any such changes were made. Scandalously, the British government and Brian Faulkner's Ulster Unionist government refused to take part, hoping to sabotage the first major television debate about the future of Northern Ireland. The Home Secretary, Reginald Maudling, idiotically and ineffectually demanded that the programme be banned.

Partly because of the publicity and also because such a major programme had never before been devoted to the subject, seven and a half million viewers tuned in, including nearly two thirds of the population of Ulster. It was unusually quiet on the streets of Belfast and Derry that night. Half of the viewers managed to stay with the programme until it finished three hours later, after midnight. Yet even the Controller of BBC Northern Ireland had to admit that the epic was 'cool, at times laborious', which, being translated, means that, by playing ultra safe, the BBC had made *The Question of Ulster* much duller than it should have been. Its phenomenally large audience demonstrated a hunger for enlightenment that the BBC failed to satisfy with such a tedious programme – and never really tried again. The courage required to make something a little more accessible to the ordinary viewer had been blunted by the constant, nervous interventions of top BBC management. As a result, apathy set in. Every move you made had to be notified to the Controller in Belfast and to every Tom, Dick and Harry at Broadcasting House as well. The inquest into Paul Hamann's *Real Lives* film, *At the Edge of the Union,* thirteen years later, typically focused not only on its subject matter but also on the procedures followed to keep both the Director General and the BBC Northern Ireland Controller properly informed. Small wonder, then, that producers of everyday programmes, which make up the warp and the weft of British broadcasting, decided not to bother to go to the Province at all.

Even when the terrorists brought the bombing more aggressively to England – nearly annihilating the whole of the British Cabinet in Brighton – the public seemed to shrug off the Troubles as a necessary inconvenience to be endured, like the wartime blitz. Some members of the Conservative government, however, regarded much of the television coverage of Northern Ireland as tantamount to treason and hasty legislation was drawn up to prevent the direct broadcast of interviews with Martin McGuiness, Gerry Adams and other representatives of eleven Republican and Loyalist organisations. The law was supposed to force broadcasters to provide only dispassionate summaries of what the banned politicians had to say but it was so badly drafted that they simply substituted the authentic voices with those of actors, making Paul Loughran (Butch Dingle in *Emmerdale*) nearly as famous as, and probably richer than, Gerry Adams, whom he imitated for the best part of six years.

How much more difficult it became to make meaningful political documentaries and balanced discussion programmes in Northern Ireland with this absurd constraint in place. Although the lack of network air time given to the Troubles after *The Question of Ulster* may have reflected popular sentiment, it was a discreditable cop-out. On Bloody Sunday we now know that soldiers fired on a demonstration in Derry without provocation and that the fourteen people who died and the others who were injured had been unarmed and were completely innocent. 'We found no instance where it appeared to us that soldiers either were or might have been justified in firing,' says the Saville Report. It completely contradicted the Widgery Report, published eleven weeks after the killing. John Simpson, who was reporting for the BBC from Northern Ireland at that time, says that he and all his colleagues knew that the dead were innocent victims. He claims that the Widgery Report was regarded by all those who knew the facts as a scandalous white-wash. You would have learnt very little of all this from watching BBC Television. Only Granada's *World in Action* kept its nerve and continued to report on Northern Ireland as prominently as such a tragedy deserved. Those of us at the BBC who were in a position to do so should have tried much harder to stimulate public interest with lively and informative programmes, to shed light on the crucially important debate. Historians will be astonished at our neglect. How could we have failed properly to reflect what we now know was one of the darkest moments in Britain's recent political history? We had a duty and we failed.

Being responsible for programmes about Northern Ireland was by no means the only way to commit hara-kiri. John Gau's, predecessor as Head of Current Affairs, John Grist, lost his job for upsetting Harold Wilson and the Labour Party. His department had made a documentary called *Yesterday's Men,* a smart title reflecting the accusation that Labour had thrown at Tory ministers in the recent election – but Labour had lost. David Dimbleby asked pertinent questions (or impertinent ones, as Wilson saw it) about how much money he had been paid for his memoirs. The ex-Prime Minister stopped the interview and insisted that the offending questions be cut out. After much internal dispute, the questions were dropped, so Dimbleby and his producer insisted that their credits be taken off the film. Harold Wilson and many of his senior colleagues then demanded, noisily and publicly, that the BBC go further and cancel the programme. However, the Director General, Charles Curran, stood firm, supported by the Chairman and the Board of Governors, who, most imprudently, had seen the programme before its broadcast. When the row continued even more angrily, afterwards, they had no one to blame but themselves. Eventually the BBC was forced to apologise for Dimbleby's suggestion, in commentary, that Wilson had benefited financially from privileged access to government papers. The Labour Party bore a grudge for years. The Annan Committee on the Future of Broadcasting later maintained that *Yesterday's Men* had cast a permanent shadow over the courage of BBC current-affairs programmes: 'Time and again people in the BBC attributed this palsy to the effect of the row over this unfortunate episode [that] was blamed for the caution, lack of direction, touchiness and unsteadiness.'

Falling on his sword, John Grist was moved to the distinctly less prestigious position of Controller, English Regions, Birmingham. Later, by way of reward for accepting the role of scapegoat, he was appointed to the zenith of cushy numbers, United States Representative, with a fine apartment in the United Nations Plaza and more or less unlimited expenses. Will Wyatt, who was my last BBC boss, rose almost to the very top of the BBC, ending up as Deputy Director General. On the way up, he was asked by the former Head of Current Affairs, Brian Wenham, if he would be interested in taking charge of a merged News and Current Affairs:

> I have thought about what has happened to heads of current affairs. There was John Grist, who took the rap for *Yesterday's Men* and was sent to the English Regions. You took a public rubbishing from the Annan Report. John Gau was tarred with the Carrickmore incident, punished by being denied the controllership of BBC1 and then parachuted out. Chris Capron is exhausted and wants out. Then there is news. Derrick Amoore cracked under the pressure, hit the bottle, was sacked and is now exiled to Radio London. Alan Protheroe has been resurrected, but was previously sacked from news. And Peter Woon has taken endless flack about the superiority of ITN and cannot be long for this world. Your kind offer invites me to be responsible for both areas. No thanks.

CHAPTER 11

Ban the Bomb

Sir Winston Churchill persuaded the BBC to avoid running any documentaries or in-depth discussions about the nuclear bomb, secret papers made public for the first time reveal. Churchill later boasted that the BBC had 'very willingly accepted' his demand that they should not broadcast even 'responsible discussion' about nuclear warfare. The ban effectively ran for more than a decade into the mid-1960s when the BBC suppressed the infamous *War Game* documentary.   BBC News, 19 August 1999

There was one other topic of the most overwhelming importance to everyone in Britain that producers of my era failed to cover properly, with what, in hindsight, looks like the most culpable negligence: the consequences of nuclear war. The reasons for this failure are at the very root of the relationship between the government and the BBC. Whose side is the BBC on?

During the Second World War the answer was pretty clear-cut. National security was paramount. But during the 1950s this cosy relationship was seen to have changed radically when Sir Anthony Eden's government controversially and deceitfully decided to invade the Suez Canal Zone. The BBC reported the significant opposition to the adventure, including that of the United States government, and invited leaders of the Opposition to state their case. There were dark threats of financial sanctions against the BBC but events moved so swiftly against the Prime Minister that nothing became of them. Eden was forced to withdraw British troops from Suez in a humiliating climbdown and he then resigned. Three years later Hugh Carleton Greene was appointed Director General of the BBC and he made it his mission to underline the importance of its editorial independence from government. So it is no surprise that there were frequent, bruising clashes between the two when their interests were at odds. Yet it was during Greene's time that the BBC first cancelled a television programme because it might undermine government policy.

The film was *The War Game*, made by Peter Watkins in 1964 and scheduled in *The Wednesday Play* slot. It is, to this day, a vivid and harrowing depiction of the effects of a nuclear weapon exploding over Kent. Shot in black and white as a drama documentary, it graphically underlines the horrors of a world where government administration and hospitals no longer exist, yet where tens of thousands have been killed and ten times as many are dying from their injuries and radiation sickness. Until Watkins's film exposed the horrors of a nuclear attack, the subject had received hardly any mainstream television coverage. Within the BBC there was much wringing of hands. *The War Game* was such a powerfully persuasive film that there was a fear that it would cause real panic if it were to be broadcast.

As it happens the government had just appointed Lord Normanbrook as Chairman of the BBC Governors. He had the most formidable track record, including simultaneously holding the two very top civil-service jobs, Secretary to the Cabinet from 1947–62 and Joint Permanent Secretary of the Treasury and Head of the Home Civil Service from 1956–62. The historian, Peter Hennessy, author of *The Secret State*, says he was the last man in Whitehall to underestimate the cataclysmic effects of a nuclear attack on the UK. 'Throughout the high Cold War, he briefed his four premiers – Attlee, Churchill, Eden and Macmillan – on the catastrophe that awaited the UK if global war came.' He would certainly have read and, perhaps, helped draft, the 1955 Joint Intelligence Committee report, 'The "H" Bomb Threat to the UK in the Event of a General War':

To render the UK useless as a base for any form of military operations the simplest and most effective form of attack would be by surface bursts effected in suitable meteorological conditions. These, besides causing local damage, would cause very considerable areas of the country to be affected by fallout. We are advised that something like ten 'H' Bombs, each of a yield of about 10 megatons, delivered on the western half of the UK or in the waters close in off the Western seaboard, with the normal prevailing winds, would effectively disrupt the life of the country and make normal activity completely impossible.

The West's nuclear defence was based on the threat of Mutually Assured Destruction, with the apposite acronym of MAD – in other words, we'll wipe you out if you try to wipe us out. The Cuban Missile Crisis in 1962 made everyone realise how real the threat of nuclear war could be. The UK was far more vulnerable than the US, being so much smaller and nearer to the Soviet Union. Normanbrook believed that priority must be given to planning a system of emergency government that could administer those parts of the country that survived a nuclear attack. This involved building top-secret regional seats of government and a vast underground bunker for the War Cabinet under the Cotswolds at Corsham in Wiltshire. The very limited accommodation available in these bombproof shelters was reserved for senior politicians, civil servants and key military personnel. There was no provision for their families, so it is very doubtful that all of them would have reported for duty had Armageddon arrived. Crucially it was decided that there was no practical way of planning for the protection of the public in the event of nuclear attack. Prime Minister Attlee emphasised, as early as 1948, that it was 'essential to avoid a situation in which the Government would be driven to devote resources to civil defence on a scale which would cripple the national economy, detract from our power of offence and alienate our allies in Europe'.

Normanbrook was, without doubt, the single most important architect of the policies to be followed after a nuclear strike. He was in a better position than almost anybody else to know that, if Britain were to be subjected to a sustained attack, total disintegration of law and order and a collapse of the nation's morale – 'breakdown', as the planners rather ghoulishly called it – would be inevitable. A principal scientific officer at the Home Office, psychologist Dr Edgar Anstey, who had made studies of the destruction of German and Japanese cities, told historian Peter Hennessy:

> We calculated that the number of megaton deliveries required to cause breakdown was about 25 for the UK, and about 450 for the USA or Soviet Union. Moreover, and this was the really important finding, this scale of delivery was well within the capacity of either the USA or the Soviet Union, even *after* it had been subjected to a pre-emptive attack by its major adversary ... A megaton delivery on a city such as Birmingham would [also] render 'ineffective' 50% of the population within a radius of about 20 miles, including e.g. Coventry, where the people would see, hear and smell what happened to Birmingham, and would either take to their cellars or get into their cars and drive to where they thought they might be safe.

It is not necessary to be the world's most contrary troublemaker to conclude that withholding from the public the critical fact that you were on your own when the balloon went up was hardly the conduct expected of a democratic government in peacetime. The BBC, of course, knew all about the Attlee doctrine since it was a component of, and party to, the government's emergency plans. But it was top-secret classified information, so the BBC connived with the government to keep it from the public. Broadcasting *The War Game*, of course, would have let the cat out of the bag.

Unusually, Director General Hugh Greene decided to consult his Chairman about the dilemma which faced him, at least partly because he was receiving conflicting advice as to whether or not *The War Game* should be shown. He almost certainly chose to seek Lord Normanbrook's advice because he had just lived through a major crisis with *That Was The Week That* Was. Then, the Acting BBC Chairman, Sir James Duff, had told Greene that he and some of the other Governors were likely to resign unless *TW3* was taken off the air: too many of their Conservative friends were really angry about the programme. Greene did cancel TW3 and there was a terrible to-do – a major public outcry about political interference and a craven BBC. Greene gave the feeble but convenient excuse that 1964 was an election year. That fooled no one and, many years later, he told me that the real reason he axed TW3 was because he doubted that the BBC could survive the relentless government interference he anticipated if there had been a revolt by the Governors.

Normanbrook decided to 'take soundings' in Whitehall about *The War Game*. Indeed, according to the BBC's official historian, Asa Briggs, the film was shown to Sir Burke Trend, the Secretary to the Cabinet, Ministry of Defence and Home Office officials and the Chiefs of Staff. According to Greene's biographer, Michael Tracey, Normanbrook feared that 'showing the film on TV might damage the national interest, might have a significant effect on public attitudes towards the policy of the nuclear deterrent and might inadvertently be considered by some to seem as if the BBC was lending support to CND'. Senior colleagues were evenly divided as to whether or not the film should be broadcast. The official reason given for cancelling the broadcast was: 'The effect of the film has been judged by the BBC to be too horrifying for the medium of broadcast' – which, perhaps intentionally, left the way open for a later cinema showing. Hugh had spent many years in Hitler's Germany before the war, as a newspaper correspondent, and the experience had left him fiercely anti-censorship. In normal circumstances it would be unthinkable for him to have come down on the side of the censorious. Many years later, I was producing a documentary about Hugh Greene's time as Director General and he still found *The War Game* uncomfortable to talk about. He could not concede that the decision to ban the film was anyone's but his own, so proud was he of his reputation for fierce independence. However, there is little doubt in my mind that the main reason Greene banned *The War Game* was in deference to Lord Normanbrook's serious concerns about the 'national interest' and his continuing anxiety that Governors might resign. We can be sure that Greene would not have shared his Chairman's worry on one score: that the broadcast might recruit new members for the Campaign for Nuclear Disarmament. CND could already boast an astonishing list of star names – Bertrand Russell, Benjamin Britten, J. B. Priestley, Barbara Hepworth, Henry Moore, A. J. P. Taylor and Peggy Ashcroft. If Hugh Greene had been in one of his particularly mischievous moods, he might even have joined himself.

However, in the long term, the events surrounding the banning of *The War Game* led to an extraordinary and all-pervasive virus of self-censorship throughout the BBC. This corporate mental block seemed to be exclusively reserved for the debate about nuclear disarmament. I cannot think of any other topic that was similarly off limits, especially one that so seriously divided the main Opposition party. (When Neil Kinnock was leader of the Labour Party, he called for all British and American nuclear bases to be closed and for Trident to be scrapped, while acknowledging that this would bring an end to the United States' protection in time of war.) Somehow, the debate about the defence of the realm had attained an almost sacred status of untouchability. Unquestioningly embracing this aura of self-censorship, most BBC producers tended not to treat CND with the respect and admiration that was its due but with disdain and even contempt, as if it were an illegal subversive organisation – as MI5 did, at least until the mid 1990s. CND was painted as the puppet of Soviet propaganda rather than respected as a proper focus for the acute disquiet so many people felt about the dreadful menace that nuclear weapons represented. Of course CND had been infiltrated by the Soviet Union. So had many organisations of crucial interest to Moscow, like MI5 and MI6. While CND's annual Aldermaston March was normally shown on the *BBC News*, the vital issues that it raised were seldom debated at length. No serious documentary series were commissioned to explore ways that we, the British, might settle our tribal differences without wiping out the world. Disarmament was never a subject for *One Pair of Eyes*.

Fifteen years after *The War Game* controversy and nearly twenty after the Cuban Missile Crisis, the Campaign for Nuclear Disarmament underwent a major revival, with its membership increasing from four thousand to a hundred thousand. This was in response to the increasing tensions between the superpowers when the Soviet bloc introduced SS20 nuclear missiles in Eastern Europe and NATO deployed Cruise and Pershing missiles to counteract them. The British government announced that it would be deploying ninety-six Tomahawk Cruise missiles at Greenham Common in Berkshire. A huge march was organised from Cardiff to London and anti-nuclear campaigners chained themselves to the railings of the air base. These were edgy times. They also turned out to be the dying days of the Cold War but, of course, none of us knew it at the time, least of all the security services. They continued to be paranoid about members of CND, bugging their telephones and even, CND alleges, infiltrating an agent into its London office.

It was in this feverish atmosphere that my friend and senior producer colleague, Eddie Mirzoeff, approached E. P. Thompson to ask if he would deliver the 1981 Richard Dimbleby Lecture, the most prestigious event of its kind on television. Thompson was a Marxist historian of international repute, probably best known for his book *The Making of the English Working Class*. He was one of the principal intellectuals of the British Communist Party, leaving it in 1956 over the Soviet invasion of Hungary. Thompson was a leading luminary of the movement against nuclear weapons in Europe. However, his lecture, entitled 'Beyond the Cold War', was by no means an anti-nuclear polemic. As he always did, Eddie Mirzoeff had sought the views of a wide range of his contacts before deciding who would be the best person to give that year's lecture. Sir Isaiah Berlin, regarded as one of the leading liberal thinkers of the twentieth century, readily endorsed Eddie's choice of Thompson. The Managing Director of Television, Alasdair Milne, was happy for his name to go forward to the BBC Board of Governors. By custom, it was always they who issued the invitation.

Sir Ian Trethowan, the Director General, returned from holiday, enraged to find a *fait accompli* – that Thompson had been chosen and endorsed by the Governors. The invitation had already been dispatched. Ever wary of an irate Mrs Thatcher, at her lowest in the opinion polls (her popularity was soon to soar with the Falklands War), Trethowan insisted that the invitation to Thompson be rescinded, regardless of the public furore that was bound to – and did – ensue. Commentators who were well disposed towards the Director General claimed that he had selflessly taken the flack, rather than allow the Governors to become the butt of Prime Ministerial wrath. As a perfect example of the BBC's left hand not knowing what its right had was doing, the charismatic Professor Nicholas Humphrey had simultaneously received an invitation from the Science and Features

Department asking him to give the Bronowski Memorial Lecture. Humphrey is a distinguished psychologist, a key figure in the anti-nuclear movement. Ironically, his lecture, entitled 'Four Minutes to Midnight', was far more radically opposed to British defence policy than anything that Eddie Mirzoeff and E. P. Thompson had in mind. There was not a squeak of protest about Humphrey's radical and persuasive lecture nor, for that matter, about E. P. Thompson's when it was eventually broadcast by Channel 4.

Perhaps emboldened by this, Mick Jackson, a bright young director in Science and Features who went on to make his name in Hollywood, decided to test the water and proposed a film for the popular-science series *QED* about the effects of a nuclear bomb exploding over London. Mick describes the film he wanted to make, *The Consumer's Guide to Armageddon*:

> It would be rigorously scientific and non-political like a public information film. After some trepidation I was given the go-ahead to shoot it, on a tiny budget, mostly at the derelict Becton Gas Works on the Thames marshes. But it was made clear to me that it wasn't to be mentioned or to appear on any schedules until it had been seen and approved.*

Mick was asked to water down the title which the sixth floor regarded as too flippant. The film was broadcast simply as *The Guide to Armageddon*:

> I was unbelievably careful to shoot the film very coolly, with measured, factual narration. But the effect of the visuals (flying glass ripping into a pumpkin, an old woman's face, a side of beef charring and melting in the window of a butcher's shop) was vivid, arresting and quite powerful. However, the scientific facts were *unchallengeable*. I think the BBC saw this as their get-out-of-jail-free card. It was science not politics. There was a slight glitch. The film's premise was of a 1-megaton warhead air-bursting one mile above the dome of St Paul's. At the last minute, somebody on the sixth floor noticed that

* *Threads* director Mick Jackson, in correspondence with the author

Mrs Thatcher was to be presiding over the memorial service for the Falklands War dead at the same venue on the same day. This seemed to be testing fate and the transmission was rescheduled.*

You can always tell when the BBC is nervous about a programme. It reaches for the comfort blanket of a studio discussion to follow the controversial broadcast. On this occasion, the amiable Ludovic Kennedy was on hand to pour oil on troubled waters. The end result was praised by the critics and judged 'effective and responsible television'. Peter Watkins, still smarting from the cancellation of *The War Game* nearly twenty years earlier, rudely dubbed the film 'The Effects of Nuclear War on a Pork Chop'. Mick was by now obsessed with the subject and he asked for the go-ahead to research an in-depth follow-up, a major film about the effects of a full-scale nuclear attack on Britain:

> The key word here, I think, for the Corporation was 'research'. If this could be seen to be coming from the respected Science Department, and to be backed by the impeccable imprimatur of the world's scientists, it could be defended as 'effective and responsible television' and maybe they'd be finally off the *War Game* hook. I guess I spent a year at least – probably closer to two – travelling through the US, Britain and Europe, talking to nuclear physicists, defence strategists, meteorologists, doctors, psychologists, agronomists, economists, political commentators, radical and establishment . . . everyone I could think of. And I read massive amounts of stuff. Massive. Again it was to be totally off the radar. I was to do all my own research and take as much time as I needed. 'Just get it right.'†

Mick collaborated with the writer Barry Hines, author of the book which Ken Loach had made into the award-winning film *Kes*. They chose to make the film about the effects of a nuclear attack, not as a spectacular disaster movie, but through the prism of two ordinary families in Sheffield. They called the film *Threads*. It is horrifying

---

* *Threads* director Mick Jackson, in correspondence with the author
† ibid.

because it is so matter of fact, so underplayed. We see the survivors steadily deteriorating physically from hunger, cold and radiation sickness, and mentally, as it dawns on them that there will be no help from outside. Much of the action takes place within one of the regional seats of government where officials are seen to be helpless victims themselves. Covering a period of thirteen years from the time of the nuclear blast, the film is punctuated by a sober narration of the chilling consequences of nuclear war. *Threads* is one of those few films that you dream about after watching it – wishing you could wake up. Although its subject matter is very similar to *The War Game,* its lack of polemic makes it less in-your-face. It convinces without trying to convert you. It's a very powerful film. When Mick showed it to his BBC bosses, they were mightily relieved not only that it was transmittable but that it was such a distinguished contribution to the nuclear debate. Brian Wenham, the Director of Programmes, told Mick, 'This is a major piece of work.' High praise indeed from that enigmatic oracle. The film was nominated for six BAFTA awards and won three, including one for Mick as Best Director.

The Home Office had allowed Mick and the writer, Barry Hines, to sit in on a Home Office post-nuclear-war exercise, training local government officials in the roles they would have to play. The two filmmakers found it deeply depressing and unimpressive but it gave them plenty of material for the screenplay. However, there was a quid quo pro. Home Office officials were to be allowed to see the film before transmission. After viewing it, the officials arrived in Brian Wenham's office at the Television Centre, Mick remembers, with a long list of apparent inaccuracies and 'lacunae':

One of the advantages of having done my own two years of research was that I was able to at least answer them robustly, in most cases rebut them chapter and verse, and in a couple of cases 'slap them upside the face' by quoting from their own publications . . . Most alarmingly to me personally, a couple of thuggish looking young guys in suits sat just behind and to each side of me, just outside my peripheral vision. I guess they were MI5 and I don't know if they were there to watch my body language, whisk me away by the shoulders, if it became necessary, or just intimidate me. If it was the latter it certainly worked.*

Allowing a government department to see a programme before its broadcast was fairly common practice. Often access was conditional on such a viewing if potentially sensitive or secret material was to be filmed. I had shown Jenny Barraclough's *Bomb Disposal Men* to the Ministry of Defence before transmission because we had been allowed to show top-secret equipment that was being deployed in Northern Ireland for disabling explosive devices. The BBC stance is that such viewings are provided solely so that the experts can check that the producer has not transgressed the agreed line; the BBC, we would recite priggishly, would only listen to comments on the factual accuracy of the programme. In other words, the viewing was *not* an opportunity for government censorship. This time, the Home Office had bartered the right to a viewing of *Threads* by providing access to its nuclear-war exercise. As it turned out, the Home Office had the best of the bargain because Mick could probably have made his film just as well without the limited help he was given. But it freed the BBC from a very sticky dilemma. Would it have dared refuse the Home Office the viewing that Lord Normanbrook had allowed for *The War Game,* two decades earlier? In the hostile climate of an increasingly strident Thatcher government, victorious in the Falklands, now within weeks of its 'victory' against Arthur Scargill and the miners, would Director General Milne have dared say 'Boo' to the goose?

To Alasdair's credit, he was determined to exorcise the shame of *The War Game* ban and he scheduled it for broadcast in July 1985 – better twenty years late than never. He had been heartened that *Threads* had received so much praise and negligible flack, a year earlier. *The War Game* was shown one night, followed by a repeat of *Threads* on the next. The two films were part of a special season of programming entitled *After the Bomb,* marking the 40th anniversary of the bombing of Hiroshima and Nagasaki. *The War Game* no longer had the shock value

* *Threads* director Mick Jackson, in correspondence with the author

that had so frightened the horses when it was first made, partly because the special effects available to a low-budget drama documentary in the 1960s now made it look rather amateurish and very dated. Also, a film that had been talked about for twenty years had exceptionally high expectations to live up to – perhaps too high. Significantly, too, the world had moved on. Mikhail Gorbachev had just been appointed General Secretary of the Communist Party of the Soviet Union and his *glasnost* was the first real sign of a thaw in the Cold War.

So this first broadcast of *The War Game* was not expected to be a trauma for the BBC. However, irony of ironies, it was pushed completely off the agenda because, the day before it was to be shown, Paul Hamann's *Real Lives* programme, *At the Edge of the Union,* was banned by the BBC Board of Governors while the Director General, Alasdair Milne, was abroad on holiday. Somehow, while Alasdair was Director General, it never seemed to rain gently when it could pour like hell. While the whole of the television industry was up in arms, denouncing the BBC Governors for censoring the *Real Lives* film – in front of the world's press at the Edinburgh Television Festival – the *Observer* exploded a quite separate but equally sensational anti-BBC bombshell. It so dominated the headlines that the BBC's first broadcast of *The War Game* might never even have happened. The *Observer*'s front page headline read: REVEALED: HOW MI5 VETS BBC STAFF.

CHAPTER 12

Cloak and Dagger

I knew how the MI5 system of vetting BBC staff worked because I had, in a way, been part of it. I so disapproved that I would talk about it quite openly in the BBC bar, half-expecting someone would leak it to the press. When the story broke, three years after I had left the BBC, my ex-colleagues were terrified of risking the sack by briefing the newspapers and, instead, proposed to the journalists that they talk to me. The *Daily Telegraph*, the *Daily Mail*, the *Guardian*, the *Observer* and *The Times* – the whole of Fleet Street was on to the story. And what a good one it turned out to be. The BBC is always preening itself on being quite independent of government, never afraid to criticise politicians and public institutions. It likes to flaunt its unique royal charter that protects its independence and guarantees, through the licence fee, the income that its competitors must struggle so hard to earn. The BBC can be a bit sanctimonious and here was the perfect opportunity for its opponents in the commercial media to pull the BBC down a notch or two and kick it in the balls.

What would happen is this. Every year the BBC did a sweep of the universities in search of bright new recruits. Those shortlisted were called for interviews in London. The Appointments Board comprised three senior production people, one from television, one from domestic radio and one from the external services at Bush House. The board was usually chaired by a gentle but steely middle-aged lady from the Appointments Department called Barbara. She always brought us her own homemade biscuits for the coffee break. Once we had chosen the people to join the Graduate Trainee Scheme, Barbara would make for the boardroom telephone. Surreptitiously cupping the dial, so that none of us could see whom she was dialling, she would read over the surnames, initials and dates of birth of the chosen candidates to her contact at the other end of the line. The information she was seeking in return was clearly computerised because the response was almost instantaneous. The other interesting clue was that Barbara dialled only a four-figure number – in other words an *internal* number on the BBC switchboard. 'That's "formalities" over and done with then,' she would beam. 'It's always so much easier when we don't have to appoint someone from Essex University, if you know what I mean.' We producers nodded sagely – innocents abroad in a very wicked world.

This was MI5 negative vetting. If there was nothing on your file, you were in the clear. If there was something on your file, you had a big problem. No one would tell you what it was – and the chances were that whatever it was was wrong – but you had no way of correcting it. The vetting 'service', if that is the right word, was directed by a retired Army Intelligence officer, Brigadier Ronald L. Stonham, who sat in a pokey little office on the first floor of Broadcasting House. It was off these very corridors that George Orwell had imagined his Ministry of Truth in his novel *1984*. Behind a door labelled, rather cryptically, 'Special Duties – Management' sat the good brigadier with three assistants. He was, it turned out, the BBC's liaison officer with MI5's Domestic Subversion branch, which stored *a million* potential suspects on its computer. At the time the whole affair became public, MI5 was vetting over five thousand BBC staff, almost a quarter of the total workforce. All a bit out of proportion, you would think, but everything connected with national security was unreal during the Cold War. There were Reds under many beds, we were told. Our intelligence services were convinced that the Soviet Union and its satellite intelligence services from Eastern Europe were out to destroy our democratic institutions by political subversion. If you worked for the civil service you knew you were going to be vetted. At the BBC they lied to you by denying that it happened. When the MI5 scandal broke, Director General Alasdair Milne and his minions pretended to be much more surprised than they really were. Security vetting had been going on at the BBC for half a century. No doubt it was a good idea to prevent Goebbels from infiltrating a cluster of Nazis into the newsroom during the Second World War, but only a sloppy and complacent management could have allowed this political hot potato to simmer for another forty years until it became a public outrage, a civil-liberties *cause célèbre* and an enormous embarrassment for the BBC.

It has recently come to light that Hugh Greene, the refreshingly progressive Director General in the sixties, wanted *more* of the staff vetted than MI5 did itself. In his recently published *The Defence of the Realm: The Authorized History of MI5*, Christopher Andrew cites the security service archive recounting that Greene and his colleagues 'did not wish to employ anyone who might damage [the BBC's] reputation for impartiality'. The security services themselves, they claimed, 'were concerned with defence interests but [the BBC] were really concerned with the avoidance of embarrassment'. To those of us who knew Hugh Greene this revelation seems astonishing. On the other hand, it is certainly true that the credibility of controversial programmes like *That Was The Week That Was* would have been severely compromised had it turned out that their production teams were crawling with traitors. What's more, Greene did know the world of secret intelligence intimately. In the fifties he had been seconded to the army in Malaya to mastermind psychological warfare against the Communists and he was very close to his brother, Graham, who worked for MI6 under Kim Philby. Hugh's widow, Sarah, recently told me that whenever they came back from an 'interesting' holiday destination, he would disappear for secretive debriefing lunches in St James's. And, by the time he married Sarah, his fourth wife, Hugh was well over seventy. In this world of mirrors nothing is quite as it seems.

Many years later, in what turned out to be one of the most active periods of MI5 vetting at the BBC, the long-retired Hugh Greene told the *Sunday Times*, 'One thing I can state quite categorically is that there has never been any victimisation of anyone for their political views at the BBC.' Ambiguous and economical with the truth. The victimisation was often not of those 'at the BBC' but applicants trying to get in. What Greene didn't say was that he was required by the Official Secrets Act to deny there was any vetting. A BBC memo recently released under the Freedom of Information Act explained plaintively, 'Secrecy of the complete vetting operation is imposed upon us by the Security Service –

it is not of our making.' Greene's Director of Administration, John Arkell, was quite boastful about the deceit. He advised a colleague, 'You might like to get a bit of credit for the BBC next time you talk to MI5 by telling them that I stuck resolutely to the brief which you prepared for me. In spite of very pointed and penetrating questions I still denied that we had any vetting procedures.' Later Greene admitted that he himself had encountered difficulties when he had joined the BBC. 'MI5 thought I was a Communist but it turned out to be a mistake.' He was one of the lucky ones who found out what was wrongly held against him and was able to have it put it right.

Anna Ford, who subsequently became ITN's star reporter, was targeted by MI5 when my successor tried to contract her as a reporter for *Man Alive*. He successfully resisted the pressure and found out that the reason she had been blacklisted was because she had once lived with a former Communist. The distinguished journalist Isobel Hilton was blacklisted by personnel officers at BBC Scotland because she was a member of the entirely innocuous Scottish-China Association. She assumes MI5 muddled it up with some more radical outfit. Stephen Peet was prevented from joining the BBC staff because he continued to meet his brother, who was a Communist living in East Germany. The veto was finally rescinded only after the persistent and prolonged intervention of his MP.

The Personnel Department did its best to prevent Jeff Perks from working on the arts series, *Omnibus*. Jeff had served as a territorial with the SAS and later became a member of the British Communist Party. As a student he had made a radical film about three building workers, jailed for picketing offences. Part of it had been shown on ITV's *This Week* and Tory MPs had complained. Barrie Gavin, the editor of *Omnibus*, took issue with Chris Storey, the personnel officer who had told him that Jeff Perks was unacceptable.

'What do you mean by unacceptable?' asked Gavin.

'Not acceptable.'

'I shall talk to the Head of Personnel. I presume that he will tell me why,' said Gavin.

'Not necessarily,' replied Storey.

'Well, if you don't tell me I'm going to do two things. One, I'm going straight to my head of department and, two, I'm going public and will make sure that every newspaper and television station knows about this.'

'I would strongly advise you not to do that,' warned Storey.

Gavin persisted and went to see the Managing Director of Television. 'I don't see what's so difficult about this,' Gavin told him. 'I am asking Perks to make a film about a poster-maker in the middle of Exmoor. I'm not sending him out on a Poseidon nuclear submarine.'

Eventually he was allowed to hire Perks, who made a good film for *Omnibus*. However, the same rigmarole started all over again when Barrie Gavin offered him a new contract. For a second time he won the battle but he was exasperated. 'The Communist Party is not a proscribed or illegal organisation and, anyway, the notion that the modern Communist Party is revolutionary is laughable.' There was worse news to come. It transpired that MI5, in league with the BBC's personnel officers, had made a concerted effort to purge the Television Drama Department of some of its star directors because of their perfectly legal but unconventional political affiliations. This was McCarthyism with a British face. In many democracies MI5's behaviour would have been illegal. It could be that it was in Britain too.

The most prominent target of the MI5 plot against BBC Drama was the unquestionably talented Roland Joffée, director of such feature films as *The Killing Fields* and *City of Joy*. He went on to win the top prize at the 1986 Cannes Film Festival with *The Mission* and a nomination for an Academy Award. BBC producer Tony Garnett signed up Joffée to direct a play about the Welfare State, called *The Spongers*. It was hard-hitting and radical, written by the left-wing playwright Jim Allen. Garnett was then told by his boss that he couldn't hire Joffée. The reason? 'He hasn't got BH clearance. It's the man in the mac at Broadcasting House,' he was told – a none too subtle allusion to the vetting people at the BBC's head office. MI5 deemed Joffée a security risk because he had attended political meetings of the Workers' Revolutionary Party. He was not a member of the party and he had severed all connections with it at the time the BBC job came up. Too bad.

In their alarming book, *Blacklist: The Inside Story of Political Vetting,*

Mark Hollingsworth and Richard Norton-Taylor described the meeting when Tony Garnett confronted Alasdair Milne about the ban on Joffée.

> Milne confirmed there was a problem and tried to placate Garnett by offering him a glass of whisky. But Garnett was seething and said he would 'go public' if the veto on Joffée's appointment was not withdrawn. 'If you want all this business to come out then it's in your hands. If you don't hire Joffée then I'm off as well and imagine what it would look like if I walked out in the middle of my contract. If this continues to happen then I won't be able to hire the people I want, which is my job as a producer.' Milne didn't argue . . . He picked up the phone. 'Hire Joffée,' he snapped. Joffée's contract was confirmed and *The Spongers* became a big success, winning that year's Prix Italia.

Besides causing an unnecessary row that drew unwelcome attention to the secret MI5 vetting process, the move against Joffée showed an unpardonable ignorance about the way film and television production works. In drama it is of course the writer who is responsible for the content of a play, along with the producer who chooses both the writer and the director. The producer, if anyone, is the person to watch. And they did that too. Personnel had earlier tried to block the appointment of Tony Garnett himself. As well as a phenomenal track record as a producer, he has to his credit one of the BBC's all-time outstanding plays, *Cathy Come Home*. They also objected to his colleague, Kenith Trodd, who went on to become one of the BBC's most respected and successful drama producers with *Leeds United, Days of Hope* and Dennis Potter's *Pennies from Heaven*. Attempts were also made to prevent Roy Battersby from directing *King of the Ghetto* for BBC2 because he was a member of the Socialist Workers' Party; and John Goldschmidt from directing a *Play for Today*. His offence, it transpired, was that he had been part of an exchange of students between his London art college in Hornsey and a Czech film school. He has never been a Communist.

While MI5 and the Personnel Department no doubt believed that they were exercising a proper restraint on the employment of subversives, it could just as well be argued that they themselves were the subversives – with their clandestine interference, undermining the legitimate creative processes of the BBC and ruining blameless careers. As the MI5 spooks searched the BBC's entrails for conspiracies to overthrow government, we now know that in their midst were colleagues who themselves were leaking state secrets to the Soviet Union and plotting to overthrow the elected government of Harold Wilson. Could those of us who managed producers and writers not be trusted to protect our programmes from the taint of Soviet propaganda? If not, why were we entrusted with responsibility for everything else?

These days the MI5 vetting of staff is much reduced, claims the BBC, and I think we can be pretty sure that it is the case. After been caught so publicly with its pants down, it seems unlikely that MI5 would attempt such media purges again. However, the objection to vetting, in principle, does not yet seem to have been addressed: if the BBC is independent why should its staff *ever* be vetted by the government, especially when those employed by other media organisations are not? And the fundamental flaw of negative vetting remains – its secrecy. Civil servants who work for MI5 are unlikely to be any more competent than their counterparts elsewhere – and we know what cock-ups they make. It is inevitable that wrong and sometimes malicious material finds its way on to MI5 files. So if we can't see the information that is kept on us, how can we ensure that it is correct and, perhaps more important, corrected? The answer is, of course, we can't. I tried. I decided to vet myself since the law, up to a point, now allowed me to do so. And I thought it would be fun. Since I had left the BBC the government had introduced the Data Protection Act giving all employees the right to see all the computer files that their employers maintain on them. Or, as it was to turn out, *almost* all the computer files.

A couple of years after I had left the BBC, I wrote formally to them asking them to release all the information they held about me on their computers. They wrote back and said that there was a fee of £10 for each file they kept on me and there were something like fifteen files. I posted them a cheque for £150. Nothing happened. I waited and then I wrote again – and again. The BBC just didn't reply. So I complained to the Data Protection Registrar and received a very speedy response. 'We are watching big organisations like the BBC,' said the officer I spoke to.

'They are just the ones who are going to try and wriggle out of their obligations.' It turned out that this brisk, no-nonsense woman was coming to London specially to interview me. 'How far is your office from Euston Station?' I was mystified. She needed to know the distance because she was bringing a massively heavy suitcase with her – all the records on me she had managed to extract from the BBC.

What a disappointment they were: computer print-outs of my travelling and hotel expenses going back years; monthly statements of my pension contributions; production costs I had properly authorised. In fact, everything you could possible want to know except what I *really* wanted to know. After much vexation and frustration – goodness, the BBC is as good at obfuscation as any government department! – I was told that my records had never been computerised. Since they were retained as paper files I had no right to see them under the Data Protection Act. As for any MI5 files, they were exempt from the Data Protection Act anyway. I doubt if they will be released in a thousand years. A pity the BBC didn't tell me all that to start with.

Years later, when the BBC gave staff the right to see their paper files (but not, of course, their MI5 ones), we learnt that there had been an orgy of shredding. Others, as suspicious as I, were equally anxious to know what dirt the BBC kept on them. They were not surprised to be told that their personal files no longer existed. It is said that Brigadier Stonham affixed an upside-down Christmas-tree sticker on the personal files of those deemed never to be employed again. I like to think that *Monty Python* made that bit up. In those days a quarter of the BBC's total budget was spent on administration. It is a wonder that any programmes got made at all.

In all my professional life I only once discovered that I was under MI5 surveillance. There might have been other times when spooks took an interest in my work, but either they were smart enough to conceal themselves from me or, more likely, they had far more pressing assignments elsewhere. Being caught out in London was a surprise because it all happened with lightning speed. We had been kicking around programme ideas in the office and one of us suggested a major documentary on a foreign embassy in London. It had never been done and we all agreed that it was a good idea to put to our bosses. I suggested that we start at the top and approach the USSR Embassy. It would be a major scoop and very apposite, since the British were deeply obsessed with Russian spy stories – from John Le Carré to James Bond. The Soviet Embassy in Kensington was known to house both the KGB and Military Intelligence and it was no secret that they maintained close links with the other Eastern European intelligence agencies.

The more we thought about it the better seemed our plan. The challenge was to persuade the Russians and our bosses of its merits. Much to our surprise the Soviet press attaché agreed to see us almost immediately. He was thoroughly agreeable to our plan, even volunteering that we could film diplomats' children at their summer camp in Hastings. This all sounded too good to be true. All that remained was to have the whole matter approved by the Soviet Ambassador, who was expected back the following day. The assistant producer and I were thrilled with the morning's events. What a scoop to offer to our programme controller! We knew he would find it hard to say no. We hailed a taxi to take us the seven-minute ride from the Soviet Embassy back to our office. I was just giving the good news to my colleagues when the telephone rang. It was the Controller of Overseas and Foreign Relations at Broadcasting House. I knew him slightly. 'What the hell were you doing at the Soviet Embassy this morning without informing this office? This is a very sensitive time . . . ' I was amazed. It was less than two hours since I had entered the Soviet Embassy – just twenty minutes since I had returned to my office – and the BBC mandarins already knew!

Much later I learnt why the BBC was in such a lather. Oleg Lyalin, a KGB agent posing as an official with the Soviet Trade Delegation in London, had just been arrested for drunken driving by the Metropolitan Police. He offered to disclose everything he knew about the KGB if he and his Russian girlfriend were granted asylum. He was the first Soviet Intelligence agent to defect since the Second World War and he sang like a canary. On the basis of Lyalin's debriefing, Prime Minister Edward Heath announced the expulsion of one hundred and five Soviet diplomats for 'conduct unbecoming of diplomats'. This was unprecedented – a big story. How pleased the press attaché would have been if we had completed our documentary on the fun-loving, Soviet-bloc citizens in Britain, going about their lawful business with enigmatic smiles while dancing their nights away around a campfire in Sussex. I suppose I should have been grateful to MI5 for preventing me from making a fool of myself. Instead I felt a sharp chill run down my spine.

One high-profile colleague who was not so lucky was Sue MacGregor, the charming and talented presenter of Radio 4's flagship *Today* programme. Perhaps to counter her rather prim-and-proper image, she confesses in her autobiography that, at the time of the expulsions, she was having a brief affair with a Soviet scientific adviser based in London. He was one of those expelled and, to her utter astonishment, turned out to be the top KGB man in London. I wonder if somewhere in the bowels of the BBC all this is scrupulously recorded in dusty files whose existence is still denied. I suspect that if I needed to gain access to such history – and my BBC staff file – the easiest way to do so would be to make a long-distance phone call to the archive department of the Lubyanka in Moscow's Dzerzhinsky Square.

CHAPTER 13

The Blockbuster

Three years is probably long enough for anyone to edit a major factual television series without becoming stale. Certainly it was considered the optimum term for a BBC controller. By 1975 I thought it was time for a change and Desmond wanted a change from presenting *Man Alive*. He persuaded Aubrey Singer, now Controller of BBC2, that he should present a major documentary series called, simply, *Americans*, and that I should executive produce it. The idea was an attractive one: a series of thirteen fifty-minute profiles of real people who reflected the legendary American characters we know from fiction – books, films and television.

Blockbuster series were a hallmark of BBC2. When his was the only channel in colour, David Attenborough had commissioned Kenneth Clark's *Civilisation*, a glorious thirteen-part essay on the wonders of our European heritage. Following its success, such major series became a regular feature of the channel – *The Ascent of Man*, with Jacob Bronowski, *The Search for the Nile, Alistair Cooke's America,* John Kenneth Galbraith's *Age of Uncertainty*; and then all those spectacular natural-history series from David Attenborough himself, beginning with *Life on Earth*.

Although these series were, almost without exception, highly acclaimed and popular with the audience, they were very expensive to produce. There were three factors that helped soften the blow. First, high-quality colour programmes were encouraging more people to buy the much more expensive colour-TV licences so the BBC's income was temporarily growing faster than inflation; secondly, Time-Life in America was pre-buying these series for substantial sums; it had spotted an opening in the US market. To break the stranglehold of the networks, the new subscription cable operators were frenetically buying all the good British programmes they could lay their hands on. The third little money-spinner was the book of the series. BBC Publications made a mint from them – as did their authors.

The first such major series to come from General Features was *The British Empire.* Unfortunately, it wasn't very good and its hostile reception was the final nail in Chris Brasher's coffin, the end of his unhappy term as a departmental head, and the occasion for his replacement by Desmond. The series was widely accused of left-wing bias, of mocking and even sneering at those who had spent their lives working in the Empire. Many high-powered letters were written to *The Times* and the Director General was forced to concede that the series was 'flawed' – a favourite management euphemism for 'a cock-up'.* The crisis was exacerbated by an angry debate in the House of Lords, where it was alleged that the BBC's financial partnership with Time-Life had predisposed the production to adopt an American bias against imperialism. Three years later, General Features was to embark on *Explorers,* again in partnership with Time-Life.

Thirteen explorers, Christopher Columbus, Henry Morton Stanley, Mary Kingsley and ten others as famous, were each to be featured in a fifty-minute dramatised documentary shot on location. Michael Latham, who had been the senior *Man Alive* producer in its early days, was put in charge although he had no experience either of drama production or of the almost insuperable logistic difficulties of shooting such epics in remote parts of the world. Michael was a secretive, even devious, man who played his cards so close to his chest that we sometimes wondered whether he had been dealt quite such a good hand as he would have us believe. He chose to prepare the series without calling on the expertise available to him in the Drama Department. It could well be that Mike realised how the costs of *Explorers* would escalate if the powerful service departments, like Costume and Make-up, came to regard the series as a drama production.

For years, documentaries had included scenes which re-enacted real events; and the arts programme, *Monitor,* had made whole programmes

---

* 'Deeply flawed' meant that a programme should never have been made and its producer needed to 'consider his position'.

using actors without upsetting the apple cart, like Peter Watkins's *Culloden* and Ken Russell's brilliant portrait of Edward Elgar. Chris Ralling's drama-documentary series, *Search for the Nile,* was the first major series that was unquestionably a drama production. However, since it was shot in Africa, using mostly local actors and local production services, it had slipped beneath the radar of the service departments. They realised they had missed out and, sensing that drama documentaries were to be a new force in the land, made portentous speeches about being the guardians of BBC quality and forced themselves on to the *Explorers'* bandwagon. They insisted on unrealistically large crews and over-elaborate costumes. One set of grass skirts was so expensive that the production team decided to use them again in another African episode. The production was charged through the nose for them – twice. The costs of *Explorers* began to soar out of control.

Mike Latham's choice of directors was, to say the least, eccentric. One of them was Lord Snowdon, then married to Princess Margaret and a very fine photographer. Michael contracted him to direct two of the episodes, and his girlfriend, later his wife, Lucy Lindsay Hogg, was hired as his personal assistant and travelling companion on the second of them. Snowdon had never directed actors in his life and not much film either. Michael must have thought that the publicity value of Snowdon's name outweighed his inexperience. A much better idea, almost a saving grace, was to contract David Attenborough to present and narrate the series.

Explorers seemed to lurch from one panic to the next. Michael found himself troubleshooting episodes that were being filmed simultaneously in different parts of the developing world, and on one occasion, he telephoned Desmond from some remote location in South America requesting a senior producer to go and sort out a dispute in some other godforsaken spot in Africa. Luckily for me, I was not chosen for this thankless task and Paul Bonner, later to become Controller at Channel 4, was sent instead. Robin Scott, who had originally commissioned *Explorers* as Controller of BBC2, had now been promoted to replace David Attenborough as Director of Programmes and he was seriously alarmed about the ever-increasing cost of the series. He was a mild and urbane man and it was a shock for Desmond to be told by him that *Explorers* was 'bleeding the television service white'. Radical action was taken and the series cut from thirteen episodes to ten but this was not enough to stem the haemorrhage. *Explorers* was considered moderately successful by the critics and a financial disaster by management. This was probably the first time that the sixth floor had begun seriously to wonder if Desmond's obsession with programme making was distracting him from keeping a firm grip on the administration of his busy department.

Time-Life sold *Explorers* to Mobil, the sponsor of *Masterpiece Theatre*, a prestigious drama slot on the public broadcasting service, PBS. The first thing that Mobil did was to repackage the whole series, replacing David Attenborough with Anthony Quinn, and retitling the series, *Ten Who Dared*. Each of their programmes contained not only an episode of *Explorers* but also a mini-documentary showing fearless Mobil oilmen, daring to drill the desert, to build oil platforms, to construct refineries. What had started out innocently as a drama-documentary series about famous explorers from the past, with no other purpose than to inform and entertain the British viewer, had become an hour-long commercial for Mobil. The message of *Ten Who Dared* was as clear as day: free enterprise unfettered by government interference is the Mobil way – the American way. Senior producers were nervously shown this travesty in London by Time-Life executives. We were appalled by what Mobil had done but we couldn't help admiring their cheek. We were also shocked that our bosses had allowed Mammon to storm the BBC citadel. None of us had ever seen such masterly media manipulation. In these black arts we were as babes in the wood. By not kicking up an almighty fuss we proved that we were also whores.

Americans was a far less ambitious affair than *Explorers* and a much simpler operation to produce than most of the blockbuster series that had preceded it. Usually such series would have an overall narrative and directors were sent to the four corners of the earth to shoot the sequences that illustrated it. The episodes of *Americans* were profiles of individuals, confined to one locality. This meant that a director didn't have to worry constantly whether the scenes he was shooting would marry with the work of other directors on the series. This was our publicity blurb:

Americans is a living social history of the United States. The series profiles a Private Eye who can trace his roots through Philip Marlowe back to the original Pinkerton Agency; one of Hollywood's long line of child film stars, Jodie Foster; a Louisiana plantation owner set against the background of slavery and Southern gracious living; the First Lady, Rosalyn, wife of President Jimmy Carter. Other profiles include the President of General Motors, a District Attorney, a Rancher, a Preacher, a Football Coach, an Indian Chief, a Teacher, an Immigrant and the General commanding America's elite 82nd Airborne Division.

It was obvious to me that almost the most important person in the production team would be the researcher. We could sit in London forever discussing whether we needed a cowboy or a rancher, a preacher or a teacher, but what mattered most was that the person we chose could sustain a high-profile, fifty-minute documentary. Sally Hardcastle was the first researcher of our team to cross the Atlantic. She was a thoroughly experienced journalist, the daughter of Bill Hardcastle, the pioneering presenter of *The World at One*. In no time she had found us our teacher. Gerri Feemster was an attractive and dedicated young black woman, living in Harlem, achieving fantastic results by motivating teenage girls and boys in one of New York's roughest and toughest schools. This was the first of the series to be completed. It lacked the glamour of many of the later films we were to make but its tough subject matter showed Desmond at his best – as a first-class interviewer.

We were lucky that the BBC's New York office had a quite exceptional television producer working for it. He was Chris Jeans on secondment from the Current Affairs Department in London. By chance, he had joined Anglia very shortly after I had left and we knew each other. He came to New York to make a film, met and married Jessica, an assistant district attorney, and decided to make the city his home. The job of New York producer was often given to someone who had blotted his copybook in London and it was seldom that the incumbent was of much use to visiting production teams. Chris was quite the reverse. He had fought for the job and he was determined to make a success of it.

Because he provided back-up to all the production departments in London, he had an incredible range of expertise from politics to pop music, Hollywood to baseball. It was he who had first contacted the Pentagon on our behalf and helped us to choose one of the top generals in the US army for our series. He knew exactly the sort of glamorous soldier we were looking for and the army surprisingly delivered the goods. Lieutenant General Thomas H. Tackaberry looked great on paper. He was commander of fifteen thousand soldiers, the legendary 82nd Airborne Division, a war hero who had received the Distinguished Service Cross for heroism three times, first in Korea, and twice in Vietnam. Sally Hardcastle flew to Fort Bragg in North Carolina to check him out. She reported back that he was our man.

The 82nd Airborne Division knew how to put on a good show for the cameras and in no time waves of planes were droning towards Fort Bragg for what turned out to be the most spectacular parachute drop ever – hundreds of men, including their commanding officer, armed to the teeth and with camouflaged faces, falling from the sky against a backdrop of military vehicles lazily floating down behind them. On the ground, the soldiers assembled into their formations; when their general was satisfied, he saluted and barked, 'Airborne!' The soldiers roared back at him, 'All the way, sir.' Then they formed into a column and jogged towards the camera, guns ready for action, chanting rhythmically, at first, and then screaming, 'Airborne,' as they came to a halt. The directors of great Vietnam war films like *Platoon, The Deer Hunter, Apocalypse Now* and *Full Metal Jacket* would have died for the sequences we shot for *Americans* that day. Desmond and the director decided that a parachute drop should also be the background for Desmond's to-camera introduction to our documentary. There were no mobile teleprompters available then so presenters had to learn and remember their words. It was hilarious at the Christmas party but dreadful at the time. Desmond kept fluffing his lines. Time after time, the parachutes were repacked, the men and equipment loaded back on to the planes. Then they would take off again, manoeuvre into formation, and slowly fly back over Desmond and our film crew, repeating the drop, goodness knows how many times. Luckily it was the American taxpayer who picked up the tab.

Our filming at Fort Bragg took place less than a year after the United States' worst military humiliation ever – the retreat from Vietnam and the fall of Saigon. General Tackaberry had been a key player in that traumatic episode and now, leading America's elite fighting force in the shadow of that defeat, his job was to restore confidence and instil patriotism in the young soldiers who would be the first to be killed next time round, wherever in the world that might be. The general told us how severely morale had been undermined by the massive popular protest against the Vietnam War. He graphically described the nightmare his troops had had to endure when they travelled through domestic airports in the United States. They were spat at and jeered, sometimes even jostled, by their fellow Americans. Thirty years later Tackaberry's boss, US Defense Secretary Robert McNamara, was publicly to regret the Vietnam War and his part in it. When we were filming the general, the wound was still too raw for any such lament.

Meanwhile, I had demoted myself from executive producer to my original role of 'bloody researcher'. Or, more accurately, I was doubling up, doing both jobs. First of all, I loved research, but, more particularly, some of the characters we needed to find for *Americans* were going to be very difficult to secure because of their near-impenetrable minders – agents, lawyers and public-relations men. Having broken through those barriers, it needed someone senior enough and confident enough to say no to a proffered but unsuitable gift horse. The three really tricky but crucial subjects were the First Lady, the Company President and the Film Star. I chose also to research another two of our thirteen films, the Plantation Owner and the District Attorney. The subjects intrigued me and they were almost sure to be found in parts of America that I had never visited. I was also a little nervous as to what the director, Ivor Dunkerton, might get up to if I wasn't around. He was a bit of a handful. On *Man Alive* he and I had worked well, if warily, together. He had good ideas and I let him go off and make them, but he had a tendency to kick against the pricks even when – or especially when – the pricks were on his side. I was fearful of letting him run amok on *Americans* with a researcher too junior to restrain his contrariness or remind him that he was part of a team. Ivor was a temperamental racehorse but, if you treated him right, there was a better than evens chance that he would gallop in first past the post. Ivor did us proud and made three elegant films for the series. I was his 'bloody researcher' for two of them.

And it was to Hollywood that I now went in search of our film star. I would probably have given up had it not been for the formidable young British journalist Barbra Paskin whom Chris Jeans in the New York office had put me on to. Later she was to move in with David Hemmings and write Dudley Moore's biography, but when I first met her she was living the life of a bachelor girl in a basement studio flat, just off Santa Monica Boulevard. She was star struck and had bravely decided to sell up in London and see if she could earn her living as a journalist in Hollywood. Fortunately the BBC had kept her pretty busy – especially reporting for Barry Norman's *Film Night*. Her energy was fearsome and nothing would throw her off the scent, but she and I very nearly drew a blank. Hollywood is a powerful machine whose sole purpose is to persuade people to part with their money in exchange for a seat in the cinema. Anything that does not directly serve this purpose is malevolently regarded as a distraction. When agents heard we were from the BBC they seldom returned our calls. 'My client doesn't need the BBC,' was the monotonous turndown if ever we got to speak to an agent at all. Everyone knew the BBC didn't pay good money. Indeed the whole television industry was regarded with the utmost contempt.

Suddenly Barbra had a breakthrough. Brandy Foster, the mother of fourteen-year-old Jodie, said she would like to meet us. Jodie was a veteran. A year earlier she had starred as a child prostitute with Robert de Niro in Martin Scorsese's *Taxi Driver* for which she had just received an Oscar nomination. Jodie said at the time, 'I feel so good after seeing myself in *Taxi Driver* that I no longer want to be President of the United States. I want to become a serious actress.' Jodie had also played Tallulah in *Bugsy Malone*, made several films for Disney and starred alongside Martin Sheen in a spooky and very adult psychological thriller, *The Little Girl Who Lives Down The Lane*. Who needed Elizabeth Taylor or Gregory Peck for *Americans* if the newest of all the Hollywood stars would play ball? We drove to the Fosters' house, an unpretentious, modern, two-storey affair with a well-tended garden, in a quiet street, not ten minutes' drive from Hollywood Boulevard. Brandy was a little bird of a woman, intent, darting about making us comfortable, while Jodie, hunched and scowling, like any American teenager, loomed in the background, sizing us up. They lived alone in the house. Jodie's two sisters were married and her older brother, Buddy, had moved out, so there was no man about the house, no father. He had abandoned Brandy just before Jodie was born. It was quite plain that the subject was off-limits but his absence had clearly been the financial motivation for Brandy to push Buddy and then Jodie into TV commercials. There had been no one to help her bring up her children and she had been forced to take her baby, Jodie, along to the shoots of Buddy's commercials. One day a producer spotted the toddler on the set and asked Brandy if she would allow Jodie to make a commercial too. She was three years old when she made her first star appearance as the 'Coppertone Girl'.

Brandy knew at once how important a BBC documentary would be for her daughter and, suddenly, we could relax. We had secured our Hollywood film star. Our director, John Bird, had started life as a cameraman and he was the most gentle soul. His production assistant, Mary, was superbly adept at putting people at their ease and keeping Desmond on his best behaviour. Soon Brandy and Jodie had adopted us all as the family that they didn't have and we often used to stay for supper to chat and watch television long after we had finished work. We were very lucky. Many visitors to Hollywood never get to leave their hotels in the evenings because its citizens are notably inhospitable to outsiders, reluctant perhaps to share the good life they have struggled so hard to achieve for themselves. John and I went to meet the director and producer of *Bugsy Malone*, Alan Parker and David Putnam. We needed to shoot an interview with them about Jodie. Our compatriots were virtually unknown in Hollywood then and we found them kicking their heels in a Beverly Hills hotel coffee-shop, impatiently awaiting the studio's call to pitch their latest project. They happily agreed to talk about Jodie. Martin Scorsese was shooting *New York, New York* with Lisa Minnelli and Robert de Niro for United Artists and he invited us on to the set to describe directing Jodie in *Taxi Driver*. He was to warn, 'Child actors are more fragile than the rest of us because they do not have normal childhoods. And for that reason, many of them hit those depths of despair when they get older.'

There was not a lot that John could film to illustrate the life of this exceptional teenager because, off the screen, she was so refreshingly normal. Jodie spent most of her free time skateboarding in the steep lanes around the house or listening to pop music in her bedroom. She also babysat her sister Connie's son and charged a dollar an hour. John was looking for sequences to film and he asked Jodie what she would most like to do. She had never been to Disneyland, she said. Jodie spent a blissful day there with John, Mary and the film crew. She was hardly recognised and, for Jodie, being anonymous was heaven. Among the thousands of visitors she was just another teenager, posing for her photograph with Mickey Mouse. Her real ambition, she told us, was to be a film director, so John lent her the film crew for a day and she created a beautiful two-minute film called *Hands* which we included in our finished documentary.

Brandy was a pushy mum with a difference. She was a remarkable entrepreneur and first-class agent but she also knew instinctively what projects would work for Jodie and which should be turned down. Jodie would never have become the huge star she is now without Brandy's aggressive but discerning shove from behind. And, unlike the mothers of so many precocious showbiz children, Brandy planned for the long term, enrolling Jodie in the Lycée Français in Los Angeles and frequently taking her for holidays to France. Jodie even recorded a couple of pop songs there and still dubs French versions of her films. Jodie easily passed the entrance exam into one of the very top American universities.

Then, while she was studying at Yale, her happiness was stolen from her. John Hinckley Jr, a deranged stalker, became obsessed with her and the teenage prostitute she played in *Taxi Driver*. In a desperate bid to attract the world's attention, he tried to assassinate President Reagan, seriously wounding him and killing a senior White House aide. He was declared insane. No one, let alone someone as gentle and generous-hearted as Jodie, deserves that. She suffered terribly from the worldwide publicity and took a year off college to let it all die down. It nearly destroyed her. But she had the strength to recover from the trauma and to go on to become an adult star and worthy winner of Oscars and BAFTAs and Golden Globes. Who can ever forget her with Anthony Hopkins in *The Silence of the Lambs*?

I still have the photograph she gave me of herself, then almost fifteen years old, looking rather butch in jeans and a denim shirt. She scrawled a note across the bottom of it, thanking me for allowing her to direct her first film. 'Just let me know if there's ever anything I can do for you in return.' Being Jodie, not just a run-of-the-mill Hollywood film star, I know she really meant it.

CHAPTER 14

Trouble at the Mill

Back in London, Desmond's life was becoming very messy. He and Esther had been living together for several years but his wife, Patsy, refused to give him a divorce. Patsy was very popular in the Current Affairs Department and her colleagues started leaking vitriolic gossip about Desmond and Esther to *Private Eye*. After a shaky start, Esther's programme, *That's Life*, had quickly found its feet. It was unashamedly a personalised version of *Braden's Week*, without Bernard Braden, of course, and it soon became one of the BBC's top-rated programmes. Peter Chafer who produced it was calm and unflappable. Years before, he had been the floor manager on *That Was The Week That Was* who rushed to intervene when Bernard Levin was attacked, live on air, by an irate viewer. He had made several acclaimed programmes with Malcolm Muggeridge, notably his profile of Mother Teresa in Calcutta. Peter was becoming increasingly irritated by the way every time he made a decision that Esther didn't agree with, she went running along to Desmond's office to have it countermanded. At his confidential annual interview he mentioned this to Alasdair Milne who was, by this time, Managing Director of Television. The next time Milne saw Desmond he told him of the complaint and, stupidly, who had made it. Desmond was naturally furious at Peter's disloyalty and it was clear that he could no longer work with Esther. Milne decided that the solution to the problem was to move *That's Life* out of Desmond's department and into Current Affairs, half a mile away, in the BBC's Lime Grove studios.

Another major problem had blown up. Mike Latham, *Explorers'* producer, had suggested to Desmond that he should write the book of the series, probably to flatter him and keep him on side through the tricky overspend discussions that lay ahead. Mike pointed out that the book would sell much better with the well-known name of Desmond Wilcox on the cover than it would with his name on it. The obvious solution would have been to choose a writer who knew the subject, perhaps one of the screenwriters on the series. There was simply no way that Desmond could or should find time for this enterprise, but vanity and probably greed for the money prevented him from saying no. Several senior producers, including Mike and I, endorsed the idea that a ghost-writer should be hired to do the bulk of the work so that Desmond could concentrate on running the department and presenting *Americans*. When the book came out the ghost-writer was not credited. Unfortunately neither were the distinguished writers whose scripts had been filleted to compile the book. The BBC had failed to buy the book rights from the scriptwriters when it had negotiated their contracts for the series. It was therefore in breach if its agreements with the Society of Authors and the Writers' Guild. The BBC was humiliatingly forced to settle in a blaze of unwelcome publicity, making what the Society of Authors called 'handsome payments' to the scriptwriters.

Private Eye had by now started a vicious campaign against Desmond and Esther who had attracted the particular ire of its editor, Richard Ingrams. The magazine nominated Desmond as 'Plagiarist of the Year', accusing him of misusing his position at the BBC to 'line his own pockets'. Practically every issue of the magazine vilified them. Later Desmond decided on the hazardous path of suing the magazine for calling him a plagiarist. *Private Eye* engaged John Mortimer QC and very nearly succeeded in defending its allegation. The judge found that copyright had indeed been infringed but that Desmond had acted 'without guile'. He was awarded £14,000 damages against the magazine – a tidy sum – along with costs of £80,000. Naturally this incited *Private Eye* to intensify its hate campaign against the couple.

While we were still shooting *Americans*, Esther had become pregnant, and now Patsy Wilcox did agree to divorce Desmond, keeping custody of their children. Desmond and Esther quickly married. Although there was a BBC rule that husbands and wives should not work in close proximity, Alasdair Milne agreed, most illogically, we all thought, that her programme could return to the General Features Department.

Milne was probably worn down by the constant nagging from Desmond on the subject; and both he and BBC1's controller, Bill Cotton, were mindful that Esther was now one of their big stars, someone who needed treating with kid gloves to prevent her defecting to ITV.

Americans was in full swing by this time, shooting more or less continuously during two summers to catch the good weather. *That's Life* continued the *Braden's Week* pattern of a punishing winter run over twenty-six consecutive weeks so Esther certainly deserved a good break. Both she and Desmond believed in taking proper summer holidays. This meant that Desmond was spending a massive amount of time away from the office. I agreed to deputise for him when he was away, but I had to spend a great deal of time in America too. While he was away in America, the department was visited by the Annan Commission on the Future of Broadcasting. Sara Morrison, one its members, who was later to become a good friend and colleague, quizzed me insistently about why I was deputising, why a deputy was needed at all and why the Head of Department was filming abroad. Years later Sara explained that she had rightly suspected that the BBC was top heavy, with too many not very busy chiefs because promotion was the only escape route for those producers who had passed their sell-by date. The committee had just visited the Arts Department where Humphrey Burton, another actor-manager, was habitually mocked by his staff for being an absentee departmental head. He presented many of the department's programmes and spent a good deal of time coaxing money out of the Germans. 'Where's Humphrey?' someone would ask. The answer, so the joke went, was always, 'He's either in Munich or in make-up.'

All these *événements*, seasoned with a pinch of bitchiness and resentment, conspired to erode confidence in Desmond, both among his staff and on the sixth floor. However, his reporting skills remained unaffected by domestic dramas and both John Bird and I were relieved that he was on top form to tackle our next *Americans* subject, the President of General Motors. During the research I had formed serious doubts that we could make a good film because the public-relations team assigned to us was so dreadful. They were grey, unsmiling and out of touch, suspicious, terrified for their own careers and determined to see that we filmed nothing that might tarnish the corporate façade. What could be more boring? The company's Detroit headquarters was a hive of conformity, buzzing with sober suits, rimless glasses and military haircuts. No one smiled. Meetings were formal and hierarchical – even the bosses feared for their jobs. Who would employ a man who had blotted his copybook at General Motors?

On the other hand, it was clearly a most intriguing time to look at the American car industry since it was confronting rapid change. Jimmy Carter was President and the government was cracking down on lead pollution. The OPEC oil embargo had finally persuaded the industry that a way of making smaller, less thirsty cars just had to be found. What finally persuaded me that we should go ahead with our film was my meeting with the President of General Motors himself. Pete Estes could have been born on a different planet from the automatons who helped him manage his empire of a third of a million underlings spread through a hundred and fifty-seven countries across the globe. He was animated, funny, argumentative and positive – the sort of character you might stumble across running the Detroit Lions football team. He was certainly not a figure you would immediately associate with running the largest manufacturing business on earth. How General Motors came to choose such a charismatic personality to be its fifteenth president, when the company displayed such a yearning for the bland, heaven alone knows.

Better still, it transpired that Estes had been head of the Chevrolet division of GM when the consumer guru, Ralph Nader, had attacked it in his book, *Unsafe At Any Speed*. It was a savage assault on the American motor industry, claiming that manufacturers were compromising the safety of their cars in their reckless pursuit of profits. Nader's severest criticism was reserved for the Chevrolet Corvair, whose engine was fitted at the back like a Volkswagen Beetle's, because it had a marked tendency to spin out of control. Nader also claimed that its steering column could impale the driver in a head-on collision. The 1961 Corvair now has the distinction of being listed as one of *The Fifty Worst Cars of All Time*. This topic, I knew, would really give Desmond something to get his teeth into when he came to interview the company's President.

However we still had a major problem with the mediocre PR men. They were horrified to discover that good documentaries dug much deeper than the conventional news coverage that they were used to manipulating. They learnt too, with growing alarm, that our approach was sometimes ironic, often critical and aimed at revealing truths that they thought it was their job to cover up. In desperation, the PR men did everything they could to block us. Where they couldn't say no they obfuscated. We insisted that we must be allowed more informal time with the President. They offered instead that we could film Pete Estes going to a performance at the Detroit Opera (big deal), but otherwise they expected us to make do with the two-hour slot that had been allotted to us for the main interview. Fortunately, they were terrified of the boss and it was he who saved the day.

Pete Estes invited us all to spend Sunday with him at his lavish home set in three acres of Detroit's most opulent suburb. There was a vast swimming pool, lots of beer and a barbecue big enough to roast a buffalo. None of the PR men had been informed, let alone invited. Estes did not suggest that we bring our cameras with us but nor was he surprised when filming began. We had an awful lot of work to do that day if our film was going to be something out of the ordinary. We were lucky. The President splashed happily in the swimming pool with a ludicrous giant rubber duck, while his wife, Connie, prepared the meal. It was quite clear that the gregarious Estes was thoroughly enjoying himself playing host to us, and he blithely answered quite naughty questions bowled to him while he was grilling us massive steaks. We had been worried that the set-piece interview that had been scheduled for the following morning would be too formal. Now the ice had been broken.

The President and Desmond were both on top form in the pre-sidential suite the next day. The interview turned out to be a good-natured but competitive sparring match. Estes was a little shamefaced when he admitted that he was quite unable to say the name of GM's main competitor, 'Ford'. He seemed to have a quite genuine block. (Yet, when we went with him to some major industry function, he greeted Lee Iacocca, the President of Ford, like a long lost buddy.) I could see the panic on the faces of the public-relations men when Desmond started asking Estes about Ralph Nader and the Corvair. Estes looked taken aback at first, but he quickly recovered his poise and responded confidently:

> It was quite a time, the Nader time. I guess now I have the feeling that in order to be a really rounded General Motors' man you have to run into some pretty severe criticism and you have to stumble and, possibly, make a big mistake in order to be really seasoned for the long pull in our industry. It is so cyclical that every three or four years we're either tremendously high or tremendously low, and to get out of your own obsession with that cycle you occasionally need a rap on the head and certainly the Nader experience was that for me.

Desmond followed up by asking Estes whether he now regretted that GM had assigned private detectives to follow Ralph Nader. The GM President at the time had been forced into the humiliating position of apologising unreservedly before a televised Senate investigation committee. Pete Estes' defiance was ill concealed: 'I don't know that even now I would regard that as a mistake,' he told Desmond. 'Perhaps the mistake was to apologise at the Senate investigation for having done it.'

Even the public-relations men had figured out by now that we BBC people were the President's blue-eyed boys and, at last, they pulled their fingers out. John was able to shoot a stunning and eerie sequence as row upon row of dummies were prepared for make-believe catastrophic accidents. Daddy dummy, mummy dummy and lots of little baby dummies – at $35,000 a piece – were hurled through windscreens, rammed into walls and set on fire. We also filmed the president trying out a beautiful little electric car. I wonder what ever happened to that project. How can it still be little more than a dream, over thirty years later? No doubt, President Obama would like to know the answer too.

The assembly line was an extraordinary spectacle too. A constantly moving belt on which cars were being built by robots to individual customer specification. A set of red doors would be followed by a white bonnet and boot lid, a four-door saloon would precede a coupé. This was the innovative 'just-in-time' technology which kept the factory in constant motion and eliminated the need for warehousing. Jonathan Gili, the film editor, cut a wonderful montage of the robotic assembly line to the opening of Bizet's *Carmen,* the opera that we had filmed Pete Estes attending. At first we thought it was just a clever pun but the spectacular sequence is one that everyone who saw it remembers. Not long after *Americans* was broadcast, the montage with Bizet's music was copied by a British advertising agency for a car commercial. It ran for ages on ITV. Imitation may be the sincerest form of flattery but it is also the easiest way for an advertising executive to earn a substantial fee.

I was concerned about General Motors' reaction to the finished film. Normally we wouldn't have given a stuff what anyone thought. We never, well almost never, gave into pressure to show films before transmission – unless the courts forced us to. But this was a delicate and different game. General Motors was the largest manufacturing company in the world, the biggest spender on television advertising. It had real clout and could force our co-production partners, Time-Life, to come into line with a click of its fingers. Ever since *Explorers,* I had reason to be nervous about Time-Life. Desmond and John Bird, the director, agreed with me. John and I decided to take the bull by the horns, fly to Detroit and show our film to Pete Estes 'as a courtesy'. It was a slightly risky operation but by no means unprecedented. More often than it would like to admit, the BBC has been forced to screen films before they were broadcast. There was a tried and tested formula to cope with all this. The mantra was that we were showing the film 'for comments on its factual accuracy'. That way, the BBC was seen to retain editorial control. The problem, of course, came when the viewing failed to mollify and instead served as evidence for a writ of restraint in the High Court.

We were in the main boardroom at General Motors headquarters in Detroit, just John Bird and me versus a roomful of important-looking vice presidents, as identical as the dummies we had filmed in the GM Test Centre. The only noticeable difference was that they didn't have hooks in their heads. We were awaiting the arrival of the President. 'Hi, fellas.' He bounded over to John and me, enthusiastically shaking our hands and giving us a broad grin. 'How's it goin'?' There was no need to answer because the lights were dimming and our film began. We certainly couldn't have asked for a more attentive audience. There was neither rustle nor cough. Suddenly the phone rang. It was for Estes. He listened for a moment and then got up to leave. 'Sorry, fellas, I have to go take an important call from Washington in my office.' The moment Estes left the room, John and I scanned the sea of subordinate faces. None of these lofty vice presidents would look us in the eye. None would speak. Estes had given no intimation of his reaction when we were interrupted. How could these high-paid coolies know what they were supposed to think?

Estes soon returned and the viewing continued. As the film finished, the lights went up and all the President's men rose to their feet in unison with him. 'Thanks, fellas,' he said. 'Glad you used so many of our commercials.' With that he swept out, followed by his minions. We were left alone with the public-relations men who veered away from us like frightened horses. The commercials Estes was referring to were either very kitsch ones, showing some of GM's early glamorous cars, or they were ads for the Chevrolet Corvair. Was he damning us with faint praise or buying time to form an opinion? Late that evening I received a phone call in my hotel from the Vice President of Corporate Affairs, a Rottweiler of a lawyer. He was used to getting his own way when he was dealing with broadcasters. He could cut off their blood supply, their advertising revenue, in the twinkling of an eye. 'We have discussed your film and we have decided you may not air it,' he began. I was not expecting that we would leave Detroit covered in confetti, but the bullying arrogance of the man infuriated me. 'Could I stop you there one minute?' I interjected. 'There is only one person who can tell me that I may not broadcast the film and that's the Director General of the BBC. Goodnight.' I put the phone down and felt ever so much better.

It worked. We never had another squeak out of General Motors. Nor should we have done. By answering difficult questions fluently and forcefully Pete Estes had greatly enhanced his company's standing. The film was a superb boost for GM's image, an admirable tribute to its President and a fine episode in a prestigious BBC series. What more could they want? Blood? The GM board wanted its President to inter-cede and stop the BBC from showing the film. Its bully boys just couldn't accept that nobody cared a damn what they thought. Pete Estes waited for tempers to cool and then made the sensible and pragmatic decision to let sleeping dogs lie. He saw no purpose in publicly fighting the BBC in a battle that he knew GM would loose. I sensed that all my clashes with public-relations men, over the years, had been intensive training for this moment. Later we learnt that General Motors was using our film to train its executives in countering ticklish questions while burnishing the corporate image. Game, set and match.

CHAPTER 15

The First Lady

We knew that the most difficult of our characters to secure for *Americans* was the First Lady. The task was made doubly so because we were forced to leave the decision until very late in the shooting of the series. The impending presidential election that brought Jimmy Carter to office looked at first as if it might well be won by the incumbent President Ford. When Carter told his mother he was running for President, she asked, 'President of what?' We couldn't count on Betty Ford being in the White House and there is nothing so *passé* as an ex-First Lady. We just had to wait until the results of the election were known. After President Jimmy Carter had been sworn in with his wife Rosalyn, we knew we would have to wait some more. Not surprisingly, there were pressing matters of state that took priority over fixing up filming for the BBC.

Chris Jeans, the BBC New York producer, was bullish. He knew quite a bit about Rosalyn Carter's press secretary Mary Finch Hoyt. She was, and is, a much-respected, high-profile journalist who had contributed to the *New York Times,* the *Washington Post* and the *Los Angeles Times.* Since this was America, he just phoned her up at the White House. She took the bait immediately. Mary could see exactly how useful it would be for Rosalyn to star in a major BBC documentary. Her problem was that we needed access early on in the presidency because *Americans* was due to broadcast within Carter's first year. Not only was the First Lady's schedule packed tight, but Mary Hoyt was worried at the repercussions if the BBC were to be given privileged access to the First Lady before the American networks, NBC, CBS and ABC. A couple of weeks later, Mary phoned Chris Jeans back. She told him to bring me along to the White House. I was in London at the time so, for once, it was not difficult to obtain special permission to fly by Concorde for the appointment. The only trouble was that Concorde was fully booked. I had made a documentary about the plane and its test pilots but I had been prevented from travelling on its maiden flight because of insurance problems. Now I was thwarted, as it turned out, for ever. I flew on a conventional British Airways flight and arrived at the White House in heaps of time.

Mary was the antithesis of the hopeless sort of public-relations men we had encountered at General Motors. She had used her journalistic contacts in Britain to find out all about us. It seemed we had passed the test and this was Mary's chance to check us out face to face. She then set about finding a positive way to accommodate *Americans* while keeping the networks happy and, a few days later, we were given the go-ahead. Instead of sending us a list of restrictions, we were sent a copy of the First Lady's programme for the months ahead. All we had to do was agree dates and let Mary Hoyt know which of the events we wanted to cover.

The East Wing of the White House contains the offices of the First Lady and we were told to report there on the appointed day. We had each filled in an elaborate security-clearance form before leaving Britain and, no doubt, MI5 had been glad to assist their friends across the water with our vetting. Happily, the talented and unflappable John Bird was the director, as he had been for the Company President and the Film Star, so my function was more flunky than producer. Courtesy demanded my presence because I was the series executive producer. You can hardly send a deputy, or plead more urgent work, when your documentary's topic is the wife of the President of the United States. John wanted me there, in any case, to ensure that Desmond was kept out of his way, and Mary Hoyt and I would have plenty to do co-ordinating the First Lady's schedule with our filming requirements.

At first it all worked like clockwork. The security people at the gate checked our passports against their computer and, in no time, we all had passes. Not so our filming equipment. Sniffer dogs were called, metal detectors produced. Intricate tools of our trade were prised from their mountings and examined minutely. It took hours and we were late for our first appointment. Mary Hoyt was quite relaxed. The First Lady, had plenty to be getting on with, she said, and we could start filming her office routine as soon as we were ready. Mary had the perfect solution to the security problem at the gate. 'Why don't I give you an office here, in the East Wing, where you can keep all your equipment and make calls?' We took over the East Wing boardroom. We were off to a great start.

When Desmond, John and I met Rosalyn Carter, for the first time, we could see that the documentary was going to work. She was an attractive woman, very soft-spoken, but as entirely self-assured as you would suppose of someone who had already served two terms as consort to the Governor of Georgia. When Jimmy was running for President, Rosalyn had campaigned for him, solo, in forty-one states. The press had dubbed her 'the steel magnolia' and she planned to play a major part in the administration, not only promoting her special interests, like mental health, equal rights and voluntary service, but acting as a formal adviser to the President, even attending cabinet meetings.

In her first interview for us she explained how very humble her beginnings had been, in the tiny town of Plains, Georgia. She was the eldest of four children. Her father, a garage mechanic, had died of leukaemia when she was just thirteen. To try and make ends meet, her mother had taken in sewing and become a much sought-after dress-maker in the neighbourhood. Rosalyn worked beside her mother, helping with the sewing, the housekeeping and looking after the three younger children:

> My mother was only thirty-four when my father died and she took over the complete responsibility for the family and never asked for help from a charity or relatives or anyone in the town. She never complained and never demanded support or help from any of us. In fact, I've frequently felt very guilty about not helping out enough as a teenager. But like all teenagers, I suppose, I was selfish and unaware because I see now that I could have been far more helpful in looking after the rest of the children in the house. But it tells you what kind of woman she was that she never once suggested to me that I wasn't doing enough and has never since talked about it with me.

Rosalyn and Jimmy Carter had four children. Their three sons, Jack, Chip and Jeff, were grown up and married but their daughter, Amy, a late addition to the family, was only ten years old. The filming of Amy had been the only concern that Mary Hoyt had raised with me at our first meeting. I undertook only to film Amy with her mother's permission and I was warned that even if we were given the go-ahead, the time we would be allowed to film with Amy would be minimal. On our second day, Rosalyn had several appointments in the capital city and our team went with her in the President's limousine. That is to say that Desmond sat on the jump seat, facing the First Lady, while the cameraman knelt on the front seat, filming her over Desmond's shoulder. The sound recordist, on the second jump seat behind the driver, also had to operate the battery light. All this is pretty standard for filming big shots in large cars. The difference here was that a sub-machine gun was clipped to the floor by the front passenger's seat. The secret service had failed President Kennedy, fourteen years earlier, and there was no way they would allow the First Lady to travel the streets of the capital except in an armed, armoured and bullet-proof car. She was accompanied by two secret-service men, one was the driver, and the other had to squeeze up against our cameraman on the front passenger seat.

The First Lady had decided that she would undertake some of the foreign visits that are normally delegated to the Vice President and we were invited to go with her to Puerto Rico in the Caribbean. Technically Puerto Rico is a 'self-governing unincorporated territory of the United States'. In fact, it is virtually the 51st state, and those of us who adored *West Side Story* needed no reminding that New York has a large Puerto Rican population – and that means votes. We were given a flight schedule for Air Force Two with the cryptic instruction, 'Depart Andrew's Air Force Base. Wheels Up 10.45 a.m.'

The passenger in front of me at the military check-in put his bulky briefcase through the X-ray machine and the alarm went off. The security men opened it up and inside were the component parts of a sub-machine gun, neatly cushioned in foam rubber, ready for instant assembly. I hoped he was a secret-service man because they let him through to the departure gate. The outside of the aircraft was impressive, with 'United States of America' painted along the length of the fuselage, but, inside, it was disappointing – not a Boeing 747, like Air Force One, but a rather shabby, medium-sized commuter jet. At exactly 10.45 a.m.

the wheels of the aircraft left the runway and, nearly four hours later, we landed at San Juan Airport. There was a big press contingent of White House watchers on the flight but Mary Hoyt had promised us another interview with the First Lady. We were given far more than our fair share of time with her. Rosalyn told Desmond about the death of her father-in-law from cancer and how Jimmy Carter had cut short a sparkling career in the US navy so that he could return to Plains, Georgia to run the family peanut farm:

> Jimmy was sacrificing everything he had worked and saved for by abandoning his naval career just as he was about to become really successful. It was the first big row in our married life. It was more than an argument it was a battle and it went on for days. I screamed, yelled and argued and did everything I could to make him change his mind but he wouldn't. So we packed up and went home to Plains. And we were poor, oh golly we were poor. In those first years we had hardly any money. We even had to apply for minimum-rent public housing, a small apartment on the edge of Plains. And we worked, and we worked, and we worked.

Waiting to receive the First Lady at San Juan Airport were the Governor of Puerto Rico and his cabinet ministers. Pleasantries were exchanged, a photocall and a press conference speedily completed, and then the whole lot of us were herded into a fleet of little propeller aircraft. In no time, we were airborne again. This time it turned out to be a twenty-minute flight and we landed on a grass strip at a luxurious golf course with its own well-appointed hotel. It emerged that the original plan, for the First Lady to stay at the American Embassy in San Juan, had been overruled by the secret service. This golfing resort, surrounded by an electrified perimeter fence, was considered the safer alternative. There was the inevitable banquet for the First Lady, followed by interminable meetings for her to chair. Early the next morning, we left, in the same small planes that we came in, bound again for San Juan Airport. On the tarmac, Rosalyn met a group of human-rights activists, no doubt a pointer to the government of Puerto Rico as to which way the new administration's wind was blowing. By early afternoon we were back at Andrew's Air Force base. 'Wheels Down', I am sure, was exactly on schedule. I forgot to check.

Not only was Amy subject to negotiation, it turned out, so was access to her father. There had been agreement in principle that we should have a chance to interview the President, but when it came to fixing a convenient time, the West Wing started playing silly buggers with the East Wing. We asked for more: we said that we needed to film the family together in the private quarters of the White House. We could tell, from Mary Hoyt's demeanour, that she wished we hadn't asked for the moon, but we knew she would bust a gut to try and deliver it. By now we had Rosalyn on our side too. She had been extremely impressed with the way our crew operated. They never shouted instructions at her, as newsmen do, never shone lights in her face. In fact, they seldom used lights at all. Because there is so little documentary tradition on American television, Rosalyn had never experienced the unobtrusive and painless way a British crew silently observes but never tries to stage-manage. Rosalyn told me not to tell any of her staff what she was about to tell me. Amy had invited some school friends around, that afternoon, to watch a new movie in the White House cinema. We could go along with our cameras. We did.

A couple of days later there was a vast evening reception on the White House lawn – our first opportunity to film the President and the First Lady together. She introduced me to Jimmy and I could tell at once that she had briefed him about the filming, the problems that lay ahead and her determination that we should be allowed to film what we had told her we needed. Late that night the telephone rang in my hotel. It was the White House on the line, a man who introduced himself to me as a spokesman for the President. It reminded me of my late night unpleasantness with the General Motors public-relations chief. Mr Spokesman came straight to the point. 'We have fixed you half an hour with the President next Tuesday in the Oval Office at twelve noon. That's all the time you're going to get. You want to film him in the family apartments? We've never allowed that before. But if you give us an assurance that you will film the President and the First Lady leaving church on Sunday morning – *and* you agree to keep that footage in your finished documentary – then we'll allow you to film the family in the White House private apartments before Sunday lunch.' It didn't sound like a bad bargain to me – although pedants at Broadcasting House would certainly have got their knickers in a twist about my committing the BBC to broadcast any sequence from a film yet to be edited, let alone one that had not even been shot. But I was in no position to bargain, so I said yes.

The Oval Office seemed more like a film set than the real thing. It was much bigger than we imagined and swarming with people. President Jimmy Carter looked very insignificant sitting in the middle of the maelstrom. There was just time to set up a few lights and then the camera was running, the milling minions dispersed, and Desmond moved effortlessly from small talk into the first question. Jimmy was not about to launch into a tirade against his wife like the ones we used to film for *Man Alive*, but if you watch a film about a First Lady, convention dictates the need for a few harmless words from the most famous husband in the world. Jimmy obliged. The following Sunday we filmed the President and the First Lady leaving church, and as bartered, in the private apartments with Amy. To our surprise, two of their three sons were also there, with their wives and children. We suspected that their mother had summoned them up to Washington especially for our filming. The steel magnolia's iron fist in a velvet glove.

Our last appointment with the First Lady turned out to be the first intimation of the calamities that then lay ahead but would eventually destroy Jimmy Carter's presidency. The Shah of Iran, Mohammad Reza Shah Pahlavi, and Empress Farah came to Washington on a state visit and all hell was let loose. It was only fourteen months before the Shah was to be toppled and replaced by Ayatollah Khomeini. Iran was already on the verge of a bloody civil war that the Shah was desperately trying to suppress with strong-arm tactics, notably the deployment of his wicked and ruthless, sixty-thousand-strong, secret police force, Savak. The CIA and Mossad had trained them to perform the most obscene and disgusting acts of torture known to man.

There were many thousands of Iranians living in the United States, entitled to enter the country comparatively easily because of the special relationship between the two countries. Oil, of course, was the bond. It soon became known that there was going to be a massive demonstration against the Shah. Since Savak couldn't prevent such a manifestation of hatred on American soil, they set about organising a pro-Shah counter demonstration. These are the games that end in tears. In this case it was the Shah of Iran, the President of the United States and their two wives who were crying. Police had tried to break up the disorder with tear gas and a vast cloud of it had drifted across the White House lawn, enveloping the two first families at the podium, along with our film crew. Neither the President nor the Shah was able to continue his speech for quite some time. This was a massive propaganda coup for the anti-Shah protestors, their cause being concurrently publicised around the world by the live television coverage.

Later Rosalyn came to our office in the White House – her board-room – and expressed complete bewilderment at what had happened. All of a sudden it was brought home to us that the First Lady of the most powerful country in the world was completely out of her depth. Now she was the farmer's wife, from a one-horse town in the Deep South, asking us to explain to her the reasons for what had just happened, in the heart of the capital of the Free World. We found an atlas and I explained how and why British and Soviet troops had overthrown the Shah's father, during the Second World War, and installed Mohammad Reza on the throne. I explained about the repressive regime and the importance of Iranian oil to the American economy. I could have been teaching her ten-year-old daughter Amy. The First Lady had learnt none of all this during her poverty-stricken schooldays in Plains, Georgia.

A year or so later, the Shah was driven into exile, aggressively pursued around the world with extradition demands by the revolutionary govern-ment in Iran. He eventually came to the United States for medical treatment. The US government categorically refused to hand over its ally to the new regime. As a direct result, Iranian revolutionaries stormed the American Embassy in Teheran and took fifty-three American staff hostage. Their four hundred and forty-four days in captivity were the worst humiliation for the United States since the fall of Saigon. An attempt by the US military to rescue the embassy staff ended in catastrophic failure. The diplomats were only released after Jimmy Carter had been defeated and Ronald Reagan sworn in as President. If Carter's administration had surrendered the Shah, the embassy staff would never have been taken hostage and Jimmy Carter might well have won his second term in the White House. But he was too honourable a man to betray someone he perceived to be a friend and ally of the United States. Ayatollah Khomeini's decision only to release the hostages to the new incumbent, President Regan, was the ultimate mortification for Carter that it was intended to be.

When the filming was complete we threw a modest party at the Georgetown Inn, where we were staying. Naturally we invited the First Lady to attend, along with the members of her staff who had helped us so much. We were told Rosalyn might come but there was no sign of her when the party began. Suddenly there was a kerfuffle in the lobby and the secret-service men had arrived with sniffer dogs. Now we knew for sure that Rosalyn was on her way. There was a black waiter serving at the buffet, the only non-white person in the room. Rosalyn made a beeline for him and shook him warmly by the hand, as if he were a long lost friend. Her political duty done, only then was she ready for the party to begin. So different from her husband's predecessor but one, Richard M. Nixon: 'Politics would be a helluva good business if it weren't for the goddamned people.'

CHAPTER 16

Let's Go Naked

Americans was scheduled for broadcast in prime time on BBC2, in the autumn of 1978, but there was no way of anticipating what mischief Aubrey Singer could get up to now he was firmly ensconced as the Controller of the channel. He had become anxious and then livid when he found that Desmond had appointed himself to be the author of the book of the series. Remembering the row about the *Explorers* book and the damaging settlement with the series' writers, Aubrey asked himself how Desmond could claim authorship when a production team had been paid to carry out all the research that was required for the series on which the book was based. Whatever way you looked at it, he concluded, the BBC must own the rights in the research and he correctly anticipated that the people who had actually done the research might ask for a cut of the action if they felt that Desmond was unfairly profiting from their endeavours. Aubrey also queried the title of the book and of the series, '*Americans* by Desmond Wilcox'. What did 'by' mean? Titles and credits are, understandably, a very touchy matter. Your standing in the industry and your market value depend on the visibility of your name on good productions. Why, Aubrey asked, was Desmond implying that both the series and the book were all his own work?

It would be normal for a Controller to resolve such an issue with one of his heads of department by phoning him up, even inviting him over for a drink. However, Aubrey was frightened of Desmond, who was a barrack-room lawyer *par excellence* and far more skilled at thinking on his feet. Aubrey had been bested by Desmond too often and too publicly in argument and he intended to win this battle: Aubrey knew he had right on his side. So he resorted to a cowardly and underhand sub-terfuge that could have been invented by *Yes, Minister*. He wrote a savage memo to Desmond, laying out his concerns, sent a copy to his boss, Alasdair Milne, and threw away the top copy that should have gone to Desmond. This, Aubrey believed, would win him brownie points with Alasdair, for wielding the smack of firm management, without hassle from Desmond who would stay in ignorance of his shafting. Had he known Alasdair better he would have spotted the danger in this deceitfulness. Alasdair immediately confronted Desmond with his copy of Aubrey's memo. Desmond had, of course, never seen the original. After that rancorous meeting which resolved nothing, Alasdair wrote a terse note to Desmond instructing him to downgrade his 'by Desmond Wilcox' credit on the series titles, give proper credit to the production team in the book and have his agent negotiate to buy the BBC research that Desmond had used.

Desmond's reply to Milne, which he copied to Aubrey – whose duplicity was thus exposed, was neither temperate nor truthful. It achieved a tactical ceasefire: the book did acknowledge the production team but the screen credit didn't change, nor was payment for the research ever offered by Desmond or demanded by the BBC. Hot air all round. But Aubrey wasn't finished yet. One of the highlights of the BBC1 winter season was the Emmy award-winning series, *Washington Behind Closed Doors*, starring Jason Robards and Robert Vaughn. Based on the book by *Washington Post* investigative journalists Bob Woodward and Carl Bernstein, it was a dramatic retelling of the Watergate scandal that had driven President Nixon from office three years earlier. *Washington Behind Closed Doors* was one of the best-ever television dramas to come out of America. It was eagerly awaited and much-hyped in Britain so, not surprisingly, it was scheduled in prime time and the Controller of BBC1 expected it to achieve the number-one position in the ratings.

Aubrey took his revenge on Desmond by placing *Americans* on BBC2 against *Washington Behind Closed Doors* on BBC1. This was criminally bad scheduling on two counts. First, a Controller should never schedule one of his 'jewels' – expensive original series – against unwinnable opposition. Secondly, it was his duty to provide 'alternative' viewing on BBC2, a nebulous concept, but it certainly meant that a Controller shouldn't schedule a high-profile contemporary American documentary series against a high-profile contemporary American drama series. Aubrey had broken the rules and damaged his channel just to spite Desmond. He paid for it six years later when he tried the same trick again, but this time his motive was competitive rivalry rather than a personal vendetta against one of his subordinates. By now Managing Director of Television, he authorised the new Controller of BBC1 to run the tacky and mindless American schmaltz *The Thorn Birds* as a spoiler for Granada's truly magnificent *The Jewel in the Crown*. If Aubrey thought he would get a pat on the back, he was mistaken. Home Office minister Douglas Hurd briefed lobby correspondents that the BBC should expect no increase in the licence fee if it continued to broadcast such trash. The Board of Governors was incensed.

Alasdair Milne decided to get rid of Aubrey and he invited him to go on a shoot one Sunday, pheasant not film. They spent a happy morning blasting away together and they lunched well and cordially. On the way back to London, Alasdair casually mentioned to Aubrey that he wanted him out – not for a month or so, because he was off to India and he wanted Aubrey to act as his deputy while he was away – but immediately after that. The following day Alasdair cheerfully relayed the news of Aubrey's brutal dispatch to his chief press officer. 'That was cruel, wasn't it?' he was asked. Alasdair responded cheerfully, 'Don't be impertinent, boy.' Three years later, when Alasdair received the same treatment at the hands of the Board of Governors, he called them 'twenty-two-carat shits'. There have always been plenty of those knocking about in the BBC.

All of us who had worked on *Americans* were bitterly disappointed by the small audiences and the diminished press reaction that were the inevitable consequences of having to compete against *Washington Behind Closed Doors*. However, I have to acknowledge that *Americans* in some respects failed to live up to the expectations of a major BBC2 series. It lacked wonder. The great series like *Civilisation* and *Ascent of Man* and all those made by David Attenborough, from *Life on Earth* onwards, gave us unforgettable insights into subjects of such extraordinary breadth and scope that we were bowled over. We marvelled in admiration and awe. *Americans* was a series that explored real-life versions of legendary characters and, inevitably, punctured the fairy tale by substituting authenticity for fantasy. *The Year of the French* and *Italians,* two far less high-profile series, made soon after *Americans* by many of the same key people, recaptured the sense of wonder that somehow had eluded us.

I was free! I still had responsibilities as an executive producer and as Desmond's deputy but, with *Americans* out of the way, he could now devote his energies to running the department and doing what he liked most, involving himself in the production in his wife's top-rating show, *That's Life,* and helping her bring up Emily, their baby daughter, Esther's firstborn. I could start making programmes of my own again. While Desmond had been away in America, Bill Cotton, the Controller of BBC1, phoned to say that he was short of a *Tuesday Documentary* and would I like to propose one? These prestigious documentary slots were much sought-after because they were in peak time on BBC1. I put in a number of suggestions to Bill and, at the very end of my note, I said, if he wanted a laugh, why didn't we make a film about the growing European trend for people to take their holidays in the nude? I should have guessed it. Bill jumped at the idea. Then I had to start thinking seriously how I could deliver. I decided that I would direct the film myself. I had not been on the road for a long time, largely through choice. Directing requires infinite patience and it takes weeks to make a film. As a producer you can agree the outlines of a film with its director and forget all about it until it's made. That way you can handle a variety of topics instead of plugging along with one. But this film depended entirely on the director and the reporter. Get it wrong and we would have a public disaster on our hands, with the Mary Whitehouse chorus screaming for the abolition of the BBC. Besides I knew it was going to be a most entertaining assignment and I didn't think many of the directors in my department would thank me for landing them with a film that they might have to direct in the nude. The first thing I did was to enlist a friend, reporter John Pitman, with whom I had worked on *Braden's Week.* John has a wicked sense of humour. He was dead keen and I knew that together we could strike the right note for a major BBC1 documentary – naughty but nice.

I had once visited some friends at one of the many nudist camps in

Yugoslavia – which is what gave me the idea for this film – so I had a rough idea what to expect. But the place that knocked your socks off, and everything else, was the nudist town at Cap d'Agde in the South of France. It is an astonishing sight – a Mediterranean beach, two miles long, populated by twenty thousand stark-naked people. To accommodate this melting pot of European sun-seekers, there are two thousand apartments, eight hundred villas, three supermarkets, fifty shops, twenty restaurants, four bars, a couple of night clubs, several beauty parlours and three banks. Even in the shopping malls, everyone goes about their business as naked as nature intended. Right next door to this immense urban complex, on the shores of the Mediterranean, is a vast campsite for twelve thousand naked people. Here, you can rent a chalet, bring your caravan or just turn up and pitch a tent.

Years before, I had made a tongue-in-cheek film for *Man Alive* about British nudists and their secretive clubs, normally situated in damp and muddy parts of the country, where heavy sweaters, umbrellas and Wellington boots would seem more appropriate than gooseflesh. These nudists – who inexplicably insisted on being called 'naturists' – were hilarious because they were invariably respectable and upright citizens who, in the real world, would tut-tut at too short a skirt, too deep a cleavage or a bikini that left too little to the imagination. They were mostly paunchy bank managers, civil servants in mid-life crisis or poly-technic lecturers, their uniformly stout, blue-rinse wives, wobbling mountains of flesh. Communal nudity was their ritual secret, carefully concealed from their neighbours, who might well have laughed at all their frolicking in some secret woodland with nothing on at all.

In Cap d'Agde it couldn't have been more different. The French and the Italians didn't give a damn. Their superbly tanned women non-chalantly strutted the beach in nothing but dark glasses, perhaps with a gold chain around their waists. The Nordic races, tall and blond, wind-surfed and sailed in the noonday sun, usually wearing the top half of a rubber suit but never anything below the waist. I always wondered what would happen if the winds and currents forced them on to a crowded conventional beach. What could they do but bury their heads in the sand? The Germans played volleyball and drank a lot of beer. So did the

Dutch and the Danes. The British, outnumbered and made nervous by the babel of languages they couldn't understand, clustered together on the beach, noses daubed white with sun lotion, somehow managing to look slightly scruffy even in their nakedness. The retired Gallic natives played pétanque or chess, or sat at one of the cafés watching this startling world go by.

Nudists call people who wear clothes when they need not, *textiles,* and, in the early days at Cap d'Agde, they used to jeer and clap the *textile* sightseers. By the time we were filming there, no one cared any more. When the two-mile nudist beach was first established, in the 1950s, a high fence had been erected to shield the *textiles* from the shameful sights and the nudists from the peeping toms. We couldn't even locate where that fence had been. It was all a bit like one of those dreams when you find yourself walking down Oxford Street, as naked as the day you were born, while the world bustles by, heedless of your indignity.

We decided that we would keep our clothes on for filming. We were lucky to have with us one of the best researchers in the department, Betty McBride. She declared there was no way that she was going to bare all. My assistant, Charmian, was similarly reluctant to take the plunge, and the four members of the film crew were adamant that they weren't going to work in the nude. So we dreamed up an elegant rationale that we would use when we were challenged about our state of dress, as we knew we would be. Our line was, 'If the BBC were to make a film about fascists you wouldn't expect us to wear black shirts . . . ' Later we learned that such nonsense would have been quite superfluous had we thought to wear BBC T-shirts. All the Europeans, it seemed, loved the BBC but were understandably wary of unidentified film crews, whose tacky films might end up on the porn market. The BBC, an unclothed delegation told us, could film whatever it wanted. *Bienvenue.* One of the most articulate of the British holidaymakers was David Frankel, a prosperous businessman from London who owned a luxury flat at Cap d'Agde and kept a large boat in the marina. David, his wife and two teenage sons spent the whole summer naked, at their Mediterranean retreat. He was refreshingly forthright in explaining his motives to John Pitman:

Let's face facts, beautiful women are beautiful women and men in a naturist environment obviously look at the girls. And they're lovely to look at. Here is a living *Playboy,* if you like. There's nothing wrong with that at all. We can't sweep away the normal sexual instincts because we are without clothes. People think it's all bottled up and hidden away and doesn't exist. Of course it exists. Probably in a way it's more prolific, but it isn't obvious. And that's what is nice about it, because it's dignified. It shows that men and women can be together naked and they can have all the sexual desires and all the sexual thoughts going through their minds. But it's obvious and that's fine. That's the normality of it.

Using the tricks of the trade I had learnt many years before on *Time Out,* we acquired local crews to film sequences in Denmark, Yugoslavia and in Germany, where the nudist movement had first started over a hundred and fifty years earlier. To round off this phantasmagoria of the implausible we decided that we needed our own footage of the Mr and Mrs Nude America Pageant at the Tree House Fun Ranch in California. Festivities always began there with naked skydivers parachuting into the swimming pool. The budget wouldn't run to the cost of us all going to California so I asked Barbra Paskin, our researcher on the Jodie Foster *Americans* film, to hire a local crew and cover the event for us. Barbra had a lot of questions. Essentially she needed guidance as to what naughty bits of the human anatomy could or couldn't be shown. It's not easy directing by transatlantic telephone line and she and I didn't get it quite right. When the film was shown, there were vociferous complaints that we had shown the Misses America fully frontal but had cut the Messrs America off at the waist, as it were. Most of the calls came from concerned feminists, complaining on behalf of the women. Duty Office told us there weren't nearly so many viewers upset that we hadn't shown the bottom half of the men.

It was not surprising that this *Tuesday Documentary* generated an enormous amount of press interest. That was the whole idea. None the less, when the *Radio Times* was delivered to our office, John and I suffered from a severe bout of cold feet. Screaming out from the page was the title, in large type, *LET'S GO NAKED!* And, underneath it, in silhouette, were a man and girl, naked, in a proud gymnastic pose. We had shown the film to Desmond and he had laughed in all the right places. He had not asked for any changes nor had he 'referred it up', asking the Controller to endorse his judgement before the film was broadcast. It was one of the great manifestations of trust, in the BBC, that no one senior to a head of department viewed a programme before transmission, unless he was asked to. Of course, when the programme was a hot potato, senior people were most reluctant to become involved. An unwritten law that was neither Murphy's nor Sod's, but something very particular to the Corporation, meant that the last person to see the film before transmission, like in musical chairs, was the one who would have to carry the can when the fireworks started. Ambitious and successful executives quickly learned this axiom for their survival and promotion. The BBC Board of Governors never did. The audience for *Let's Go Naked* was phenomenal, probably the highest-rated *Tuesday Documentary* ever. It may not have done my reputation as a serious programme-maker any good but the very fact that it attracted millions of viewers, gave them plenty of laughs and caused hardly anyone to complain, meant that the Controller of BBC1 was a happy man and a very satisfied customer.

Meanwhile there was much rejoicing in the world of television that Aubrey Singer, the BBC2 Controller had been promoted to be Managing Director of Radio. That he knew nothing about radio hadn't prevented the important promotion, incredibly putting the buffoon within a hop, skip and a jump of becoming Director General. Fortunately, as we have seen, he was sacked before this calamity could come to pass. Desmond had been a candidate for the BBC2 Controller's job, vacant because of Aubrey's promotion, and he was also considered for the highly sensitive post of Controller, Northern Ireland. He told the world that if he landed the job, he would take *That's Life* with him to Belfast. Its production team was not amused. It is an indication of how Desmond's star had waned, at least in Alasdair Milne's eyes, that he was turned down for both these important posts. Brian Wenham, the enigmatic Head of Current Affairs, assumed the controllership of BBC2. We all liked him immediately despite his inscrutable ways. He was anxious to encourage good programmes and was a lover of the arts. It turned out that he was much more in tune with them than he had ever been with current affairs. It also turned out that he was a great fan of John Pitman and he later commissioned two major series from him that I was to executive produce.

I already had a pet project that was cheap, involved John Pitman and would, I knew, appeal to Wenham. My proposal was to make a short documentary film about the eighty-five-year-old waitress at the Oriental Club, in London, who had been serving drinks to members for well over sixty years, since the First World War. You couldn't mistake Alice. Her hair was tied back in a neat bun, enclosed in a white linen cap. Over her long black dress she wore an elaborately embroidered white lace pinafore with cuffs to match. She looked like a character from a turn-of-the-century West End play. The members adored her, some it is rumoured, when she was young, passionately. She never married.

I had joined the club some years earlier, partly, I have to admit, to amuse myself observing the habits of the last survivors of the Raj before the species became extinct; but also partly because it was a joy to have a comfortable meeting place in palatial surroundings just off Oxford Street. It is a watering hole that serves enormous double measures of gin and Scotch, provides good food and boasts a front desk that never reveals to outsiders whether or not you are in the club. There are quite a few grander clubs in London but the Oriental is far less stuffy than most. Those who have lived and worked in the East have had to learn how to get on with ordinary people and take advantage of unexpected encounters with strangers. The purpose of a top London club, of course, is to protect you from just such eventualities. The whole point is to exclude people that you don't know or wouldn't want to know. When I had been put up for membership of the Oriental, I had hoped and prayed that none of the Election Committee associated me with the BBC series *The British Empire*. It was dinosaurs like these who had hated it most and complained the loudest.

'Met your BBC chap in Beirut. A bit left-wing, don't you think?'

I had been told to report to the bar of the Oriental Club at 5.30 p.m.

exactly, to mingle with members of the Election Committee and the other candidates for membership. The first of the questions that would decide my fate was the easy one. In a cowardly way I murmured my assent to his opinion that my colleague in the Lebanon was a bit of a leftie.

Now the old buffer had a trick question for me. 'Hear you've been to Calcutta. Where did you stay?'

There is only one correct answer and I gave it. 'The Bengal Club, sir.'

'And was that in the main building or the chambers?' he asked.

'I stayed in the chambers, sir, because the main building was demolished six years ago.'

Of course he was testing me. Had I not known that the clubhouse had been demolished I would have been an impostor and rejected for membership. The Election Committee was pretty suspicious about my application anyway. I was a television producer, not a captain of Indian industry or a retired judge from the Calcutta High Court. What was my social standing? Was I one of them or a Trojan horse from the gutter press? The debate went on behind closed doors. I had two things going for me. The people who had proposed me were respected senior members of the club and, frankly, there was a shortage of new members so vital to make the books balance. I was accepted.

Now I had to face a kangaroo court to ensure that the old boys would allow us to film Alice. Television was not something that elderly Oriental Club members had much time for. Like Harold Macmillan, they probably thought it was only invented for the benefit of those below stairs. I had to explain the plan in detail to Sir Arthur Bruce, one of the club's most venerated grandees, and his antique chums. We met in the smoking room and Alice herself served our drinks. After courteous and prolonged pleasantries, Sir Arthur took the bull by the horns. 'There is one thing that we will absolutely not allow the BBC to film,' he decreed. 'If you are to depict us having drinks before lunch, you most certainly may not show us taking port afterwards.' I was slightly taken aback. Although the rest of the world had long before learnt to live with the medium of television, I had been expecting all sorts of worries when the old gents realised that this was for real. A ban on filming the consumption of port after lunch was not one of the restrictions I had anticipated. I must have looked puzzled. One of Sir Arthur's companions decided to enlighten me. 'Now look here,' he ventured boldly, but with a twinkle in his eye, 'what Sir Arthur means is this. He doesn't want us to be portrayed as the drunken old farts we really are.'

I asked my friend and favourite director from *Americans*, John Bird, to direct the film. I knew he would do it brilliantly. If the club didn't like it, I joked, they could hardly ask him to resign because he wasn't a member. In any case, I judged, I would be of more use acting the diplomat, smoothing ruffled feathers, while he got on with making the film. Alice gave a wonderful interview to John Pitman, who had a special rapport with wicked old ladies like this. She was feisty, indiscreet and nostalgic and she gave us a remarkably vivid and touching account of what it was like to be in service, when she was young, between the two World Wars. Her boyfriend had never returned from the Somme, she told us, and she had never wanted to marry anyone else.

'Did any of the members ask you to marry them?' John Pitman enquired.

Defiantly Alice replied, 'It's none of your business. If any of them did want me to marry them, I'm not telling you.' Then she put her hand in front of her mouth, in a mock expression of horror, pretending she had over-stepped the mark, forgotten her station in life. But then she chuckled wickedly.

Our film, *Alice at the Oriental*, was a little gem that was broadcast many times. It is good to hear that the Oriental Club has just acquired a new copy of the film from the BBC. The old one was quite worn out.

CHAPTER 17

Mutiny

I may not have earned a long break in Sri Lanka but I was off there for the winter of 1971/2 just the same. Some time before I had applied for and been awarded a Leverhulme Fellowship to study the paradox reported by the United Nations International Labour Organisation that 'the more a young person has been educated in Sri Lanka, the greater the likelihood that he or she will be unemployed'. I had shown no ambition or aptitude for academic study when one is supposed to, at school and university, but now I found it absorbing. I was intrigued and saddened that the country I knew quite well seemed to be falling apart.

However, I was looking forward to getting back to work in London because Brian Wenham had given the green light to another proposal of mine, *Battles of Broadcasting,* a film offering the prospect of a good deal of mischief-making, which is certainly why Wenham found it attractive. My plan was to produce a television autobiography with Hugh Greene, who had retired a decade or so earlier. He had been Director General for the first five years of my BBC career and he was probably the most admired DG after the very first one, Lord Reith. Everyone in the Corporation remembered Greene's bold, liberal touch, most with nostalgia, affection and admiration.

I had a secret agenda too. I had become increasingly gloomy about the calibre of the people who seemed to be rising to the top at the BBC. *Battles of Broadcasting* was intended as a parable – to show that caution, vacillation and kowtowing to the aggressive Thatcher government were not the way it had to be. It is debateable whether I should have been doing any such thing, using precious air time to propagate my views. But hey-ho, I thought, this is a worthy cause if ever there was one. I was not so naïve as to think that *Battles of Broadcasting* could change anything overnight. But out there, in the big wide world, I fondly hoped that opinion formers and influential policy gurus might be watching and noting. A good start would be for the Home Secretary, William Whitelaw, to get rid of the chum he had installed as BBC Chairman, the patrician George Howard, owner of Castle Howard, made famous on television by *Brideshead Revisited*. This gentleman-amateur caused havoc in the higher echelons of the BBC by arrogantly vetoing the management's candidates for top jobs – like John Gau for Controller of BBC 1 – and insisting on the promotion of ne'er-do-wells like Aubrey Singer.

Arriving back at my office in Shepherd's Bush after three months abroad I was in for a most unwelcome shock. To my dismay, there was mutiny in the air – and anger. In my absence Esther had unquestionably twisted Desmond right around her little finger. The *Sunday Times* described the couple as 'a mutual admiration society, succumbing to *folie à deux*, feeding each other's illusions of grandeur and pushing the limits of BBC conventions'. So infatuated was Desmond with Esther that he would use any of the considerable powers bestowed on him as head of an important BBC department to please her. This was nepotism gone mad. This was the time of year when trouble always brewed. People were tired after the long winter runs of their programmes, impatient for the summer holidays to arrive. Yet this time it was quite different from anything I had experienced. I didn't seek to canvas opinion. It came to me in bucketfuls, from senior producers to the youngest trainee. They were frightened because Desmond and Esther could be dangerous when crossed. Some of the junior people were on short-term contracts that they feared might not be renewed if they fell from favour. Others complained to me that they suspected unjustified promotions were being handed out to the 'loyal' at the expense of better, less obliging people.

Although Desmond could get way with almost anything because of his charismatic charm, Esther lacked his magnetism and his powers of persuasion. The malcontents compared her to Lewis Carroll's Queen of Hearts, to Marie-Antoinette and Imelda Marcos. They prophesied that Esther's influence would bring Desmond's golden empire crashing down. The sentiment directed against her wasn't professional jealousy, as she and her supporters claimed. It was fury, almost hatred, that she had stolen their champion who had fought and won their battles for them on the sixth floor and supported them when the lawyers and the politicians were baying for their blood. Esther had taken their fearless commander, they said, and made him into her domestic pet.

Producers now felt inhibited from discussing programme and personnel matters in Desmond's office over what had been a customary drink after work. The office had become a crèche for his baby and her nanny, a refuge, indeed a nest for his wife. My colleagues had become convinced that Desmond had lost interest in promoting their programme proposals – he was their only conduit to the Controllers of BBC1 and BBC2. Worse, they suspected that he was not putting their ideas for new programmes forward, in order to preserve a larger slice of the financial cake for his and Esther's projects. While there had been a grudging acceptance of Desmond presenting *Americans,* despite his long absences abroad, there was fury that he was now planning the department's next major series for himself as well. Desmond knew there was serious trouble in the ranks. Although he was seen as a maverick, he was also a clandestine admirer of the BBC management tradition and a master at exploiting it ingeniously and effectively to stave off trouble. Now he had taken the department to breaking point. In exactly the same way that the infatuated Edward VIII would brook no criticism of his adored Wallis Simpson, Desmond rode roughshod over his colleagues' counsel with an uncharacteristic disdain. In the abdication crisis the new king had been a bit of a wimp, ineffectually trying to see off his formidable opponents. Desmond was not. He fought like a lion for the lady he loved.

Tim Slessor, now running *Man Alive*, was one of the most senior producers in the department. We had always been friends and I utterly trusted his judgement and discretion in the situation that we were now facing. He was logical and unemotional, as affectionate towards Desmond as I and as solid as a rock. We agreed with what we were hearing from our colleagues: it had been a wrong decision of Alasdair Milne's to allow Esther and her production team to return to Desmond's department, three years earlier, and it was one that urgently needed to be reversed. Tim and I knew that we would get nowhere by confronting Desmond personally. After the thunder and lightning subsided nothing would change except that we would have become sidelined and resented as enemies of the court. To go behind Desmond's back would undoubtedly be disloyal to him, but Tim and I resolved that our wider loyalty, even our duty, was to our resentful and embittered colleagues.

I discussed the matter with Hugh Greene one evening when we were filming *Battles of Broadcasting.* I explained to him what had happened earlier to Peter Chafer, the editor of *That's Life*, when he had complained about Desmond in a confidential talk with Alasdair Milne. His grievance had immediately been passed back to Desmond. Another senior producer who had made an identical complaint, and suffered a similar outcome, managed to arrange a transfer to another department. Hugh was quite clear what needed to be done. It was a personnel matter, he said, and we should make a formal complaint to the executive responsible for senior staff, in our case, Robin Scott, Alasdair Milne's Deputy Managing Director. 'He is duty-bound to act on a complaint from staff as senior as you two. In any case,' Hugh said, with a knowing smile, 'I think you will find that Robin is a better operator at this sort of thing than Alasdair.' It so happened that the opportunity to act came more quickly than Tim and I were expecting. By chance, Desmond and Esther were going off on holiday at the same time as Alasdair. Esther's spin-off series, *That's Life Reports,* was a long way behind schedule but due for broadcast in just a few weeks. No producer would think of taking leave at such a critical time so her departure triggered a further wave of discontent. Tim and I asked for a meeting with Robin Scott. We outlined the problem to him in confidence and sought his assurance that nothing would be said to Desmond unless effective and determined action was going to be taken. Dear old Robin was about to retire. He needed this like a hole in the head. He chickened out and passed his notes of our meeting to Alasdair for him to read when he returned from holiday. When he did, Alasdair phoned me to say he was about to talk to Desmond. 'What are you going to say to him?' I asked. 'I'm going to tell him to sort it out if he can – which I think is deeply unlikely. If he can't, either Esther will have to go or he will.'

When Desmond was called to the sixth floor, Alasdair just handed him Robin's notes of his meeting with Tim and me. Thanks a lot, Alasdair. Of course we were rather expecting this pusillanimous performance so we had taken precautions to stiffen Alasdair's resolve, to prevent him shoving the whole unsavoury business back under the carpet yet again. Within days, an article appeared in the *Daily Telegraph* demanding, 'Is Aunty Losing Her Grip?' It criticised Alasdair for failing to tackle the Desmond problem and leaving it to senior producers to do the dirty work. By way of a bonus, the article also attacked Aubrey, now Managing Director of Radio, for his thoughtless handling of the financial cuts to BBC orchestras. The tabloids soon made the Esther and Desmond drama their front-page stories. Now the matter was out in the open, Tim and I were sure that Alasdair would be forced to act.

The next stage of the showdown was painful. If you are a politician, you become a seasoned practitioner of disloyalty for the common good. Even so, it seemed to drain quite a lot out of the hardened ministers whom Margaret Thatcher called upon to support her when instead they told her it was time for her to go. Loyalty is a bond of trust between two parties. When there is a conflict of loyalties, the easiest option is to do nothing. That's why the tyrannical Robert Maxwell was able to steal hundreds of millions of pounds from his employees' pension funds. Far too many who took the Maxwell shilling looked the other way. Tim and I had been loyal to Desmond through thick and thin. Now it was his staff that needed our support.

Thinking that the Desmond problem was now Alasdair's not ours, Tim went off on his family summer holiday. No such luck for me. For sure, my fate was negligible compared with that of Joan of Arc, Claus von Stauffenberg or St Sebastian, but for days on end I was called into Desmond's office, more in sorrow than in anger, and given the *Et tu, Brute?* treatment. Anger would have been easier to deal with. The stream of consciousness never seemed to touch on the merits of the issue that had brought all this to a head. Instead, Desmond explored every possible avenue that might allow him to keep Esther and her programmes in his department. Finally, in her presence, he suggested an ingenious solution to me that might well have saved their bacon. It was that I – of all people – should take on the editorship of *That's Life*. On one level of course it made sense. I had produced *Braden's Week,* the forerunner to Esther's programme, but I knew that she would never forgive me for what had now happened. How on earth could we work together now? Michael Leapman, the respected journalist who later chronicled the events of the mutiny in his book *The Last Days of the Beeb,* describes what happened next:

> It took hardly any time for Clapham to reject the suggestion. To begin with, he was surprised it was acceptable to Rantzen. She replied that she would go along with the plan . . . But, most important of all, it did not answer Clapham's and Slessor's main point, that the argument was about the Wilcox/Rantzen domination of the whole department, not just that one programme. It was as much about her influence on her husband's job as about interference on *That's Life*. Clapham said he would not go along with the notion. 'It's the Managing Director's instruction,' Wilcox told him. 'If that's so I reject it,' Clapham replied. Wilcox sagged back in his chair and said quietly: 'We're finished, then.'

Matters now came swiftly to a conclusion. All ten of the department's senior producers signed a letter to Alasdair strongly supporting Tim and me. In the tabloids, predictably, they became the 'Gang of Ten'.

> DEAR ALASDAIR – We are increasingly concerned with the situation in General Features. We would like to assure you that there is widespread support in the department for the staff regulation 'Relatives of Staff' which begins: 'In principle a member of staff should not be directly or indirectly in authority over a relative. This rule should be strictly observed with a near relative, e.g. spouses . . . ' Like Tim Slessor and Adam Clapham, we senior producers feel this regulation should be observed. We have not asked junior, and possibly more vulnerable, members of the department to sign this letter, but know that it reflects the general feeling of our colleagues.

As was the standard practice by now, Alasdair passed the buck straight down the line to Desmond who immediately sent for the Gang of Ten and me. If he didn't believe it before, he was now persuaded that he had completely lost the support of all his senior staff. The Gang of Ten's letter finally convinced Alasdair that he had to act. He told Desmond that he was moving *That's Life* permanently to Current Affairs at Lime Grove. Desmond called a meeting of the whole department, hoping perhaps that enough of the junior staff would support him to justify a last-minute appeal against Alasdair's decision. He might have been encouraged by an unconvincing anonymous letter of support from 'the silent majority' that was circulated in the department, but I doubt it. It just didn't ring true. Michael Leapman could have been a fly on the wall:

> At 4 p.m. about fifty members of the Features Department huddled round a long table in a conference room . . . Wilcox and Rantzen sat at either end of it. Wilcox did what the *That's Life* team had expected, appealing to their loyalty to him and the Features Department and painting a lurid picture of how unpleasant things would be in Lime Grove. 'This is a result of your actions,' he declared, seeking the eyes of Clapham and his supporters.

I could sense that the meeting was getting restive, impatient with Desmond's argument for maintaining the status quo. I decided to produce the letter I had written to Desmond explaining why I had gone with Tim to see Robin Scott and why I had done it behind Desmond's back. It was very generous in acknowledging Desmond's and Esther's talents and achievements, but it also made it very clear that Tim and I were resolute that things could no longer continue in the same unhappy fashion. There weren't many doubts about the mood of the meeting before the letter was read – and none after. It was quite apparent that Tim and I had overwhelming support. Michael Leapman again:

> It was a difficult meeting, lasting just over two hours. Wilcox and Rantzen, still at bay, learned how little support they could count on in the department. But if it had achieved no other purpose, the session had cleared the air, and when it was over the participants

were infected with a quite irrational sense of exhilaration. All of them – including Wilcox and Rantzen – trooped to the bar . . . and enjoyed a companionable hour. There was a feeling that the matter was now out of their hands, that things were moving remorselessly towards a conclusion that would depend on decisions taken elsewhere – taken, to be precise, on the sixth floor of the Television Centre.

Things moved even faster now. Unusually, Desmond played his cards badly. Until this point in the drama, it seemed to me, he had got off quite lightly, compared with what Alasdair had told me might happen. *That's Life* was to go back to Current Affairs but Desmond's own position was secure, even if his image was somewhat dented by all the brouhaha. Normally he would noisily push confrontations to their limits and then back off, just before plunging over the precipice. This time he foolishly and disastrously misjudged his opponents. First, he fired off insulting memos to his bosses on the sixth floor, disputing their decision to move Esther's programme from his department. Then, he let it be known that he and Esther were in talks with Michael Grade about transferring *That's Life* to London Weekend Television. He called in several of the researchers, asking if they would go with him and Esther to LWT, and, off his own bat, offered them fifty-per-cent pay increases to defect. Sickened by Desmond's conduct, but distrusting Alasdair Milne, one of them decided to complain to the Director General himself.

Bill Cotton, the Controller of BBC1, was almost certainly tipped off by Michael Grade about Desmond's overture to LWT. He and Michael were close family friends, as Desmond well knew. In the end, the discussions with LWT came to nothing but Desmond had committed a fundamental transgression by conspiring to steal one of the jewels in the BBC's crown. Bill Cotton had been Esther's strongest supporter on the sixth floor. In his world, the stars and their programmes mattered more than anything else. He was determined not to be out-manoeuvred into losing one of BBC1's most important weapons in the ratings war. Now he and his colleagues were united in blaming Desmond for this calamitous turn of events. Suddenly it was all over. *That's Life* did go back to Current Affairs but Desmond was gone. The offices the next day were eerily quiet and no one knew quite what was going to happen next. There was an overwhelming feeling of loss, that the wrong fox had been shot, that a popular head of department had been sacrificed while the perceived culprit had expediently been spared because of the millions of viewers *That's Life* attracted. Desmond's staff had been prepared to forgive him almost anything. Now it was too late.

Tony Isaacs, the executive producer of the travel and exploration series, *The World About Us,* came to see me. He was one of the most senior producers in the department, a towering, bearded figure. It wouldn't be hard to imagine him leading a nineteenth-century expedition up the Amazon or down the Nile. He had worked as a director with the Shell Film Unit in Nigeria and at Associated Rediffusion with Desmond. Tony had just received a phone call from Alasdair Milne asking him to take over as acting head of the department. It would take some time, he was told, to find and appoint a permanent head. It was an inspired choice – I suspect, Brian Wenham's idea. Although Tony was one of the now legendary Gang of Ten, he was popular in the department. He looked rather apologetic when he gave me the news. I was delighted. Neither Tim nor I was expecting to be asked to take over the department and neither of us would have accepted. The struggle had been too bitter. Now it was time for the wounds to heal.

Tony asked me to replace him as the executive producer of *The World About Us* while he was running the department. This turned out to be a six-month stint of pure, uncomplicated pleasure. The producers were, predictably, travellers and explorers themselves and they seldom appeared in the office. If they weren't in remote parts of the globe making films, or in a cutting room, they were probably digging their allotments or lying on the beach in the sun. Why should I care? Tony never did. When he was running *The World About Us,* he was hardly ever in the office himself. You were more likely to track him down fishing in Kashmir, or buying a priceless Buddha for a song in Mandalay, than sitting in his office, twiddling his thumbs, like a house-trained BBC executive. It was hardly a full-time job. Luckily I had plenty on my plate.

The first thing that had to be sorted out was the transfer of the *That's*

Life staff to Current Affairs. Bill Cotton had called each one of them into his office and asked them whether they were happy to change departments. Fortunately, the mutinous mood had dissipated so swiftly that nearly all of them were willing to go. Although *That's Life* itself was moving, lock, stock and barrel, the budgets and the producers for *The Big Time* remained with the General Features empire. That was all part of the immutable way the BBC worked. Tony decided that I should be responsible for the next series of *The Big Time*, because I had already been involved as Desmond's deputy, and I knew all the people. Pat Houlihan had come to General Features after working for Michael Parkinson and on *Monty Python*. She had been the first to spot the potential of Sheena Easton, who had become a huge pop star following her appearance on *The Big Time*. Pat had also talent-spotted Paul Heiney and Chris Serle, who had made such successful partners for Esther on *That's Life* but were now looking for a new assignment. The other regular director on *The Big Time* was Nick Handel. He had swiftly made his way up the ladder, directing wistful and quirky films for *That's Life*. As well as being a smart director, he was always bubbling over infectiously and regaling us with tales of the most unlikely encounters he had experienced when out researching his films. We all regretfully agreed that *The Big Time* had run its course. We needed to invent a replacement – similar but something fresh. Although it took us some time to come up with the right title for the show, we instinctively knew its format. Paul Heiney and Chris Serle were now accomplished presenters, game for anything, so we made them the subject of each programme as well as the presenters. The title suddenly became obvious. We kicked ourselves for not thinking of it sooner, sparing ourselves many nights of lost sleep. It was *In at the Deep End* and it ran successfully for several years.

Without a doubt, the best of the first series was Patricia Houlihan's production *Ballroom Dancing*, with Chris Serle. He had to learn his waltz and his paso doble, his quickstep and his rumba, from scratch. Chris was a complete novice but he made astonishing progress, rapidly picking up the tricks of the trade from the experts of the ballroom-dancing world. Producer Pat Houlihan threw a couple of extra stars into the mix – Darcey Bussell and Wayne Sleep – to add bling to the glitter. After weeks of arduous training, Chris was ready to compete in *Come Dancing,* the naff but popular Saturday-night television show that had been running, on and off, since 1949 – and sometimes looked like it. Chris won the competition, in prime time on BBC1, watched by a huge audience. Our programme brought such a boost to the ailing *Come Dancing* that it's hard to believe it took a BBC1 Controller twenty-three years to wake up to the potential and commission its successor, the compulsive *Strictly Come Dancing.* Often it attracts an audience of over ten million viewers.

And Desmond Wilcox, whatever became of him? Tim and I took him out to lunch once the dust had settled. We collected him from his home where an icy Esther sat like a statue with a migraine. She didn't join us for lunch and we didn't expect her to. It was a surprisingly affable meal but, in the interests of domestic harmony no doubt, Desmond never proposed a return match. He was full of plans for the future. He had never lacked courage or perseverance so he was swiftly back on his feet, selling a long-running documentary series to ITV – no easy task – and another to BBC Scotland. Because he still retained an uncanny eye for a good story and the finely honed skill of delivering enthralling television, his work as a freelance film-maker attracted a good deal of attention. He set up a small production company defiantly called the Man Alive Group and acquired a licence from the BBC to use Tony Hatch's memorable *Man Alive* theme as the company's signature tune. Desmond's support for Esther had been vital in the early days. Who else would have had the chutzpah to replace an established star and a major peak-time series with an ersatz version featuring his mistress? But once *That's Life* was up and running, Esther no longer needed her husband to hustle for her, and after he was gone from the BBC, she sensibly confined herself to the full-time job of producing and presenting her programme. *That's Life* gathered its own extraordinary momentum and, thanks to Esther's talent and determination, it ran for an astonishing twenty-one years.

CHAPTER 18

Aristocrats

When the name of the new Head of Department was announced, we all had to phone around our friends in other parts of the BBC to find out who exactly this Will Wyatt was and what he had done. It was a quart-size job he was taking on because the sixth floor had decided to amalgamate the Documentaries Department with its arch-rival, General Features. Since Documentaries was being evicted from its Television Centre stronghold and sent across Shepherd's Bush Green to join us in Kensington House – also the production offices for Sport, Science, Religion and Arts – it looked to the Documentaries people more like a General Features takeover than a merger. Not only was Kensington House a most awful building in a horrid place, it had quite unjustifiably acquired a reputation as a hotbed of radical rebellion. The Documentaries people were fearful that they would be treated as pariahs by their erstwhile colleagues and bosses in the Television Centre, fifteen minutes' wet and windy walk away through heavy traffic in garbage-filled streets.

Will was anonymous-looking, more the provincial academic than the trendy producer. He was in his late thirties, always good-humoured but without much of a sense of humour. Hyperbole was not his middle name. He trained as a journalist, joined BBC Radio News and started his television career, as I had done, in the Presentation Department. Like me, his first assignment was *Points of View* with Robert Robinson. He worked on the highly successful *Late Night Line Up* and produced several notable documentaries and series, the most remembered being the BBC2 weekly review of television, *Did You See?* presented by Ludovic Kennedy. Promoted to assistant head of Presentation, Will was also responsible for Barry Norman's *Film Night*, *The Hollywood Greats* and *The Old Grey Whistle Test*.

As soon as he took over the new department, Will quietly set to work integrating the two rival groups and arranging early retirement for a significant number of distinguished elderly war horses grazing in the Documentaries Department. They had once made their mark but now, it seemed, seldom films. Will never raised his voice but quietly got his own way, without even the most excitable of his subordinate colleagues losing their tempers with him. We soon learnt, on the grapevine, that Will had prepared for his preferment during his twelve years at the Television Centre. He was an ambitious but deceptively quiet operator, on good terms with all the sixth-floor bosses and – an important bit of gossip – he had been 'noticed' at a get-together with the BBC Governors. Senior management discouraged such intimacy, partly from paranoia but also from bitter experience of their meddling ways. Information was shared with the Governors only on a 'need to know' basis. So they welcomed Will's more open approach and marked his card 'should go far', lest the management was too incompetent to do so for itself.

Will spent longer than is customary at Documentary Features because, surprisingly, he was never chosen to be Controller of either BBC1 or BBC2. However, he quickly made up for lost time when, after eight years, he was appointed Assistant Managing Director of BBC Television, then Managing Director and, finally, Deputy to John Birt, the BBC's most unpopular Director General of all time. Will supported Birt loyally and almost certainly saved him from being kicked out when the murky terms of his employment contract became public. Yet no one ever held it against the amiable Will that he had served as aide-de-camp to the devil incarnate. Dirt never stuck to him and he made no enemies. He was just what the sixth floor wanted, a safe pair of hands. Just what the new department most needed. Will Wyatt was the antithesis of a drama queen.

Will weighed me down with documentaries and series to supervise, perhaps hoping to keep me out of mischief, but also because the new department had a vast number of programmes in the pipeline. Many of the younger directors from the old Documentaries Department resented having an executive producer thrust upon them, especially one from the former General Features Department. Too bad. They needed one.

An old dog like me knew many tricks of the trade that they had never even thought of. I was trained to smell burning and stamp it out before it became a fire. The brighter directors soon grudgingly accepted that I might not, after all, be a malevolent fiend, hell-bent on censorship of all things sensitive and meaningful. Occasionally they even thanked me when a ruse of mine improved their precious films.

My television biography of Sir Hugh Greene, *Battles of Broadcasting*, had by now turned into something of an epic, seventy-five minutes long. Somehow it had survived the mutiny and the change of captain on the bridge. By good luck a young academic had just started writing Hugh's biography. Michael Tracey knew the subject backwards and we took him on as the interviewer. The director, Tristan Allsop, and I had decided that it would be wrong for Hugh both to present the programme and conduct the interviews. Many of the people we wanted to film held opinions on him that were far from complimentary and, confronted by Hugh, we thought they might either clam up – or hit him. Out of curiosity, I accompanied Michael, Tristan and the film crew when they filmed Mary Whitehouse of the *Clean-Up TV* Campaign. I wanted to know what she was really like, this ogre who spent her time complaining, not only about Dennis Potter's plays, but also about *Dr Who, Jackanory* and the dancers on the *Benny Hill Show*. Shortly after we met her she had mounted a vicious private prosecution for gross indecency against a National Theatre director, yet she presented herself as the prototypical Essex housewife, caring and hospitable, deferential to her subdued, standard-issue husband. How could this wolf in British Home Stores' clothing have accumulated such political clout that the liberal-arts establishment dreaded arousing her wrath? Hugh had always obstinately refused to meet her on the grounds that she was an unelected nobody. She, of course, thought otherwise, having collected half a million signatures on a petition demanding that he be sacked. Had he been more accommodating when she had first appeared on the scene, he might have defused a lot of her wrath – but that was not Hugh's way.

Hugh ended the programme by describing his nemesis. To teach him a lesson and clip his wings, Prime Minister Harold Wilson had moved Dr Charles Hill from the Independent Broadcasting Authority to be

Chairman of the BBC, prompting the now famous quote that 'it was like inviting Rommel to command the Eighth Army on the eve of Alamein'. As an inducement for him to resign as Director General, Hill offered Hugh a seat on the Board of Governors. He succumbed to the flattery – no previous Director General had ever been a BBC Governor. Almost immediately Hugh regretted giving way to his vanity and he resigned well before his time was up. How could a flying ace sit calmly in club class while a novice pilot wrestled with an emergency in the cockpit?

After the sixth-floor screening of *Battles of Broadcasting*, the director of News and Current Affairs opined pompously to me that it was a 'fine piece of narrowcasting'. I suppose he meant that the programme would only be of interest to a media elite. Screw him. True to form Alasdair Milne soon did and Dick Francis, by then the Managing Director of Radio, was sacked ignominiously, the second of Alasdair's three managing directors to bite the dust. The BBC owed him better treatment than that. He had served as Controller, Northern Ireland for over five years, through some of worst of the Troubles, hardly putting a foot wrong. The third managing director, the saintly John Tusa, survived Alasdair himself, being safely tucked away in Bush House. If only he had been made Director General instead of Alasdair the BBC might have been spared John Birt too. Some years later, Brian Wenham admitted that he had expected to be next for the chop so, when he had seen that there was a vacancy for the Head of the British Council, he cut out the advertisement and kept it. When Alasdair surprised everyone by firing Dick Francis and appointing him Managing Director of Radio in his place, Wenham claimed that he had passed the job advertisement on to the redundant and despondent Dick Francis. It sounded like one of Wenham's apocryphal yarns to me – but Dick Francis really did become Head of the British Council.

In fact, *Battles of Broadcasting* was well received and much talked about. And, perhaps just as important, it turned out to be the only filmed record of that great Director General talking about broadcasting and I still keep hearing parts of it in programmes on Radio 4. Soon after the broadcast, Hugh bumped into Ian Trethowan, the Director General at the time. Instead of congratulating him, Trethowan asked Hugh, sarcastically, 'Do you think *every* Director General should be given a major segment of air time to rewrite history?' Is it any wonder that Trethowan never made the grade as a great Director General? After Hugh Greene left the BBC, he joined the board of the family brewery, Greene King and, at the age of seventy-four, married for the fourth time. He co-edited *The Spy's Bedside Book* and the *Penguin Book of Victorian Villainies* with his brother Graham. They enjoyed making mischief together. When the *New Statesman* ran a competition for the best parody of Graham Greene, both brothers submitted anonymous entries. Hugh won.

I had now embarked on a major new production. Brian Wenham, the Controller of BBC2, had accepted my proposal that we make a series about six of the great stately homes of Europe. We were going to call it *Castles and Palaces* and it was unapologetically aimed at the American market as well as our own. The BBC could not easily have afforded such an opulent project without co-finance, but since the subject matter was not one that would require creative compromises we were happy to accept Time-Life's offer to co-produce. I suggested that we approach the popular historian Robert Lacey to present the series. He had become a high-profile public figure following the publication of his massive biography of the Queen, *Majesty*. He was good looking, and he wrote elegantly. He proposed that the focus of the series should be more on the historic families than the castles and palaces they owned. He was right. We rechristened the series *Aristocrats*, and away we went.

Ruth Jackson, one of the bright young directors in the department, was dying to work on the series. She was married to Kevin Pakenham, so her parents-in-law were Lord Longford and the much admired historian and author Elizabeth. The Longfords knew everybody. This bonus, added to Ruth's own extraordinary contact book of top people, gave her entrée into some of the grandest families in Europe. She came to see me and we struck a bargain. She would find the six aristocrats if she could direct two of the six films. She and I started making a wish list. We clearly needed a British aristocrat and we could hardly leave out France, Italy, Spain or Germany. So there was only one slot going begging. Ruth already had possible aristocrats pencilled in for France, Germany and

Italy but she wanted to check them out before proposing them to me; and, of course, she had to make sure they would agree to take part.

Our first choice as the aristocrat to bat for Britain was the Duke of Westminster. Nobody thought much of his family seat in Cheshire, a 1960s' mock French château with a mini-Big Ben standing beside it. But His Grace the 6th Duke, Gerald Grosvenor, was then the country's richest man. Now he's worth about £6.5 billion, owning vast estates in Lancashire, Cheshire and Scotland; and more of Mayfair and Belgravia than anyone is ever likely to win in a game of Monopoly. The duke had just turned thirty years old when we asked him if we could feature his family in *Aristocrats*. He had an attractive wife, Natalia, and two pretty young daughters, Lady Tamara, aged three, and Lady Edwina, aged one. A couple of weeks later Ruth reported that the Westminsters were willing to play ball.

Next Ruth told me that I needed to travel with her to Austria to check out an aristocrat she hoped could be persuaded to be the subject of the sixth film in our series, His Serene Highness the Prince of Schwarzenberg. Everyone called him Prince Karel. We were invited to lunch at his eighteenth-century palace in the centre of Vienna. It was big enough to accommodate a restaurant and a hotel without unduly disturbing the royal family. The prince had arranged to meet us at one o'clock in the restaurant, one of the smartest in the city. If, like me, you sometimes get given the bum's rush by a bolshie maître d' who doesn't fancy the cut of your jib, try telling the one at the Schwarzenberg Palace Restaurant that you are lunching with the Prince of Schwarzenberg and see what happens – in a trice you will have him bowing, scraping, fawning and walking backwards in front of you bent almost double, low enough to lick your shoes. The forty-five-year-old prince made his entrance dead on time. He was dressed in a smart blue-grey serge jacket edged with green piping and matching jodhpurs, and he bore a strong resemblance to a Prussian army officer. He wore the shiniest of black riding boots and carried a riding crop.

Prince Karel was charm itself, the food and the service quite un-rivalled. His family had fled Czechoslovakia after the Second World War, leaving behind their huge estates and dozens of palaces including another Schwarzenberg Palace in Prague. What we didn't know was that he was secretly a leading member of Czechoslovakia's freedom movement and a great friend of Václav Havel, who would be the country's first President after the collapse of the Soviet Union, then still eight years away. When the country did become free, Prince Karel was elected a senator and Václav Havel appointed him Minister of Foreign Affairs, a position he still holds. Sadly, the prince turned us down. The reason he gave was that he was going through a sticky patch in his marriage to Princess Therese. She would allow neither herself nor their three children to be filmed, he said. I suspect the prince may also shrewdly have judged that *Aristocrats* would give him quite the wrong image for the political career on which he was soon to embark.

John Bird, my friend and colleague from *Americans* and *Alice at the Oriental*, had now joined the *Aristocrats* team. He came back from a research trip to Spain with good news. Doña Victoria Eugenia, Duchess of Medinaceli, the most titled woman in the world and the owner of ninety castles, had agreed to take part in the series. Meanwhile, Ruth and I flew to meet the family she had chosen for Italy. The Frescobaldis are one of the oldest and noblest families in Tuscany. They have been wine makers for thirty generations since 1308 and claim to have sold wine to both Michelangelo and Henry VIII. Their family home is a stunning thirteenth-century Florentine palazzo on the River Arno. At that time, rich and famous Italians were being kidnapped and murdered almost on a daily basis, so we were half-expecting the Frescobaldis to turn us down. Instead they said yes.

We were not expecting any such difficulties in France. Jean Louis, the Marquis de Ganay, and his wife were of a generation that remembered the BBC as a beacon of hope during the German Occupation and they welcomed us with open arms. In any case, they weren't in the slightest bit shy of publicity. On the contrary, they seemed to feature permanently in the international gossip columns. Wealth tax had forced them to open the château to the public and their friend, the Duke of Bedford, had impressed on them the importance of maintaining a high profile. Their home, the sixteenth-century Château de Courances, is a fabulous, moated palace, surrounded by some of the loveliest gardens in France.

It is exactly how a French château should be. The de Ganays were a delightfully entertaining couple who spoke perfect English. Now we had four of our six aristocratic families signed up. There was a front-runner for us to check out in Germany and a gap that we were later to fill, most satisfactorily, with Prince Franz Josef II of Liechtenstein and his family.

The aristocrat we had our eye on in Germany was a Bavarian prince whom Ruth described as the joker in the pack. She warned that some of our other aristocrats might pull out of the series if they knew that Prince Johannes von Thurn und Taxis was to be part of it. She wouldn't say why. She told me that I would find out soon enough for myself. John Bird was to direct and I went with him to Regensburg to meet the prince. We were cautious and intrigued. The mediaeval city is an hour or so from Munich, a beautiful drive through Bavarian forests and farmland. Some sixty-thousand acres of it, along with several breweries and seven magnificent castles, belonged to the Thurn und Taxis estate. The postal monopoly that had enabled the family to accumulate its astounding wealth had been awarded by the Holy Roman Empire in the sixteenth century. Serving Italy, Austria, Germany, Hungary, Spain, Holland, Belgium and Luxembourg, the dispensation survived for over three hundred years. The Thurn und Taxis mail coaches bearing the family name also carried passengers. That's how taxis got their name and how the family made its fortune, estimated to be more than two billion US dollars. *Forbes* magazine claimed that it made him the second richest man in Germany. When John and I arrived in Regensburg, the prince's father had only recently died and Johannes had just inherited this unbelievable legacy.

Prince Johannes was fifty-six years old and not in the best of health. He was also a bachelor, so who would inherit the riches when he was gone? To remedy this predicament he proposed marriage to a beautiful, wild but penniless aristocratic girl, much less than half his age. She was properly addressed as Countess Maria Gloria Ferdinanda Gerda Charlotte Teutonia Franziska Margarethe Frederike Simone Johanna Joachima Josefine Wilhelmine Huberta of Schönburg in Glauchau and Waldenburg. Everyone called her Gloria, except those who used her English nickname, 'Princess Punk'. She acquired the sobriquet in London on account of her multi-coloured hair, psychedelic lifestyle and her penchant for roaring up and down the King's Road on a powerful and noisy motorbike. Prince Johannes had met Gloria on the international bacchanalia circuit and chimed with her heterodox high jinks. No wonder Ruth had been worried about what the other aristocrats might think. All the same, royalty from all over Europe and beyond had flocked to Regensburg to attend the wedding of the decade, along with some extraordinarily uncommon commoners. We were shown film of the event. It had been a fairytale spectacle, more Disneyland than House of Windsor, and as outlandish as befitted this most curious couple. A baby girl appeared without delay and, shortly after our visit, a second daughter was born. More pertinent was the birth, fifteen months later, of a son, Albert, the twelfth Prince Thurn und Taxis. At last, an heir.

John and I approached St Emmaram's Castle, the Regensburg home of the Thurn und Taxis family, with disbelief. It was colossal. It seemed to us as big as the Louvre in Paris, itself once a sumptuous palace for the Sun King, Louis XIV. The castle had been built as a Benedictine monastery twelve hundred years earlier and acquired by the Thurn und Taxis family early in the nineteenth century. We were escorted towards the royal apartments through a staggering kaleidoscope of baroque. First the library, all mahogany panelling and gilt; next through the eleventh-century cloisters to the chapel, a masterpiece of rococo: life-size plaster angels and scintillating candelabra. There was a vast Titian-esque painting hanging above the altar – probably a real Titian, come to think of it. The ballroom glistened with acres of newly polished dance floor. On its walls hung priceless tapestries, illuminated by gargantuan chandeliers. The setting cried out for an orchestra and a hundred or so couples in full evening dress to bring it all to life. The banqueting hall was straight out of Versailles, with priceless oil paintings in every alcove, spotless linen tablecloths on mile-long tables. On either side were ranged perfectly aligned rows of delicate gilt chairs. And so to the private apartments.*

* Gloria von Thurn und Taxis' video tour of St Emmaram's Castle:
  http://www.thurnundtaxis.de/en/intro/

In the drawing room a footman in a pale-blue tailcoat and breeches offered us exotic cocktails. Just like in the movies, he was wearing a white wig with a black ribbon tied in a bow at the back. The prince and princess made a theatrical entrance. Had John and I strayed into the wrong studio just as a recording of *The Borgias* was about to begin? Prince Johannes immediately put us at our ease in almost faultless English. He was thoroughly practised at dealing with over-awed mortals – urbanity itself. The ex-punk princess, now a real Cinderella, was a picture of expensively dressed modesty. We were joined by the prince's recently widowed mother, the dowager Princess Maria Anna. The five of us went in to lunch.

We were ushered to our gilt chairs, the prince in the middle, beneath a giant oil painting of some imposing ancestor, his mother on his right and the princess on his left. John and I sat opposite. There were five be-wigged, liveried footmen hovering silently behind us, one each. The prince was a raconteur *par excellence*. I suppose you can't really call it 'name-dropping' when a cosmopolitan and gregarious prince drops names. He seemed to know everyone, have been everywhere, done everything. Bette Davis said this, Princess Grace whispered that. The constant stream of anecdotage knew no bounds until His Serene Highness tired of toying with the particular dish in front of him. Then he would put down his fork and, immediately, we would all have our plates whisked away. No matter that we had hardly started eating, the prince had finished. Luckily there were many courses, each accompanied by a superb wine. Our host had patently modelled himself on Noël Coward, who, 'naturally, dear boy', had been a great friend. The jokes with which he punctuated his narrative could indeed have been delivered by the Master himself – except that there was something slightly awry with the prince's idiom. It was as if one of the instruments in a string quartet was playing slightly out of tune.

Suddenly, without warning, as the royal trio folded their napkins and made to leave the table, priceless Ming porcelain plates of enormous diameter were placed in front of us. They must have been worth a king's ransom; indeed they may once have served that very purpose. It was a signal that it was all over. Just like the end caption of *Tom and Jerry,* here was a message to the dilly-dallying guest, 'That's All Folks.' John and I had hardly spoken during lunch. The two princesses had kept pretty mum too. Now we reaped the reward for our obsequiousness. His Serene Highness gave *Aristocrats* his benediction. When he came to see our finished film, his near-perfect command of the English language alerted him to the possibilty that Robert Lacey's commentary was mildly taking the piss. So his regal appraisal meticulously ignored the narration. 'You must congratulate your cameraman,' he beamed. 'He has taken quite beautiful pictures of our castles and palaces.' Hang on, wasn't that the title I suggested for the series in the first place?

CHAPTER 19

Mission to Explode

As it turned out I had left the BBC before *Aristocrats* was broadcast and John Bird was appointed executive producer to complete the series in my place. That year, 1982, was one of quite extraordinary turmoil in the television business. On the ITV network, Central Television replaced ATV in the Midlands and Southern Television lost its franchise to a new company, TVS. Channel 4 had been given the green light to start broadcasting and David Frost's TV-am consortium had won the new franchise for breakfast television. Most imprudently, the BBC decided, at very short notice, to start a breakfast television service of its own, as a spoiler for the new TV-am. Only someone as agressively competitive as Aubrey Singer could have sanctioned such foolishness. He had just been promoted to the plum job of Managing Director of Television on the insistence of the Board of Governors under its feudal Chairman George Howard. The board had overruled Alasdair Milne, the new Director General it had just appointed. Alasdair had wanted Bill Cotton to run the television service. Instead he was given the buffoon.

The BBC move to sabotage TV-am was wrong on several counts. First the BBC was pleading poverty, demanding cuts throughout the Corporation of between five and eight per cent. Secondly, in its bid for the next licence-fee increase, the BBC had identified several priority areas for new funding and breakfast television wasn't one of them. Thirdly, it was a widely held view that the BBC was already trying to do too much, especially with its aggressive expansion of local radio. As far as the general public was concerned the arrival on the scene of TV-am was extremely popular because of its promise to feature the Famous Five, David Frost, Angela Rippon, Anna Ford, Michael Parkinson and Esther Rantzen, not to mention Robert Kee who was, in many ways, the most estimable of all. (Esther cannily dropped out of the consortium before TV-am went on air.) The press supported TV-am's claim that BBC sour grapes fuelled the intended sabotage. As it turned out, BBC Current Affairs produced something even better than a spoiler. *Breakfast Time* went on air, a couple of weeks before TV-am launched, with Frank Bough and Selina Scott presenting and the trusty Ron Neill producing. It was a great success from its very first day.

I had received two discreet approaches about leaving the BBC to join the expanding world of television and I was seriously tempted by one of them. I had been working at the BBC for nearly twenty years and I was in the most senior job it was possible to hold and still have a direct role in programme making. The route on upwards, if anyone should choose to promote me, was not one that appealed. Certainly, being Controller of BBC1 or BBC2 was prestigious. They are important and creative jobs but they are what I call 'front-of-camera' jobs – an awful lot of your time is spent showing the public face of your channel – and I am a much better back-room boy. In any case, there was no reason to suppose that I would be offered either of those two plum jobs, for which I might well have had to labour in the vineyards for many more years. And, if I failed to become a Controller, I probably should have been destined for a Sideways Move – in *Yes Minister*, to be chairman of the War Graves Commission, in BBC terms, to be head of staff training. I had started at Anglia only months after it went on air. I was one of the first to join BBC2. Now I fancied another little adventure, another flutter on life's wheel of fortune. This was probably the last chance to make a fruitful career move before middle age gave way to early retirement, second childishness and mere oblivion, sans teeth, sans eyes, sans taste, sans everything.

My close friend since schooldays, Michael Deakin, had also made a career for himself in broadcasting and we met regularly for lunch to exchange professional gossip. He had started off working on Radio 4's *Today* programme, with Jack de Manio, where he found the shift system gave him plenty of time off to dabble in other enterprises. One of them was Editions Alecto, an art gallery in Kensington, which specialised in making lithographs with up-and-coming artists like David Hockney. The upstairs of their building was vacant so when Michael heard that Donald Baverstock and Alasdair Milne had left the BBC and planned to start their own production company, ever the canny Samaritan, he offered them sanctuary.

Donald Baverstock wasted no time in joining a consortium to bid for the new franchise, Yorkshire Television. It won and Donald invited Michael to join the new company. He went on to become one of its top documentary producers, best remembered for *Johnny, Go Home*, a film about the dangers to runaway children of sexual predators. The man accused of wrongdoing in the film, dubbed 'the bent bishop', was duly sent to gaol. There he studied law in the prison library and he was successful in bringing a very rare private prosecution against Michael and YTV for criminal libel. Michael ended up in the dock at the Old Bailey before the Attorney General stopped the case. This had been a terrifying ordeal, possibly with a prison sentence at the end of it. The overwhelming publicity the case attracted brought Michael notoriety – and he loved it.

Michael was great friends with David Frost and the journalist MP Jonathan Aitken, who both made programmes for him at YTV. Indeed Michael had been an important witness for the defence when Jonathan had earlier been charged under the Official Secrets Act with leaking highly sensitive and politically embarrassing information to the *Daily Telegraph*. Jonathan was acquitted and he was truly grateful for Michael's help in keeping him out of prison, at least that time. David Frost had known Michael at Cambridge – they had both been involved in theatricals – and David continued to find Michael entertaining company, a quick wit, bubbling over with clever ideas that could transform a run-of-the-mill programme into something special.

David, Jonathan and Michael signed up their galaxy of stars for TV-am in a blaze of publicity and appointed Peter Jay Chairman and Chief Executive. Peter was chosen from David's capacious stable of influential friends who gathered each summer in a marquee in Chelsea to celebrate David's birthday. Failure to be invited was ominous: it could mean that you were no longer a man or woman of substance. To refuse an invitation was unheard of. Only those detained at Her Majesty's pleasure, like Jeffrey Archer and Jonathan Aitken later were, could excuse their absence with impunity. Peter Jay was at that time married to James

Callaghan's daughter and he had recently returned to Britain from a stint as Ambassador in Washington. By all accounts his appearance before the Independent Broadcasting Authority, on TV-am's behalf, had been a masterpiece of bamboozlement. John Birt of Weekend World had been brought in to coach him. With fine words and phrases he seduced Bridget Plowden, by now the IBA Chairman, already bedazzled by the stars, with his electrifying vision of the future, his 'mission to explain'. To the surprise of the whole world the TV-am bid won.

The new station was starting from scratch, looking for experienced production staff who could be persuaded to leave the comparative security of the BBC or one of the existing ITV companies. Michael asked me if I would like to join him. His top priority was to find an executive producer to run their daily, two-hour flagship programme, *Good Morning, Britain*. They needed someone with experience of live, rolling news and current affairs but such producers were few and far between and I wasn't one of them. What finally made me decide not to take on this daunting assignment, if it were offered to me, was my meeting with Peter Jay. He didn't appear to know the first thing about television and, more worryingly, he didn't seem to think it mattered. I knew that even if I had bitten the bullet and taken on the job, there was a serious downside. Four of them, in fact. The first was that I would have to get up at five o'clock in the morning, seven days a week, at least for the first few months, until the programme was running smoothly. Secondly, if I made a success of the programme, what would I do next? There was nowhere else to go in a TV station with only one major programme. Third, if *Good Morning, Britain* failed, it would be such a high-profile disaster that I might never find work again. Even if I didn't cock the production up myself, there were plenty of factors outside my control to suggest most strongly that catastrophe was looming on the horizon. And, most important of all, there was TV-am's fundamental design fault. It promised that the Famous Five, all shareholders in the company, would have a major say in editorial policy. This was a recipe for disaster. Egos are difficult enough to deal with at the best of times, let alone at dawn. Would the stars choose with whom they were to be paired, the interviews they would conduct, the editorial line? Who would referee a dispute between two stars, between the producer and a star? There are very few top presenters who successfully produce their own programmes. (Melvyn Bragg of the *South Bank Show* was one of them.) Nearly always the dual role of actor-manager leads to tears before bed-time, as I knew only too well. However, there was no way for TV-am to get around this commitment. The concept of the Famous Five as share-holders and creative partners was the one aspect of TV-am's proposal that distinguished it from all the others and helped it to secure the franchise.

Quite separately, Michael had been approached by a consortium of business friends who were interested in setting up a production company to make programmes for Channel 4. The backers were looking for an experienced producer to run the company and to be a shareholder in it. Michael couldn't take the job because he was totally committed to TV-am so he proposed me. The chairman of the company, Sir Kenneth Cork, was an ex-Lord Mayor and, ominously, the best-known company liquidator and bankruptcy lawyer in the land. He was, of course, a big cheese in the City and he had brought in the Midland Bank to finance the new company. The bank's logo was a much-promoted griffin so, without over-taxing their imaginations, the consortium had decided to call their new company Griffin Productions. I had endless meetings with them before I convinced myself that this wasn't all just pie in the sky. I talked to some contacts at Channel 4 and I was advised that a nod and a wink would soon be forthcoming, so I said yes.

Before I told Will Wyatt of my plans to leave the BBC I had under-taken an unusual assignment. There was to be a major cultural event in London, the Festival of India, prompted at least partly by Indira Gandhi's anxiety to rehabilitate her international reputation. Some years before, she had declared an Emergency that had led to flagrant abuses of human rights with many of her political opponents ending up in gaol. There had been international condemnation of her and, when she did go to the polls, the voters had rejected her decisively. Now she had been re-elected and was Prime Minister again. The Festival of India was to be a flamboyant exposition of the country's culture and BBC2 had decided to reflect the event with an Indian season – documentaries that had recently been made about India and some serious Indian feature films like Satyajit Ray's *Pather Panchali*. I had volunteered to coordinate the scheduling and propose a couple of new documentaries to augment BBC2's Indian season. The BBC2 Controller, Brian Wenham, agreed that we should mark the festival with a major documentary about contemporary India, presented by the BBC's correspondent there, Mark Tully. I asked the distinguished producer Jonathan Stedall to direct it. He had already made some superb documentaries in India and he had worked with Mark. I went with Jonathan to Delhi to discuss the project. Mark proposed that we concentrate on the go-ahead state of Gujarat, where its rapid industrial development demonstrated that India did have the potential to join the modern world. We called the film, simply, *From Our Delhi Correspondent*.

Mark and I also came up with an ingenious and complementary idea. The BBC was always being criticised in India for showing documentaries in Britain that supposedly denigrated the country by concentrating on poverty. Of course there were films that showed scarcity, calamity, floods, earthquakes, famine and, yes, poverty. However, India's image was much enhanced by the large number of documentaries that were always being made about its spirituality, its culture and the strides the country was making in science, technology and achieving self-sufficiency in food. Compared with other developing countries in Africa, Asia and South America, for example, the BBC served India exceptionally well. Mark and I proposed that we take advantage of the Festival of India in London to stage a return match, showing off some of the many positive documentaries the BBC had recently made about India, screening them in India's four main cities. The big bosses in London approved the plan and the British Council agreed to co-host our peripatetic documentary festival, inviting the audiences and arranging suitable premises for the showing of the films.

Back in London, one of my earlier Indian programmes now needed attention. Michael Deakin had been asked by the *Spectator* to review Alan Whicker's autobiography and Michael had used the opportunity to excoriate him. Michael had produced Whicker for Yorkshire Television and he had not enjoyed the experience; indeed, it was quite clear, from his review, that he had come to detest him. Michael told me that Whicker had used his autobiography to mount a thinly veiled attack on my charming and inoffensive *Man Alive* documentary, *Indian Summer,* about the British who had stayed on in India. Michael claimed it was actionable. Like an elderly colonel in Tunbridge Wells, Whicker had launched into an intemperate attack on the distortion and bias he claimed were regularly to be found in documentaries and current affairs programmes, particularly on ITV:

> *World in Action* is usually a sort of Marxist party-political, *TV Eye* the predictable protest of the militant Left. On occasion they lay aside their political message and produce powerful and energising investigative journalism. More often they peddle the same old repetitive line and struggle to knock the pillars down; ridicule the Establishment, show the police as stumbling buffoons or brutal Fascists, support the wreckers working to bring down our freedoms to whom any riot or strike is a victory, attack all Centre and Right governments anywhere, avoid a constructive word about the US or a hurtful comment on a Communist state. Industriously, they scour the world for some enemy of Britain to encourage, lavishing sympathetic understanding on the masked man with the rocket.

Whicker then praised BBC documentaries in general but claimed that one of them had been maliciously edited, totally distorting the meaning of an important interview. Whicker didn't name the film but it was quite clear from the context that he was referring to our *Indian Summer* documentary. By implication he was suggesting that our motives were as base and our methods as fiendishly as those he had just berated in ITV. The film's director, Philip Geddes, was hopping mad when I showed him what Alan Whicker had written. So was the film's reporter, Jack Pizzey, who was by this time living in Australia. He agreed that whatever action we chose would have his full support.

It is true that what Alan Whicker had to say was damaging nonsense – and Philip and I wanted to press for amends – but what most attracted me to the idea of suing Whicker was that the episode contained the most wonderful potential for hilarity and mirth. The delight of it all was that the disputed interview, with a redoubtable British memsahib called Irene Herbert, took place on the back of a massive elephant in the Indian jungle. It was quite clear, even to the layman, that there was no way we could possibly have edited the sequence. Mrs Herbert claimed that she had taken a pot shot at a man trying to steal the branches off her trees. Whicker claimed that we had cut out a question and an answer to make it look as if she was confessing to attempted murder when, in fact, she was talking about shooting at an animal. We hadn't cut out anything. She *was* confessing to attempted murder – or at least grievous bodily harm. The transcript we gave to our lawyer made that quite clear. It is true that Irene sometimes referred to the thief as 'it'. But that was the way such people spoke of the Indian lower classes, I'm afraid:

> I didn't kill it. I shot at it. But, there again, it was destroying all my trees. They climb up the trees and cut off all the branches to feed their cows, for timber, for anything. And I shouted at him and said, 'Go away.' He took no notice . . . So I lost my temper and I went up [into] the jungle – there he was, cutting at this tree – and let fly. He leapt off the tree, sort of slid down like a monkey and disappeared, made the most frightful noises as if he'd really died. So I really got a bit frightened and dearly hoped I hadn't got him in the eye or something. [My gardener] went and harangued the man and said, 'Madam says that if you want a bandage put on or anything like that, she will look after you.' 'Oh no, no, I'm not coming near that madam, she'll shoot me again.' But still, they didn't come and cut any more trees after that.

Obviously Whicker had never seen the programme, indeed he was later to admit as much. Instead he must have been listening to the frightful sort of people who inhabited the golf-club bar in the tax haven where he lived – gin-driven tittle-tattle. At Michael Deakin's suggestion, Philip and I consulted Patrick Swaffer, the brilliant lawyer who had defended him and Yorkshire Television against criminal libel over *Johnny, Go Home*. First Patrick sat Philip and me down and became very solemn. Had either of us any dark secrets that we didn't want revealed? He pressed us hard and both of us looked rather shifty while we mentally did a fast rewind through our past lives. Patrick explained that the defence barrister might try to show that our reputations were already so sullied that he could argue Whicker's book had done us no further damage.

Irene Herbert, guns blazing, was prepared to come to England and give evidence in the High Court on our behalf. Yes, she said, she had shot at a human and, given the same circumstances, she would jolly well do so again. Telexes started chattering between Patrick's office and Hamish Hamilton, Whicker's publishers. We were asking for an apology, damages and an undertaking that Whicker's defamatory remarks would be removed from subsequent editions of his book. I had mischievously proposed to Patrick that we insist that the copies of the book already in the shops be pulped. Sensibly, he advised against it, warning of the risk of a counter claim from the publishers. More chattering of telexes and Alan Whicker asked to see the film. I didn't fancy viewing it with him, so my secretary did. 'Good film,' was all he had to say. In no time, Patrick called us to announce a victory. Hamish Hamilton had agreed to delete the offending passage from future editions and to pay Philip and me a modest tax-free sum in damages and fund our legal costs as well. Whicker was forced to write us each a letter of apology. What fun! Jack Pizzey then mounted his Antipodean high horse, forcing Whicker and his publishers to pay him damages too. What's more they agreed to take advertisements in *The Listener* and the trade press, apologising to Jack for Whicker's dastardly slurs. Hamish Hamilton must have been a little aggrieved to discover that their fearless, award-winning reporter made it up as he went along.

Leaving the BBC was much easier than I had thought it would be. Will Wyatt showed no surprise or regret. That was his style. He asked me when I wanted to go and I told him that I would like to be free by the time Channel 4 launched, in three months' time, but that I would stay to see through the screenings of the BBC documentaries in India. Will said he wanted to come too. He had never been to India and saw this as the perfect opportunity to dip his toe in the water. We had chosen for the screenings half a dozen BBC documentaries about India that had recently been broadcast and, of course, *From Our Delhi Correspondent,* the documentary Jonathan Stedall was making with Mark Tully as a salute to the Festival of India. Suddenly there was a major glitch. A technicians' strike at the BBC prevented us from mixing the soundtracks of any films that were in production. It was difficult enough completing *From Our Delhi Correspondent* in time because the film was being edited in London yet Mark Tully who had to write and record the narration was four thousand miles away in Delhi. I tried every trick in the book to obtain an exemption for our film. It was not scheduled for broadcast until some time later, so the mixed soundtrack for the broadcast could wait. My deadline was the screenings. I could hardly show an incomplete documentary to the movers and shakers of India.

The managers refused to seek special dispensation from the union because they were toughing it out. So I asked if we could mix the soundtrack abroad, perhaps in Holland or Germany, and export it directly to India – and, if necessary, leave it there. When the strike was over we could easily mix the sound again in London for the later BBC2 transmission. Permission denied. It would aggravate the conflict, I was told. Too late I realised that I never should have asked. It is hard to credit it but Mark and I decided to chance it and put a live commentary on the film for each of its showings in Delhi, Bombay, Madras and Calcutta. We managed to acquire a lip mike, a microphone that excludes all extraneous sound, and Mark sat with me, high up above our audience in the projection booth, reading the commentary as the fifty-minute film was running, while I watched the screen through the projectionist's window and tapped Mark on the shoulder to cue him when to narrate and when to shut up. No footage counter, no cue lights, it was a *tour de force* of belt and braces. Only old warhorses like Mark and I would ever have known how to add live commentary. The need had long since been overtaken by technology. It may well be that you can't teach an old dog new tricks but this pair exhibited its old ones immaculately.

One of the documentaries we showed was a superb film called *Return to the Punjab,* made for the *World About Us* series. It followed a Sikh family from Gravesend in Kent travelling to India, with children who had never been there, to visit the village of their ancestors. It chronicled their journey from their grim home on the wretched Thames Estuary to a tiny village in the Punjab – by jumbo jet, train, taxi, bullock cart and, finally, on foot. The amazement of the London-born Sikh children had to be seen to be believed. We screened the film first at the India International Centre in New Delhi. It was a time of big political trouble in the Punjab that would soon lead to fanatic Sikhs seizing the Golden Temple in Amritsar, the army storming it and Prime Minister Indira Gandhi being assassinated in reprisal. The week of our screening in Delhi was a particularly tense one.

When the lights went up, after the film, the atmosphere was electric. There were already hands up to ask questions. Mark Tully, Will Wyatt and I, along with some panjandrum from Broadcasting House, were there to answer them. A be-turbaned Sikh in the middle of the audience was very agitated. We took his question first. Why had the BBC made the teenage Sikh boy from the Gravesend family remove his turban and cut his hair? Mark turned to me and we had a hurried whispered conversation. 'No way had they told him to cut his hair,' I told Mark. In fact, I was shocked at the suggestion. I had not been responsible for the production of this particular film but no *World About Us* director would have contrived such a distortion. Almost certainly the boy had cut his hair to avoid teasing at school or, perhaps, to annoy his parents. Thousands of British children of Indian parents swam with the tide of their contemporaries. Millions were the children of immigrants who did the same all over the world. How lucky the BBC was to have Mark on the platform that day. Politely he answered the irate Sikh in the audience with a question. 'Sir, can I ask you if that is a relation of yours sitting beside you.' 'Yes,' replied the Sikh, in Hindi. 'He is my brother.' Everyone in the audience turned to look. His brother was clean-shaven with neatly trimmed hair. It was as dramatic a denouement as in those courtroom dramas when the lawyer unexpectedly produces evidence conclusively proving his client's innocence. 'How on earth did you know?' I asked Mark over a drink in the bar later. He said nothing. He just winked.

Delhi, Bombay, Madras, Calcutta – like viceroys we came, we saw, we conquered. For once, maybe for the first time, our audiences and the press loved BBC Television. It went without saying that the BBC World Service on radio was cherished. In India's wars with Pakistan and, especially, during Mrs Gandhi's Emergency, it was almost universally perceived that only the BBC could be trusted to tell you what was really going on. But hardly anyone had ever seen any of our television pro-grammes. There were no satellites, precious few video recorders; even black-and-white television sets were few and far between. Our reputation relied on hearsay; some of it had plainly been unflattering. Now people could see for themselves the variety of outstanding documentaries we made. Admittedly the films we had brought were chosen with some care. For this operation, at least, we had no qualms about shoving the trickier ones under the carpet. We were on a hearts-and-minds mission, for goodness' sake.

When I got back to London there was only one week to go before I left the BBC for ever. My departure was as low-key as I could make it. Not for me a farewell extravaganza, awash with crocodile tears, insincere speeches and promises of eternal friendship, to be forgotten as soon as the party was over. Instead there was an informal booze-up in the BBC Club at Kensington House, just like any other evening, with a good turnout to wish me *bon voyage*. In my pocket I had a handwritten letter from the unlovely Aubrey Singer, thanking me for all the good programmes I had made, and another from Jeremy Isaacs, the Chief Executive of Channel 4, with the cryptic words 'Be Welcome' scrawled across the new company's swanky headed paper. I had intended to come back the next morning, a Saturday, to sort out my office and clear away the files. But as I left the party I decided that I didn't ever want to come back. Alone I went up to my office, opened the filing cabinet and removed the very few private documents I would need if I ever wrote this book, dumping the rest of my papers, eighteen years' worth, in black plastic refuse sacks. The memos in my files had always been copied to absolutely everyone. That was the BBC way. I doubted there would be any comeback. There wasn't.

CHAPTER 20

Please, Sir, I Want Some More

Channel 4 went on air on Monday 1st November 1982, three days after I had left the BBC to run Griffin Productions, so it was something of an accomplishment that Griffin managed to broadcast three productions during the new station's first week. When word had reached Chief Executive Jeremy Isaacs at the new station that I was seriously considering joining a new production company, he saw Griffin as a way out of a dilemma. Channel 4 had no plans to make programmes itself, except for *Right to Reply*, its weekly audience-response programme, and it planned to make that in-house in its small presentation studio. Most of the commissioning editors had deliberately been chosen from outside mainstream television with the result that the channel employed no experienced executive producers who could supervise complex live programmes or rescue disasters in the cutting room. This was the gap that Griffin was contracted to fill. And, even before the channel went on air, it was plain to see that the Independent Broadcasting Authority was going to insist on balancing studio discussions to follow some of the more blatantly megaphonic films that Channel 4 was planning to broadcast. Two of the early problem children were *The Animals Film*, an attack on humans by animal liberationists, and *On Our Land*, a Palestinian diatribe against Israel.

Jeremy Isaacs gave Griffin an eighteen-month contract to establish an 'instant-response unit' for such eventualities and we were given two regular weekly series to justify its cost. The first was special because it was Jeremy's baby, much trumpeted by him. *Opinions* was a half-hour essay by a distinguished figure in public life, shot simply as an austere talking head. The contributors were chosen because they were controversial: no one had ever been allowed to deliver unchallenged such radical opinion on television before. To make the point the very first *Opinions* was delivered by E. P. Thompson whose Richard Dimbleby Lecture had been cancelled so shamefully by the BBC. The producer whom Channel 4 had chosen to run *Opinions* was a political journalist with experience on both sides of the Atlantic. He didn't know a great deal about television production so he was cuckooed into the Griffin nest. One day he brought a chum of the commissioning editor's to the office to see me. The young man's pitch was original, at least it was to me. Since Channel 4 was obliged to cater for minorities, he pitched, why shouldn't he be commissioned to make an unapologetically right-wing current-affairs series for the channel? Would we produce it with him as the presenter? If he didn't actually put his leather boots on my office desk, he certainly did so metaphorically. Throughout the meeting he exhibited such arrogance that I assumed he was taking the piss. Little did I know he was soon to become a legend of evil in the land. His name was Michael Portillo and he was about to be chosen as the Conservative candidate for Enfield Southgate; he was to ascend to the pinnacle of politics as Secretary of State for Defence before his electors famously showed him the boot, the whole world delighting in his humiliation. I too would have loved to have kicked him hard where it hurt, but, frustratingly, my role by then was to ingratiate myself with commissioning editors not to assault their chums.

Our second regular series was an ingeniously cheap idea of Channel 4's to cater for the Irish community in Britain. Called *Irish Angle*, it became a long-running and popular strand. Each week the programme would rebroadcast an edition of the topical magazine programmes produced by Ulster Television in Belfast or RTÉ in Dublin. The commissioning editor would decide which programme would be used that week and Griffin would then edit it, bookending it with *Irish Angle* front and end titles. One Saturday I stood in for our regular director to give him a weekend break and I went myself to Channel 4 to supervise the recording of the appropriate programme. That week the commissioning editor had chosen RTÉ's report on the general election in Eire which had just been shown live in the republic so our feed from Dublin was much later than usual. From the presentation suite in Channel 4 we could hear that some sort party was going on at RTÉ. However, the normal identity caption with the RTÉ symbol appeared on our monitor, correctly labelled 'Election Special'. The RTÉ clock began the count down from one minute to zero so we started recording in London.

I wasn't paying much attention to the content of the progamme because of all the chatter and confusion at the Dublin end. Suddenly a horrible thought struck me. I felt sure that I had heard on the car radio that Garrett FitzGerald's Fina Gael had won the election, yet we were seeing Charles Haughey declaring victory for Fianna Fáil. We could get no response from master control and it was now ten o'clock at night. We called the main switchboard number for RTÉ. A sleepy commissionaire eventually answered. 'They're all in the pub next door, sir. Would you like the number?' Soon we had tracked down the videotape operator whose machine had just finished playing the election down the line to us. I told him of my concern. 'Oh, that must be last February's election we were sending you. Is it this week's election you'ld be after? That'll be no problem. I'll call the tape library and see if we can get something to you in half an hour or so.' And he did, bless him. He fed us the right election, down the line, and we were all finished in Channel 4 by midnight. The next morning I edited the tape ready for the *Irish Angle* transmission at 3 p.m. I shuddered at the thought of what might have been. Can you imagine what fun everyone would have had at my expense – the high-powered troubleshooter who had broadcast the wrong election?

Though hardly professionally over-taxing, these programmes gave Griffin just enough work to cover its overheads and that, in turn, gave us a breathing space to drum up new business. I was extremely lucky that my fire-fighting role entitled me to a staff pass into the Channel 4 building. I could pop in to meet the commissioning editors who were mostly unknown to me. It didn't take long for me to realise that there was a severe crisis looming for independent producers. Thousands upon thousands of programme proposals had already poured in by the time Channel 4 went on air. Each commissioning editor was receiving literally hundreds more every week. The arrival of Channel 4 had seemed to promise untold opportunities to all the freelancers and casual workers who made up the media industry. In addition, the channel was attracting established producers from ITV and the BBC, like me, who welcomed the freshness of the channel's approach and saw it as a chance to do something new. Jeremy had foreseen this problem, advising people not to give up their salaried jobs, but the distant vista of El Dorado compelled otherwise rational people to throw caution to the winds. This was a gold rush without nearly enough gold to go round. It was as if there were only one book publisher in Britain, and every author, from Booker Prize winner to amateur scribbler, was knocking on the only door.

At that time, both the BBC and ITV were extremely hostile to the idea of commissioning independent producers so the new channel was the only broadcasting customer in Britain. Those directors who were happy making commercials, training films and corporate videos found a rather crowded niche for themselves, but the overwhelming number of factual-programme producers, especially documentary-makers, who were counting on C4 to earn themselves a living, were in a pretty pickle. There turned out to be two other major flaws in the C4 approach to the independent sector. First, it was not possible for inexperienced commissioning editors to sort the wheat from the chaff. A well-written programme proposal, written by a scoundrel, could look attractively plausible unless you knew that its proponent was a blackguard, a thief and a liar who had landed his previous employer deeply in the mire. Without knowledge of the industry folklore, commissioning editors were flying blind and often into trouble. If they were clever or lucky, they might discover an innovative and exciting film-maker like Phil Agland, who made astonishingly beautiful documentaries like *The People of the Rainforest*. More often than should be, what the commissioning editors had ordered turned out to be rubbish. It was inevitable, then, that commissioning editors began to stick with people they knew or those who had already established a reputation. This led to accusations of favouritism and of playing safe – denying new programme-makers a chance. The problem was compounded by the progressive reduction in the number of documentaries that were commissioned over the years. The channel needed to build audience figures. Conventional factual programmes seldom deliver them.

The second big flaw, from the independent producers' point of view, was that Jeremy Isaacs understandably favoured one-off commissions in order to keep the front door ajar for newcomers. He was most reluctant to give guaranteed output deals, except where he was forced to in order to achieve economies of scale. He did make such contractual arrangements, for example, to ITN for *Channel 4 News*, to Phil Redmond for *Brookside*, to Diverse Productions for *The Friday Alternative* and to YTV for *Countdown*. Yet the financial rewards for single factual programmes or, indeed, short runs of them, were so minute that no production company could afford to employ even the core staff necessary to generate the ideas that win new commissions. Eighteen years later, Jeremy Isaacs conceded as much in a little-publicised *mea culpa*.

> The socio-political beliefs that I had about Channel 4 hindered the growth of the independent sector. I wanted the individual voice. I felt I was doing them a favour by allowing them to make programmes that they proposed to us, not that we proposed to them. Through my attitude and the cost-plus basis of commissioning I was not allowing the business to develop.*

Companies without long-running strands were therefore compelled to work as one-man bands from home. Being a freelance producer like this is a perfectly honourable profession but it is not independent production, a business with properly paid permanent staff to kick around new ideas, in an environment where such talent can be trained and developed. Over time, big companies like this did evolve, usually built round front-of-camera talent like Lenny Henry, Victoria Wood and Graham Norton. However, in factual programmes, the expertise of most independents, few long-term commitments were made and those that were in no way satisfied the voracious demand of increasingly frustrated and penniless producers. David Elstein, one of the key champions of the fourth channel, was refused guaranteed air time by his friend Jeremy Isaacs, so he announced that he was going to close his company. He

---

* Sir Jeremy Isaacs interviewed in 2000 by Michael Darlow for his book *Independents Struggle*, Quartet, 2004. Michael Darlow was one of the key lobbyists who successfully campaigned for independent producers to receive twenty-five per cent of all new BBC and ITV productions.

returned to the mainstream, as Director of Programmes at Thames Television. As Sir John Harvey-Jones put it so pithily, 'Independent production isn't a business, it's a lifestyle.'

Luckily Griffin had a new customer, my old friend Tony Isaacs who ran *World About Us* at the BBC. A young Indian cameraman and his Swiss film-school friend had been to see him to try and sell a film they had shot in the southern Indian state of Kerala. Tony told me that there were some beautiful sequences, but that the whole film needed a tremendous amount of work by someone who knew a good deal more about film-making than these two young students. If I would put the film right, Tony said, he would buy a licence for *World About Us* and Griffin could take the rights for the rest of the world. The film was indeed brilliantly shot. There were magical images of Kathakali dancers in their gigantic masks and headdresses, their faces daubed with lurid scarlet and green make-up. These sequences had been intercut with evocative shots of sleepy buffalo working the paddy fields, egrets perched on their backs, while gnarled old men shouted encouragement to them from the shade of the coconut trees.

Instead of hiring a pokey cutting room in the West End of London, we found a way to edit the film for free. In a picture-postcard village near Zurich, the Swiss boy's father ran a commercials company. Inside his seventeenth-century Alpine barn he had built a thoroughly modern film studio and editing suite. Lunches and suppers in the village inn were long drawn-out affairs. If this was the lifestyle Sir John Harvey-Jones deplored, too bad. Cheers. The film needed a big name to make it marketable so I wrote to Sir Richard Attenborough and asked him if he would narrate the film, now called *Shiva's Disciples*. I hinted ever so politely to the great actor-director that he had recently done pretty well out of India with his Gandhi film – how about putting a little something back? Although I knew his brother David, of course, I had never met Richard, so I was delightedly surprised when he said yes. He arrived at the dubbing theatre in Oxford Street exactly on time, leaving the Roller in the care of his chauffeur, just around the corner in Soho Square. There was a good deal of commentary for Attenborough to record because it was a fifty-minute film with no interviews. He had obviously rehearsed very conscientiously with the copy of the film that I had sent him. The recording was completed with hardly a re-take, and as I thanked him, I told him that his fee had been sent to his office, as I had agreed with his assistant. He looked genuinely surprised and hesitated. 'I didn't know there was a fee,' he said. Damn, I could have saved a few bob for the company there.

Out of the blue, I was telephoned by a BBC Current Affairs producer whom I knew, telling me that he was responsible for planning the replacement for *Nationwide,* BBC1's early-evening magazine programme. He was thinking of employing Desmond Wilcox and Nick Ross as presenters for this new programme, *Sixty Minutes.* His question to me was, would Nick Ross and Desmond be able to work together when Nick had been part of the mutiny against Desmond some years before? Entirely the wrong question. Both were professionals who had long since put those differences behind them. The right question to have asked me would have been, did I think Desmond would make a good presenter for the programme? To which the answer was undoubtedly no. He simply wasn't any good at talking to the camera convincingly and this was to be a daily, live and technically tricky programme. Since I wasn't asked, I was not tempted to lie. Like all his erstwhile colleagues, I wished Desmond well and the last thing I wanted to do was to sabotage his chances of landing a good job. It seemed to be odd that the producer hadn't looked at a few of the *Man Alive* programmes that Desmond had presented and reached this conclusion for himself. *Sixty Minutes* staggered along for eleven months and was a debacle. Desmond looking unhappier with every edition. Knowing he was no good, he offered to resign to save the programme. He was pretty angry though because he knew that the blame was by no means all his. So serious were the design faults that *Sixty Minutes* was deemed beyond redemption. I tentatively proposed to my fellow directors that we should invite Desmond to join Griffin. They turned me down, suspecting, perhaps rightly, that my motive was too tainted by sympathy for my old boss.

Inside Channel 4 I soon made friends with Liz Forgan, the Director of Programmes. It's not easy to deputise for someone as hands-on as Jeremy Isaacs and she was superb at publicly defending the indefensible transgressions that were endlessly broadcast by the new channel. She was good fun to work with. One of her responsibilities was *Right to Reply*, the equivalent of a newspaper's letters page. From time to time she would ask me to come in to Channel 4 and produce it. The presenter was Gus Macdonald, a one-time arch-rival of mine from the days when he edited Granada's *World in Action* and I was editor of *Man Alive*. It was a dream team. Without being boastful, it is fair to say that *Right to Reply* was a doddle for producers of our experience. Gus would write the script on the train from Manchester and we would record the programme to length, in half the allotted time, and retire to some bar for a drink and a chat. *Right to Reply* made use of one ingenious innovation, the walk-in Video Box, available for anyone to use at the Channel 4 studios in Charlotte Street. It was a cubicle, like the ones you used to find at every supermarket for passport photographs. All you had to do was enter the Video Box, follow the instructions and say your piece. There had been some particularly strident feminist documentary on the channel that prompted an unusual contributor to the Video Box. Chad Varah was founder of the Samaritans, by then in his mid-eighties, a humble but famous and charismatic priest. How he had managed to operate the recording machine for his complaint about the feminists, God alone knows. I had first come across him more than twenty years earlier when Bob Wellings had interviewed him on *About Anglia*. I knew that he was superb on television and I proposed to Liz that we should ask him to confront the two producers of the feminist rant, solo. At first she was incredulous at my suggestion. She couldn't see how he could hold his own against two such hard-boiled and aggressive protagonists. In the end I convinced her.

First she and I had to meet the feminist producers who had demanded their right to discuss their right to reply to the viewers' right to reply on *Right to Reply*. The whole morning was a teach-in, aimed at me, about the horrors of men ever since the garden of Eden. Liz had edited the Women's section of the *Guardian* in her previous incarnation, so she was on familiar territory. She engaged the pair in vigorous debate while I listened, amazed. Our cocktail of two angry young women versus a benign but articulate old priest made a wonderful programme because the casting was so bizarre. Gus Macdonald hardly had to say a word. He sat back like a tennis umpire as Chad Varah, his liberal credentials unimpeachable, skilfully demolished the strident feminist argument in a soft-spoken and good-natured manner. Poor Liz was thrilled but schizophrenic. As Director of Programmes she was delighted that we had produced such a cracking edition of *Right to Reply*, but, as a high-profile defender of the feminist cause, most uncomfortable that the politically correct sisters had been bested so convincingly by an old buffer in a dog collar.

I also made friends, inside Channel 4, with a real rascal, the commissioning editor for multi-cultural programmes, Farrukh Dhondy. Indian by birth, he was a properly paid-up radical, with a pedigree of protest around the UK that must have put him on the watchlist of every Special Branch and MI5 officer in the country. He knew who I was because *Man Alive* used to invite him and his ilk to ginger up studio discussions. A talented playwright, Farrukh had returned to celebrity with a superb sit-comedy he wrote for Channel 4 called *Tandoori Nights*. As soon as he was appointed commissioning editor at Channel 4 he boldly cancelled two major factual series made by London Weekend Television. The best known was the magazine programme, *Eastern Eye*, which catered mostly for the Asian middle class, and *Black on Black*, serving the same purpose for the black community. Both were anathema to a commissioning editor as radical as Farrukh. LWT was not amused to be rejected by this brash and determined upstart. The ITV companies had never really accepted that the new channel wasn't their ITV2, yet they were forced to guarantee it financially. It was with considerable dismay that they found they had to compete for commissions, on equal terms, with the scruffy independent producers they so despised. Farrukh was delighted by the turmoil he caused, and especially by the wound he inflicted on the company's pride: LWT was going through a phase of particularly insufferable arrogance and self-satisfaction at the time.

Farruk's plan was to replace LWT's cosy shows with a radical, multi-cultural, current-affairs series called *Bandung File*, produced and presented by two of the most notorious left-wing public figures in the land. Tariq Ali, once an International Marxist and co-author of *Trotsky for Beginners,* was world famous for his vociferous opposition to the Vietnam War. Darcus Howe, a Black Panther in the 1970s, had been tried and acquitted at the Old Bailey, as one of the 'Mangrove Nine', for riot, affray and assault; later he served three months in prison for assaulting a police officer. But, hang on a minute. There had recently been a monumental bust-up between Jeremy Isaacs and the Channel 4 Chairman, who detested the radical current-affairs programmes Jeremy was commissioning, especially *The Friday Alternative.* The Chairman demanded a clean-up. Jeremy stood his ground. Eventually, overruling the advice of Jeremy and Liz Forgan, the Board ordered the cancellation of *The Friday Alternative.* Jeremy immediately replaced it with *Diverse Reports,* made by the same production company.

So it was not surprising that the Board threw a wobbly when Farrukh's plan for *Bandung File* was presented to them. They insisted on a period of probation. First Tariq and Darcus should be allowed to make a short series of documentary films under the guidance of an experienced executive producer. If those programmes were satisfactory then the Board would look favourably on Farrukh's pet project, *Bandung File.* It was not long before Farrukh invited me to the nearby Light of Kashmir restaurant for his favourite lunch, curried brains and Cobra beer. 'What's in it for Griffin?' I heard myself asking – the proper question for my brave, new commercial persona. As it happened, this was the sort of language that Farrukh appreciated. We horse-traded. If I agreed to be the executive producer for three of Tariq and Darcus's films, he would commission Griffin to make an expensive documentary which would attract a healthy production fee. I suggested a film about young Asians from Leicester exploring their African roots – big budget stuff. The deal was sealed with another round of Cobras.

The first of the probationary films that Tariq and Darcus made was an investigation into vote-rigging in Roy Hattersley's Birmingham constituency of Sparkbrook. Hattersley was at that time deputy to Neil Kinnock, the leader of the Labour Party in opposition. Tariq and Darcus showed me the rough cut which included an interview with an Indian Labour Party worker, conducted in Hindi. The shot was so badly framed that I thought the cameraman must have gone to sleep. I smelled a rat. The Indian girl reporter on the film translated for me. The Labour Party worker was explaining how he increased the Labour vote by registering people whose names he collected from the cemetery, and by adding to the electoral roll relatives of Asian constituents who had never left their villages in India. Tariq and Darcus rather sheepishly – and very reluctantly – let me in on their guilty secret. The Labour Party worker spoke good English, but while the camera was turning, he denied any involvement in vote-rigging. So the production team had decided to stop filming for a fictitious tea break. The cameraman locked off his camera but left it running and the sound recordist did the same with his tape machine. With only the reporter and the party worker left in the room, the latter boastfully spilt the beans, in Hindi, as to how he and his cronies fraudulently inflated the Labour vote. Obviously, he thought he was talking off the record. Naughty. I knew better than to play silly buggers with top politicians. I muttered to myself, like some geriatric soothsayer, 'Remember *Yesterday's Men*.'

I explained the BBC rule about secret filming to Tariq and Darcus. I said I didn't know the IBA rules off by heart but I was sure they were much the same, namely, that you may only film people surreptitiously if you have prior written permission from the top. This will normally be withheld unless there is some pressing public-interest justification – for example, if it is the only way you can expose a major crook. I told them that the very least that could be done, now that the film had been shot, was to seek permission to broadcast it from Paul Bonner, Channel 4's programme controller. He had been a colleague of mine at the BBC and I thought he just might be persuaded to give retroactive permission so that the problem sequence could remain in the finished film. Farrukh not surprisingly thought I was being old-maidish and undertook, rather shiftily, to talk to Paul. I didn't trust him for an instant, so I made my case in writing and copied the letter to Paul Bonner.

Nothing then happened until the film was broadcast. When the bullets started to fly, Roy Hattersley kept his head well below the parapet. Who needed this sort of publicity? He well knew that a film like this was best ignored. It would attract a small audience on Channel 4; to make a stink would be a clarion call for Fleet Street to dig deeper into this most unsavoury business. Instead, top Labour Party officials took the matter up discreetly with the IBA. So there I was on the carpet, in Jeremy Isaacs' office, with Farrukh, Tariq and Darcus, lined up like naughty schoolboys. Paul Bonner was also there and, rather satisfactorily, he seemed to be on the receiving end of the high-octane bollocking too. Not one of them owned up to the livid Jeremy that I had warned them, in writing, of what they should have done. I didn't say, 'I told you so.' I didn't say a word. Would Farrukh or Paul ever have given me work again if I dropped them in it? But hang on, what about my reputation, lying in tatters on the Chief Executive's floor?

Jeremy must have concealed this unfortunate little affair from the Channel 4 Board because Tariq and Darcus were commissioned to make *Bandung File* and Farrukh gave Griffin the documentary he had promised. The production fee? Exactly thirty pieces of silver.

CHAPTER 21

Not a Penny More

The failure of TV-am was total, sudden and catastrophic for all the high-profile people who so proudly, and often so patronisingly, boasted that they knew a better way of making television than the rest of us. It was doubly painful because the BBC's *Breakfast Time* with Frank Bough and Selina Scott had been so effortlessly successful from the very first day it went on air. My friend Michael Deakin who had hoped I would join him at TV-am clung on almost until the bitter end. Peter Jay, the Chairman and Chief Executive, had been forced to resign in a boardroom coup. Jonathan Aitken took his place, but, because he was a Member of Parliament, the IBA insisted that his appointment could only be a temporary one. Within months, Jonathan handed over the reins to his aggressive merchant-banking cousin, Tim Aitken. Vengefully, he immediately sent for Anna Ford and Angela Rippon and sacked them, claiming that their public attack on the management had breached their contracts. It took them both a very long time to receive even paltry compensation. Goodness, Esther must have been purring that she had elected to stay with the BBC.

David Frost was shattered by the fallout among his friends and his legendary self-confidence was badly shaken by the poor ratings his own performance commanded. The only survivor of the Famous Five who managed to struggle on for a while was Michael Parkinson. He had intended to walk out in sympathy with Anna and Angela but Tim Aitken persuaded him to stay with the offer of a seat on the Board. Meanwhile, cousin Jonathan managed to poach Greg Dyke, the chirpy editor of LWT's popular *Six O'Clock Show*, to take over as editor-in-chief. He chucked out everything that the old guard had stood for – and pledged to the IBA – dragging TV-am to the bottom of the market where his instincts told him the audience for breakfast television lay.

The Australian television tycoon Kerry Packer pumped in more money and sent Bruce Gyngell over from Channel 9 to ensure that no high-falutin programme ideas came between Packer and his investment. Not surprisingly, the ratings improved the further TV-am departed from the brief that had won it the franchise in the first place. It was a bitter tale of love's labours lost, drowned in recrimination. Everyone's reputation was at least tarnished by the TV-am debacle; some never recovered from the experience. It certainly didn't help the egos of the wounded that so many colleagues crowed, 'I told you so.' Like everyone else, my very bruised friend, Michael, was looking for a job. Although he had survived the bloodletting he most understandably wanted to put the whole disaster of TV-am behind him. I welcomed him to Griffin with open arms. It was, after all, he who had introduced me to the businessmen who had founded the company. Michael was just the partner I needed to bring snap, crackle and pop to our programme proposals and to look farther afield for customers, beyond the distinctly over-crowded reception lobby at Channel 4.

Michael and I had already discussed the possibility of Griffin branching out into the production of international children's drama. Nearly every television station in the world had quotas for children's programmes and budgets to go with them. We hoped to cash in on Britain's high reputation in this field. Michael had recently introduced me to Joy Whitby who had been a colleague of his as Head of Children's Programmes at YTV. She had started her career at the BBC inventing the phenomenally successful and long-running programmes *Playschool* and *Jackanory*. Then she was unlucky, joining Michael Peacock in that other disastrous failed start-up venture of David Frost's, LWT. The similarity with TV-am was uncanny: brave new ideas for serious pro-grammes that the audience wouldn't watch. Like TV-am, LWT was saved from financial disaster by an Australian. That time it was Rupert Murdoch. Now Joy was running her own small production company and Griffin had agreed to invest in one of its projects, a delightful series for young children called *Emma and Grandpa*. Joy had been chairman for the European Broadcasting Union's children's drama panel, making friends with practically all the movers and shakers in children's television throughout the world. By this time she was also a director of Channel 4. She became a very good friend of mine and a staunch ally of Griffin's. It was she who put us in touch with high-profile high-flyer Michel Noll of Revcom Television in Paris. Michel and I spent a lot of time together while I tried to persuade him that Revcom should co-produce some of our children's drama projects. He seemed more interested in buying the company.

Michel Noll's priority was to acquire international rights in television programmes. Revcom had foreseen that the new age of cable and satellite would create a hunger for inexpensive product; that the owners of programme rights would be in a seller's market. To this end Revcom had set up a production company in Australia where generous pro-duction subsidies meant that Revcom could acquire the foreign rights of television productions for a song. Michel Noll had also spotted that cash-strapped British broadcasters were willing to sacrifice foreign rights for modest cash injections into their budgets. So Michel needed know-how in each country where he was buying foreign rights, a local pro-ducer who knew where the treasure was buried. In Australia he hired two former ABC drama producers, and in the United States, a top children's producer from PBS. Michel had contacts too in Germany, Italy, Spain and Scandinavia. Griffin seemed to fit the bill for Britain. That was why Michel decided that Revcom should buy it. There was another much more interesting reason. He was having an affair with Carol Drinkwater, the star of the BBC's popular series, *All Creatures Great and Small*, and her flat in Kentish Town was less than ten minutes from the Griffin office. Michel's office was in Paris but his weekend recreation was in London so, if Griffin became part of Revcom, hey presto, his weekly return airfare became a business expense. Michel Noll was greatly impressed by the newly-arrived Michael Deakin, a class act with outrageous stories, fluent French and boundless creative ideas. The lawyers moved in and a deal was clinched. Out went the ex-Lord Mayor of London and the Midland Bank. In came a massive French conglomerate with a head office on the Champs-Elysées.

Our group chairman, Antoine de Clermont Tonnerre, was a leading member of the French aristocracy, forty-something, handsome, haughty, tall and bilingual. He was a graduate of the École Nationale d'Administration, an Énarque, as near to God as a Frenchman can be. His suits were from Savile Row and his socks, ties, handkerchiefs (and probably his underwear) from St James's. Before he joined the group, Antoine had been audiovisual adviser to President Raymond Barr, an all-powerful civil servant with considerable influence as to who would receive the generous government subsidies doled out to the French film industry. As well as being Chairman of Revcom, Antoine was also responsible for Les Films Ariane, one of the most distinguished film production companies in France. Another of his responsibilities was Éditions Mondiales, a major magazine publisher. There was more. It turned out that Revcom had acquired its name from Revillon Frères, the luxury furs and perfume business with fiendishly expensive boutiques all over the world. Revillon Frères, in turn, owned Karl Lagerfeld, the world-famous Parisian fashion house, and Parfums Caron. The cash cow that drove this mighty business was the pan-European supermarket group, Cora. It was a highly secretive family business, worth more than a billion dollars, presided over by the almost invisible Philippe Bouriez, always referred to mysteriously as 'the Shareholder'.

The immediate effect for Griffin was that we had generous funds to invest in the foreign rights both of programmes we wished to make ourselves and of those made by broadcasters and other independents. We made another film for the *World About Us* series, invested in a BBC *Forty Minutes* documentary and co-produced a two-part portrait of the Indian maharajahs with the BBC. More important, we persuaded Channel 4 to commission *Odyssey,* a classy travel and exploration series, made in partnership with Revcom and National Geographic. But this was all small beer compared with what Revcom had in mind for Griffin. They wanted us to branch out from factual programmes into fiction where there was real money to be made. Already Michel Noll was mounting a major co-production with the ABC in Australia of *Captain James Cook,* starring the Australian actor Keith Michell. There was also a role for Carol Drinkwater as Captain Cook's previously rather inconspicuous wife, Mrs Elizabeth Cook. It was our job at Griffin to identify similar epics that could bring financial benefits to Revcom.

Michael Deakin and I both liked Roger Laughton, the head of co-
productions at the BBC. He was well disposed towards us too so, when
Michael told him we were in the market for drama co-production, Roger
knew exactly what to offer us. It was a four-hour adaptation of Jeffrey
Archer's best selling novel, *Not a Penny More, Not a Penny Less*. There
had been talk of Paramount co-producing it with the BBC, but, after an
unhappy partnership on *Tinker, Tailor, Soldier, Spy*, there had been a
parting of the ways. Although the series had been much applauded in
Britain it had been utterly incomprehensible to the American audience.
Our new chairman, Antoine, had extravagantly ambitious plans to make
Revcom a global force in films and television so he was spending a good
deal of time in Hollywood, getting to know the movers and shakers
there. He mentioned Revcom's interest in *Not a Penny More, Not a
Penny Less* to Mel Harris, the Head of Paramount. 'We might be
interested if Revcom is involved and if the script is right and there's a
big American star,' he was told.

At once, Michael Deakin jumped on a plane to Los Angeles, the first
flight of what was to become a regular commuting run for him, and
presented himself to Lucy Salhany, the President of Paramount Domestic
Television. Lucy had made her name with the astonishing international
success of *Star Trek: The Next Generation*. She was renowned for her
electrifying tantrums. Michael doesn't scare easily and he soon disarmed
her with anecdotes and jokes. Just as well because Michael loved being
part of the Paramount family, lunching in the staff canteen, once even
with the legendary writer and director of *Some Like It Hot*, Billy Wilder.
Lucy's underlings were uneasy because no one knew Michael's status.
Was he a vice president, a senior vice president or no sort of president at
all? To establish the answer they needed to find out which hotel he was
staying in, the one reliable indicator of rank. The Bel Air or the Beverly
Hills would have put Michael on the same level as the gods and Lucy
Salhany but he chose always to stay with friends – and he had no
intention of revealing to Paramount that the mighty Revcom's London
office contained no vice presidents at all, just two producers, him and
me. When later I took Michael to meet the BBC executive producer in
the Drama Department's offices he was horrified at the squalor of the

jerry-built block over the post office on Shepherd's Bush Green. 'We can't bring the Paramount people here,' Michael was rattled. 'They'll never believe this is the BBC.'

It was common knowledge that the BBC owned the TV rights to *Not a Penny More, Not a Penny Less* because Jeffrey Archer never stopped telling everyone that he had sold them to Michael Grade for £1 or, in some versions, a gold sovereign. Like so many of Jeffrey's outlandish tales, one of which was later to land him in prison for perjury, this was quite simply untrue. Archer failed to mention that, some years earlier, he had sold the TV rights to a Hong Kong businessman for $200,000. The only way that the BBC could acquire these rights was to repay that sum. The BBC copyright lawyer, with surprising naïvety, was shocked to the core by the lie *direct* from a man who had been deputy chairman of the Conservative Party. That was just the first of many glitches that would have brought the whole edifice crashing down had it not been for Michael's unsuspected fount of emollience. The BBC was used to calling the tune since it normally paid the piper in full. It was reluctant and truculent when it came to sharing creative control with partners who expected to have a say in exchange for their large cheques, and Paramount was as demanding as Hollywood gets. Michael skilfully brought the temperature down. Come on, this is only Jeffrey Archer, not the complete works of Shakespeare.

Paramount didn't like the adaptation that the BBC had commissioned but both were happy to start again with a stylish and sophisticated New York screenwriter, Sherman Yellen, who sensibly decided that Archer's naïve and laboured plot would best be redeemed if it were played as light comedy. Next came the bright idea of asking Clive Donner to direct. He had worked for the BBC before making his name in Hollywood directing Peter Sellers in *What's New Pussycat* – a perfect choice. Paramount wanted Ed Asner to play the lead American. He was known, the world over, for his portrayal of the title role in *Lou Grant.* The rest of the cast swiftly fell into place, including Jenny Agutter, an actress the BBC itself had first made into a star with *The Railway Children.* Jacqui Davis who normally produced *Rumpole* agreed to take on *Not a Penny More* while her series took a summer break. There was one French composer we were all agreed should be commissioned to write the music, Michel Legrand. He had scored dozens of memorable films, like *Les Parapluies de Cherbourg* and *The Thomas Crown Affair,* with Faye Dunaway and Steve McQueen. Everyone can hum its Academy-award winning song, 'The Windmills Of Your Mind'. Legrand had also written the music for the last of Sean Connery's Bond films, *Never Say Never Again* – and that clinched it for Paramount. Since there were two major roles for French actors and a large part of the action took place in the casino at Monte Carlo, Revcom was able to make a lucrative pre-sale to French television. Hey presto, we had three major broadcasters committed for this insubstantial work and we were in profit before we had even begun.

Our masters in Paris persuaded us to move to much bigger offices in London, somewhere that would serve as an appropriate headquarters for Revcom. We found just the place, a three-floor converted garment warehouse at the centre of the rag trade, just north of Oxford Street. In fact, it was hardly ever used by our colleagues from the Paris office so Michael and I started looking out for amenable tenants to share it with. We were under no pressure from our bosses in Paris to earn money by renting out part of our building. It just seemed wasteful to turn potential tenants away. Yet there are times when it is better to throw prudence to the winds than screw up a lifetime's reputation. I know now. Channel 4 approached us because it needed a large space for a new weekly youth programme. The series also needed an executive producer with experience of live programmes. Channel 4 put two and two together and appointed me in charge of what was to be one of the most disastrous television programmes of all time. I suppose by the law of averages I was bound to take a lethal pratfall sometime, but, dear God, *Club* X was the mother of one.

The concept for the show came from a youngish pair of graphic artists, Nichola Bruce and Michael Coulson, joint proprietors of Muscle Films and Kruddart. They had teamed up with Pete Townshend of The Who. His company had no experience of television production so we agreed to form a joint-venture company which Channel 4's Stephen Garrett commissioned to make *Club* X. Stephen was a most unlikely figure. He read jurisprudence at Merton College, Oxford, and now, as if to purge himself of that unfashionably bourgeois past, he had flung himself into the grunge end of graffiti and performance art. When you phoned him, knowing the sort of programmes he had commissioned, you were convinced that you had got the wrong number. This gentle, well-spoken and courteous man would have been far more at home in the staff common room of some ancient public school than here, on the street, where it all hangs out, man.

We all met to discuss the new programme. Nichola and Michael had made a large model of the fantasy which was, apparently, the concept for the series that they had sold to Stephen Garrett. It looked rather like the inside of a cave where stalactites and stalagmites might grow. No words went with it. When I tentatively asked what it all meant, two sets of lips simultaneously curled in contempt. Stephen was diplomatic but unwilling to articulate the programme concept lest he got snarled at too. It was madness. The plan was to mount a weekly, live programme, containing diverse little films, commissioned by Stephen, from an assortment of quite separate production companies. *Club X* was to be the amorphous cloud of linking material which might, but probably would not, blend it all together. This was a recipe for catastrophe, ninety minutes a week, live, for five months. The very thought of trying to get any sense out of this commune of chippy people induced nausea and dizziness. I felt like a Pavlov's dog for whom the bell never tolled.

As the number of weeks before the first programme remorselessly diminished, everyone was becoming panicky. With good reason. Stephen Garrett had not yet found the right producer. There seemed to be only one man in Britain who we all agreed was likely to save the day. Charlie Parsons started life as a journalist on *New Musical Express* and made a name for himself with the startlingly original and radically casual *Network 7* programme that he had produced for LWT. His legs were slightly too short and he startled with the most alarming pop eyes, but he had a calm and reassuring manner which belied the turmoil in his soul. He looked surprisingly old-fashioned, always dressed, like a sixties' public-school prefect, in ill-fitting baggy trousers and a sadly geriatric sports jacket. But Charlie was a very smart operator indeed. He went on to produce *The Word* for Channel 4, and, in partnership with Bob Geldof, *The Big*

Breakfast, the channel's phenomenally successful and long-running morning show. They sold their company for £15 million. Charlie played his cards far too close to his chest for my liking, while trying to give the impression of transparent openness. It was only when he needed heavies to support him that he turned for advice to senior colleagues. Quite soon he realised that Nichola Bruce and Michael Coulson were so opposed to everything he was trying to do that either they had to go or he would – and Charlie was no quitter.

Stephen Garrett prudently kept well out of the way when the boil burst. Admirably, Pete Townsend came down to the office to support me and he read the riot act with great panache. I suppose if you have lived through intoxicated tours with *The Who* you must know how to shout and scream effectively. Nichola and Michael left the building, never to be seen again, their programme concept still an unlocked secret in their bitter minds. Charlie rolled up his sleeves and set to work in the few weeks left before we went on air. He was a fearsome taskmaster. His researchers were all young, mostly new to the business, and they worked like hell. Charlie had found an exceptionally talented assistant producer who really knew the world of experimental performing arts. For each edition of *Club X,* she would deliver some quite beautiful and memorable spectacle. The one that is best remembered was a re-creation of Yves Klein's 1960 performance piece 'Anthropometry', featuring nude female models daubing their bodies in blue paint. It sounds Pseuds Corner but it was fantastic.

Yet even these rare moments were lost in the confusion, the technical breakdowns and the noise. Of the presenters, Murray Boland, Martine Attille and the drag artist Regina Fong, only Murray knew how to conduct meaningful interviews. He became the rock on which Charlie built the whole show and indeed he went on to become a Channel 4 commissioning editor himself. In later programmes, the London *Evening Standard*'s art critic, Brian Sewell, bravely became an unlikely and erudite contributor with his high-class marshmallow vowels. However, the most extraordinary character, without a doubt, was the four foot-six, balloon-shaped, Fou Fou L. Hunter. Always costumed like a ballerina and decorated with a pink feather boa, she became a cherished icon to the growing number of *Club X* fans who perversely delighted in the show. One week, she was shot with an air gun, live on air. No one knows who fired the shot or whether it was deliberate. So great was the characteristic confusion that we only learnt about it after the show was over. Luckily it was only a flesh wound and Fou Fou, bless her, had plenty of that.

For reasons that were never convincing, Charlie decreed that we should not control the programme from anything so *passé* as a control room. This was a pity because control rooms are soundproof. Instead, we all sat in the kitchens of the Vauxhall Community Hall, the regular home of *Club X*, crouched in front of lashed-up TV monitors and a portable vision-mixing panel, straining to hear what we were broadcasting while virile pop groups like the Pogues performed only feet away. For only the second time in its history, the Crystal Palace transmitter broke down, while we were live on air, blacking out Channel 4 in the London area. We kept on broadcasting to the rest of the country just as if nothing had happened. On another occasion – a jinx too far – the main fuse box in the Vauxhall Community Hall exploded while we were on air, leaving the control room useless. We had no connection with the studio, with Channel 4 or with anywhere else in the outside world. Our wise outside-broadcast electricians had brought a generator with them so the studio lights stayed on and *Club X* continued noisily. But its efforts were in vain because our viewers throughout the United Kingdom, like all of us in the makeshift control room, were watching mute blank screens. Since there was nothing I could do I sat quietly in the corner while those who could sought to repair the fault. Stephen Garrett was beside himself with anxiety. 'You've got to do something,' he wailed at me. But that was the heart of the problem. I could do nothing, nothing about this awful, awful programme.

The idea of commissioning editors was a novel one to broadcasting, borrowed by Channel 4 from the publishing world. In those early days of the channel no one was yet quite sure who was ultimately responsible, who should carry the can when it all went horribly wrong. Because I was the executive producer I accepted most of the blame for the disaster – there was plenty flying around – yet how I wished I had been allowed to halve the length of the programme, chuck out all the film inserts that Stephen Garrett had so haphazardly commissioned and bring some coherence to the whole enterprise. That's what an executive producer would have done before commissioning editors were invented. It's what Stephen sensibly did himself when he replaced *Club X* with *The Word* a year too late. I recently spotted this press release about him from the University of Oxford:

> Television and film producer, Stephen Garrett, the man who brought *Spooks* and *Life on Mars* to our screens, has been named as Oxford University's News International Visiting Professor of Broadcast Media. His first lecture is entitled 'How to Grow a Creative Business According to the Laws of Chance'.

CHAPTER 22

There's No Business Like Show Business

Not a Penny More, Not a Penny Less was shown on BBC1 over four consecutive weekday evenings in peak time. It was a fast moving and entertaining production that had generated a good deal of pre-publicity. The BBC bosses were pleased with the viewing figures but a bit touchy about the critics who ridiculed the BBC's decision to waste air time and money on Jeffrey Archer's lightweight, literary endeavours. *The Late Show* on BBC2 broadcast a hilarious send-up of our production, demonstrating that the story of the four-hour serial could perfectly well be told in eight minutes flat.

Paramount knew how to announce to the world that the circus was coming to town. They took over the Monte Carlo Television Festival to launch the series. It was not theirs to take over, of course, but rather like the Americans invading Iraq, it didn't really matter to them what other people thought. They went ahead anyway. Paramount plastered the place with gigantic posters, unilaterally declaring the screening of *Not a Penny More, Not a Penny Less* a 'World Premiere'. Programme buyers from practically every country in the world showed up. Our job was to deliver Jeffrey Archer. He flew in for the event from London, on the last leg by helicopter from Nice to Monte Carlo. He was extremely aggressive and bossy, treating us all as if we were a potentate's slaves. Later I read that he always behaved like this on book tours. After the screening Archer praised the production warmly, repeated the fiction about selling the rights to the BBC for a gold sovereign, and then set about convincing all the buyers in the room that they simply couldn't leave until they had signed a contract for what was now 'his' production. He was good. Almost all of them signed up for *Not a Penny More, Not a Penny Less*, charmed by a fellow you shouldn't trust to sell you a second-hand bicycle.

By now Michael and I had acquired, as chairman for Griffin, the formidable Sara Morrison who had asked me some difficult questions at the BBC when she was a member of the Annan Commission on the future of broadcasting. She had been introduced to us by our mutual friend, Joy Whitby, the producer of *Emma and Grandpa* in which Griffin had invested. Joy had sat with Sara on the Channel 4 Board and, now that Joy's term was ending, she though it would do Griffin no harm to have another ally on the board. Michael and I agreed and we also felt the need of a strong chairman to preserve some autonomy for Griffin in London by matching the weight of Antoine de Clermont Tonnerre, the chairman in Paris. Sara had been in politics all her life, a deputy chairman of the Conservative Party in Edward Heath's time. She was a director of GEC and the Abbey National as well as Channel 4.

Sara regarded her Griffin appointment as no more than a fun diversion although it soon became a lot more onerous than that. Sara was the first to temper the sense of achievement that Michael and I both felt. We were chuffed that *Not a Penny More, Not a Penny Less* had actually been made – and at a healthy profit. Sara wondered if we were wise to be self-satisfied with such a lightweight endeavour when both of us were known in the business for producing high-quality programmes. It was exactly to pose such questions that we had asked Sara to become chairman of Griffin. Her maiden outing was to attend the screening of *Not a Penny More, Not a Penny Less* in Monte Carlo. She was horrified to find that she was booked on the same flight as Jeffrey Archer, whom she knew and distrusted from her time in politics. She hated the thought of sharing a helicopter with him. 'If it crashes, all anyone will remember will be the death of Archer,' she complained.

To celebrate the Monte Carlo screening of *Not a Penny More, Not a Penny Less* Paramount organised a banquet, at the Hôtel de Paris. It was a glittering affair with grand folk from French television, Paramount and the BBC. Speeches were made and the party didn't break up until very late. The next morning, Jeffrey Archer caught the eight o'clock helicopter back to Nice *en route* to London. Shortly after he had checked out of the hotel, Michael Deakin received a concerned call from reception. Although the bill on Archer's room had been settled in advance, the extras on it hadn't. There was a colossal sum due for Archer's mini-bar, Michael was told. Would he please settle it? It was clever of the management to find Michael because he and I were not staying with Archer in the Hôtel de Paris but in a no less smart hotel, L'Hermitage. Both, it turned out, were owned by La Société des Bains de Mer, a company that controls practically everything in Monte-Carlo, including the casino. If there was one thing the Société really knew how to do well, it was to recover unpaid debts.

Over breakfast Michael and I speculated as to how on earth Archer had run up such an enormous bill. He had come straight to the screening from his London flight. There was hardly a break before the banquet, which finished well after 1 a.m. Now he had left, checking out before eight o'clock in the morning. There had been so little time for Archer to indulge in a boozy party and none at all to make the arrangements for it. Had he perhaps emptied the mini-bar into his suitcase? There is no doubt that quarter bottles of champagne were offered at an obscene price but surely not *that* much. Later we learnt that some luxury hotels use 'mini-bar' as a euphemism for a paid lady companion. Now, after his high-profile perjury trial, everyone would suspect Archer of being the villain of the piece; he had, after all, been sentenced to four years in prison for telling lies. Yet, Michael and I were not entirely convinced of his culpability. The mystery remained but the unpaid bill didn't. La Société des Bains de Mer duly debited Michael's credit card for the full amount, not a penny more, not a penny less. In France they called our production *La Main dans le Sac*. Exactly.

Michel Noll, our immediate boss at Revcom, was now exploiting the crock of gold he had found in Australia. He had stumbled across a invaluable source of funding and, more important, how to access it. The Australian Film Finance Corporation had initiated a scheme to encourage private investment in films and television programmes. Known as '10BA', after a clause in the Australian Income Tax Assessment Act, it allowed wealthy taxpayers to claim a hundred and fifty per cent tax relief on funds they invested in production. Gaining access to these riches was a laborious process, involving lawyers, merchant banks and prospectuses, but Michel had the staying power. Soon he had a large number of television series in production, especially children's drama programmes which crossed international boundaries more easily than mainstream fiction. Since Revcom was a sales and distribution company, making its money from charging commission on sales, Michel took a relaxed attitude to recovering the investment. The risk was taken by the Australian taxman. Revcom was by no means the only production company to jump on the 10BA bandwagon and, eventually, the day of reckoning dawned when the Australians quietly turned off the tap.

This wheeler dealing was a completely new world to Michael and me. We both came from broadcasters who paid the full cost of programmes, once we had convinced our bosses they should be made. In the real world it was virtually impossible to make money legally from the sale of programmes because, for historical reasons, the people who bought them for the broadcasters had tiny budgets. Second-hand American series had always flooded the market. Since they had already been paid for, they were very cheap. For the first time we realised the absurd paradox of our new business: if you make a film and then try and sell it to British television you will be lucky if you get a tenth of your money back – in the unlikely event that you can sell it at all. However, pre-sell an idea for a film – no more than a dream – and the customers will pay the full cost with a profit margin built in. We learnt to by-pass the programme acquisition people altogether and focus on the broadcasters' production departments. That's where the money was. We had to convince the heads of drama that the film or series we wanted to make would be better, or considerably cheaper, than something that could be made in-house. Sometimes a really wonderful script could tip the balance. More often we would be told 'yes' if we were bringing serious money to the table. Invariably such a dowry came with strings attached. Perhaps it would be an insistence on some quite unsuitable American star; maybe a partner wanted you to shoot the whole film in Germany. Certainly there would be a fight about the director, the budget and the net profits. Retaining editorial and artistic control of a project like this was nothing less than a miracle.

A bright and pushy producer called Nick Evans brought us a screen-play he had co-written with Michael Chaplin for a film called *Act of*

Betrayal.* It was a superbly taut drama about a hit man sent to track down and kill an IRA terrorist who had turned police informer and then been given a new, secret identity in Australia. Nick had already found a possible British customer, always one of the most difficult pieces of the jigsaw to put in place. What Nick was now seeking was a partner who could help him raise money for the filming in Australia, and who would fund the budget deficit. Nick's British partner was TVS, the new and energetic ITV company for the south and southeast region of England. TVS realised that *Act of Betrayal* was exactly the tool it needed to lever more of the company's drama on to the ITV network. It happened that Michel Noll had already established a special rapport between Revcom and TVS – they were co-producing children's drama series together – so it was natural that TVS and Revcom should become co-production partners of Griffin for *Act of Betrayal*.

By another stroke of luck, Michel Noll had recently persuaded the ABC in Sydney to co-produce his blockbuster series, *Captain James Cook*. The ABC welcomed co-productions as a way of enhancing its budgets and broadening the scope of its output. The co-producer brought cash and the ABC provided its superb technical facilities. Hailed as a success, *Captain James Cook* had been directed by Lawrence Gordon Clarke, a friend from my BBC days. We now agreed that he should direct *Act of Betrayal*. Nick Evans had meanwhile been to Ireland to look for locations – Northern Ireland was too difficult and dangerous at that time – and he persuaded RTÉ, the national broadcaster, to join our co-production. What's more, while he was in Dublin Nick found the perfect actor to play our IRA terrorist, Michael McGurk. Patrick Bergin was utterly unknown outside Ireland at the time. As a direct result of his performance in *Act of Betrayal* he became a big Hollywood name, perhaps best remembered as Julia Roberts's scary husband in *Sleeping with the Enemy* and, more recently, as *Dracula*.

Towards the end of the filming, our chairman, Antoine de Clermont Tonnerre, decided to visit the set in Dublin, on his way back to Paris

---

* Nick Evans was later to write a novel, *The Horse Whisperer,* which Robert Redford made into a film.

from skiing at Aspen. I don't think he had any idea what to expect. We were filming in heavy rain on one of the city's most down-at-heel, grey and grimy housing estates where the production manager had been forced to hire the local 'football team' to protect the crew. Antoine swept in, wearing an ankle-length, bottle green overcoat and the most fashionable après-ski boots, while Michael and I, with colleagues from Paris, formed his entourage, partly to protect him. A voice yelled out from a balcony of the flats, 'Here come the fokking actors!'

Stitching co-productions together required ingenious minds, using parts of the brain that we producers didn't even know existed. The legal and tax experts at TVS and Revcom had a ball coming up with a financial structure which, to this day, I only partly understand. There were three objectives. The first was to keep the production profitable for all the interested parties, regardless of the budget. The second was to arrange that TVS would make no paper profits on the production but, rather, a significant 'loss' to set against the whopping returns it was making from its advertising revenue. Thirdly, of course, there had to be enough money sloshing around to fund the two-million-pound budget. Formally, *Act of Betrayal* was an independent production by Griffin for TVS and the ITV network. The ABC in Sydney and RTÉ in Dublin were co-producers, providing the lion's share of production facilities, in exchange for domestic broadcasting rights and a share of the profits. But, beneath the surface, smothered in mounds of legalese, in both French and English, the much more complicated arrangement emerged. At that time ITV companies were subject to a punitive levy on their profits that could only be avoided by spending them on programmes. The whole financial deal for *Act of Betrayal* was based on this fortuitous loophole, known cynically in the business as 'the levy wash'. It meant that TVS was able to claim levy relief for the whole budget of *Act of Betrayal*, while only contributing the licence fee that it received from the ITV network. Since, at that time, TVS was making profits in the region of a million pounds a week, it regarded a substantial paper 'tax loss' as a godsend. Then, with one hand TVS sold Revcom distribution rights in the production, claiming tax relief on the foreign sale, while, with the other, paying Griffin a production fee. Are you still with me? The lawyers loved it.

The whole edifice of the co-production was like a Rubik's cube. Move one element and the whole thing went awry. Change one variable and all the others figures had to be amended to keep the model in balance. Michael was forced to take an interest in the legal and financial arrangements because it was he who went with Michel Noll to Australia to finalise the deal. Michael is the least numerate person I know. He can't even claim his expenses, let alone fiddle them. Luckily he found the sophisticated concept a stimulating challenge that he was determined to master. The head of production finance at Channel 4 was a personal friend and she spent many weekends explaining the whole concept to him. Everyone made money. As a bonus, TVS earned brownie points from the IBA for commissioning an independent production company.

The production was most unusual, in one respect: there was no American money in it. Michael and I were yet to learn what a supreme blessing that was. None the less, all the partners agreed that a couple of Hollywood 'names' should be cast as leading characters to improve the chances of an American sale. Lisa Harrow is a fine New Zealand actress with a background in the Royal Shakespeare Company but, as far as Hollywood was concerned, she was Kate Reynolds in *Omen III – The Final Conflict*. In *Act of Betrayal* she played the wife of our terrorist, Michael McGurk. He, in turn, was played by Nick Evans's discovery, Patrick Bergin. And that old warhorse from *MASH*, Elliott Gould, starred as the assassin hired to hunt him down and kill him.

In the conventional sense, there was very little producing for Griffin to do. The hard work was virtually over once the deal had been done. We only had to organise the filming of the fictitious Christmas bombing of Hamleys toyshop in Regent Street – the incident that persuades our terrorist to abandon the IRA and turn police informer. Everything else was filmed either in Dublin or in Sydney, where the ABC also provided the post-production. The four-hour *Act of Betrayal* was an object lesson in professional film-making that more than justified its place in peak time on ITV over two weekends. It performed very well in Australia and in Eire too. It was immediately picked up by Turner Network Television in the United States and it sold well throughout the world.

This co-production model with TVS was one we were to use again, a couple of years later, for another screenplay by Nick Evans. However, Michael and I knew that we would have to look to America if Griffin was to become a major player in the TV movie business.

Our first attempt to mount an American co-production that was a little more demanding than *Not a Penny More, Not a Penny Less* was a total failure but an invaluable lesson. Its working title, stolen from George Bernard Shaw, was *The Devil's Disciple.* The first President Bush had ordered the invasion of Panama to overthrow the deeply unpleasant dictator, drug dealer and CIA agent, Manuel Noriega. As we were to learn when the Americans tried the same tactics in Iraq, the shock and awe are the easy bit. Capturing the baddie is a whole lot more difficult. Noriega sought diplomatic immunity in the Apostolic Nunciature, the residence of the Papal Nuncio in Panama. He showed a marked reluctance to comply with the invaders' wishes and give himself up. The US military played deafening pop songs outside his refuge, twenty-four hours a day, but nothing would persuade the dictator to come out and face the music. He knew he would spend the rest of his life in prison, or possibly lose it altogether in the electric chair.

In the end, after ten days, it was the Papal Nuncio who persuaded Noriega to surrender. We had a bright young assistant producer working for us at Griffin who happened to be a Roman Catholic. We sent him to Panama where he was commendably pushy and managed to charm the Papal Nuncio and then debrief him, recording in detail the long debates that had taken place between Noriega and the priest about the morality of the dictator's predicament. The Nuncio explained the arguments he had used to persuade Noriega to give himself up. A great film we thought, back in London. We tried the idea on Ted Childs, the Head of Drama at Central Television. He liked it. Home Box Office, the most prestigious cable station in America, agreed to participate too. Together we commissioned John Mortimer to write a screenplay. There was no writer better fitted to capture the real theatre of this morality play, the debate between the wicked but God-fearing dictator and the representative of Christ on earth. We would intercut the scripted scenes inside the besieged Apostolic Nunciature with the real news footage of the military invasion, named, as only the Americans could, Operation Nifty Package.

John Mortimer served us proud – and quickly. It was a brilliant script, a superb vehicle, we suggested, for Sir Alec Guinness as the Nuncio. For Noriega, we proposed Raúl Juliá, a fine Broadway actor, well known for his performance as Harrison Ford's attorney in *Presumed Innocent,* and much loved as Gomez in the *Addams Family*. Then, to our surprise and considerable dismay, HBO turned Mortimer's screenplay down flat. Too much talking, not enough action. Central Television suffered similar difficulties with the Network Centre, despite the phenomenal success that Mortimer's *Rumpole* had achieved for ITV – too highbrow. We couldn't offer the project to the BBC – perhaps its natural home – because Central Television owned a large share in the screenplay and regarded the BBC as a competitor. So the film was never made. A magnificent screenplay by one of Britain's very top writers languishes unseen because it was judged too sophisticated for the audience. We were beginning to learn the hard way that however many horses we led to water we were quite powerless to make any of them drink – even the very best equine champagne.

CHAPTER 23

Heads You Lose

Fancy an all-expenses-paid weekend in Paris? Every month there was a Monday-morning meeting that Michael Deakin and I had to attend at Revcom's head office on the best part of the Champs-Elysées, from which you could view the Arc de Triomphe, the Eiffel Tower and, immediately opposite, Fouquet's, one of the oldest *grande luxe* restaurants in Paris. ('Le prix moyen pour le déjeuner est de €120 par personnne, boissons non comprises.') It is the place to be seen if you are an actor, a singer or a director, rather like The Ivy in Convent Garden but with gilt furniture, red velvet curtains, chandeliers and much snootier. There are pokey tables for those whom the maître d' deems riff-raff. Our boss, Antoine de Clermont Tonnerre, was treated like a lord there, bowed and scraped to by staff and customers alike. (Gerard Depardieu paid obeisance to Antoine while I was lunching with him.) Everyone knew Antoine's reputation as a key figure in the industry. Now it was the talk of the town that he also had access to the Cora supermarket millions, perhaps even tens of millions, because the secretive owner, Philippe Bouriez, was investing like crazy in the movie business. The newspapers were full of Antoine's plans to celebrate the bicentennial of the French Revolution with the most expensive film ever made in Europe. It was to be produced by Alexandre Mnouchkine, the seventy-nine-year-old doyen of Les Films Ariane, now owned by the Cora-Revillon group.* Antoine was to be the executive producer, fitting

---

* Alexandre Mnouchkine had founded Les Films Ariane over forty years earlier, producing over a hundred classic films like Claude Lelouche's *Un home qui me plaît*, with Jean-Paul Belmondo, Jean Cocteau's *Les Parents Terribles*, Fredrico Fellini's *Fred and Ginger* and Jean-Jacques Arnaud's *The Name of the Rose*, starring Sean Connery.

235

really since his ancestor, Jules Charles Henri, the Duke of Clermont-Tonnerre, and his grandson, Gaspard Charles, ended up, just like Louis XVI and Marie-Antoinette, in tumbrils bound for the guillotine.

La Révolution Française mushroomed into two extravagantly expensive feature films, *Les Années Lumière* and *Les Années Terribles*, each nearly three hours long. They took six months to shoot, with a cast of two hundred and with thirty thousand extras. Thanks to Antoine's connections with the government's high and mighty, the production had an unprecedented free run of the Château de Versailles where so much of the action had really taken place. The budget was in the region of $25 million dollars, a record for Europe at the time. The actual cost was never revealed. Everything took longer than it should and the costs inexorably mounted. Controlling the budget is a problem as old as film-making itself. One of Hollywood's most famous names, David O. Selznik, who had produced *Gone with the Wind* just before the Second World War, expressed his frustration at the escalating costs of his next movie, *Rebecca*:

> I am personally sick and tired of working my head off to support a lot of people who won't give a thought as to how to save money . . . If there is going to be any extravagance in our picture-making, it is going to be indulged in by me personally to improve the quality of the pictures, and I am not going to have it thrown away by sloppy management. I can't tell you how very deeply upset I am to be faced with this at a time when I am overwhelmed with creative and editing work.*

In order to finance the project Antoine entered into co-production agreements with film distributors and television stations in France Germany, Italy, Canada and Britain. He also hoped to make a substantial sale in the United States. Understandably each co-production partner expected *La Révolution Française* to utilise actors from its own country in prominent roles. Why else would they commit money in advance to the project? So a cosmopolitan medley of movie stars was assembled to enact

---

* *Memo from David O. Selznick*, Samuel French, Hollywood, 1989

the eighteenth-century French royals and revolutionaries. Jane Seymour was cast as Marie-Antoinette, Klaus Maria Brandauer as Danton, the Polish actor, Andrzej Seweryn, as Robespierre, the Swiss Jean-François Balmer as Louis XVI. There were roles for Sam Neill, Claudia Cardinale and Peter Ustinov – to name just three more from one of the longest-ever lists of credits.

There were great moments, wonderfully dramatic scenes, superb lighting and photography. The highlight for me was the fabulous musical score by Georges Delerue and his opening and closing theme, 'Hymne à la Liberté', belted out by the stunning Jessye Norman. Yet this lavish epic lacked that elusive quality which transforms the ambitious idea into a magical experience. Critics described it as 'sombre', 'magisterial' and 'didactic'. It was the official French film for Bicentennial Year and perhaps just too respectable and all encompassing. But the cardinal sin of *La Révolution Française* was that it was not ready in time. The first of the two films, *Les Années Lumière,* reached the French cinemas only at the very end of Bicentennial Year – by which time everyone in France was heartily sick of the subject. The second film, *Les Années Terribles,* wasn't ready until early in the following year and sank without trace. The films were hardly shown in cinemas at all. Those who had invested in this huge project were left severely out of pocket. Central TV, for example, never managed to sell the films to the ITV network. Television companies that were yet to buy the films cried off. This was a financial catastrophe. In retrospect it was easy to trace the roots of the folly, to see how this enterprise had been allowed to spin out of control. The astonishing outcome, despite all this, was that the Shareholder was about to allow Antoine almost unlimited funds to expand the empire into the heartland of Hollywood.

Back in London, Michael and I were given a new screenplay by Nick Evans. This one was called *Secret Weapon* and told the true story of Mordechai Vanunu. He had been a technician at Israel's top-secret Negev Nuclear Research Center at Dimona. Vanunu decided to blow the whistle, to tell the world that Israel was manufacturing nuclear weapons. An enterprising journalist realised at once that this was a major international scoop and sold the story to the *Sunday Times*, which printed it on the front page. Shortly before the story became public, Vanunu was befriended by a young woman in London, a Mossad agent. She lured him to Italy where he was kidnapped, smuggled to Israel and sentenced to eighteen years in prison for treason.

Because *Act of Betrayal* had taught us how to set up these convoluted co-production deals, it was much easier this time round. TVS was happy to participate again, making a handsome profit once more before we had even started shooting. No one begrudged them their money since Ann Harris, their energetic head of distribution who had sold *Act of Betrayal* to Turner Network Television, now managed to pre-sell *Secret Weapon* to them too for a very good price. The ABC in Australia agreed to co-produce with us again, providing all the facilities to shoot the Australian scenes and those that were set in Israel. The Negev Nuclear Research Center was ingeniously built in a disused factory outside Sydney.

Secret Weapon was another important step on the ladder of Griffin becoming 'acceptable' in the United States. The decision-makers there are a cautious lot, understandably so. If something they have decided on proves to be a commercial failure, they will be looking for another job. Wise executives stick to what has been successfully tried before. That way they can hardly be blamed if anything goes wrong. This immutable law, try-nothing-new, applies across the whole spectrum of movie-making in the United States, not only to actors and directors. It includes, for example, the employment of production companies like Griffin. The obverse of this constraint is, of course, that if you have a winner's reputation, the studio bosses may take your call. Michael and I knew all this instinctively and he made very frequent trips to Los Angeles to ensure that everyone knew who Griffin was and what we had produced. He was a superb ambassador, visiting all the main studios, reminding them that Griffin had been Paramount's partner for *Not A Penny More, Not a Penny Less,* the producer of *Act of Betrayal,* and was now producing again for Turner with *Secret Weapon.* One of Michael's best friends in Los Angeles was a prominent journalist on *Variety.* He happily wrote stories as overblown about Griffin as those the major studios embellished about themselves. So successful was Michael at the showbiz hype that

Variety once trumpeted that Universal Studios was about to 'ink' a six-picture deal with Griffin. Unfortunately, like so many such announcements, nothing ever came of it. But we were amused when a team from the BBC was told by one studio that if it wanted to break into the TV movie business it should work through Griffin. At that time Griffin had a permanent staff of five, the BBC twenty-five thousand.

Casting was the really tough job on these TV movies. The Americans always crowed the loudest, demanding the impossible. They usually wanted a star so big as to be quite out of our price range or too busy, or too grand to 'do' television. So we were always on the lookout for stars that were on the way up or on the way down, or who had acted in a film so memorable that its title alone assured that its participants had a box-office value. The two key people we always employed in America to assist us with this crucial part of the film-making process were a casting director and a Hollywood lawyer. The casting director could reach the agents who would not dream of talking to an out-of-town production company they had never heard of. We have to thank Antoine for introducing us to our lightning-quick and informal Los Angeles lawyer, Peter Grossman. He was so well known by all the big players that his very presence as our representative gave little Griffin instant respectability. To our surprise he was considerably cheaper than run-of-the-mill media lawyers in London and, of course, ten times as effective because he was a part of the great Hollywood machine.

Nick Evans had almost limitless energy for casting his *Secret Weapon* screenplay. It was he who found the right American actor to play Mordechai Vanunu, spookily with his first name the same as our company. Griffin Dunne looked the part exactly, fragile, vulnerable and Levantine. He was best known for his role in *An American Werewolf in London.* Turner Network Television, our American co-producer, needed a couple more big names so we cast Karen Allen as the Mossad agent who seduced Vanunu (she had played opposite Harrison Ford in Steven Spielberg's *Raiders of the Lost Ark*); and John Rhys-Jones, the Welsh actor best known for his roles in the *Indiana Jones* movies, was chillingly convincing as the Mossad chief who masterminded the kidnap of Vanunu. This time the director was Ian Sharp, a very bright cookie, who had worked with me at the BBC directing one of the *Americans* series and had then gone on to direct *Minder* and *The Professionals* for ITV. His boss there described him as the 'master of directing mayhem'. He gave us a very classy looking *Secret Weapon* with terrifying interrogation scenes, convincingly spooky Israeli kidnappers and breathtakingly fresh vistas of Sydney, Rome and London. This was a film to be proud of, applauded by its customers in America, Australia and Britain. Complacently, Michael and I thought we had cracked the system, found a formula that would keep us gainfully employed for ever.

But by 1993 the British media world was changing fast, and for the worse, thanks to Margaret Thatcher's 1990 Broadcasting Act, which threw excellence out of the window and awarded ITV contracts not to those who promised to make the best programmes but to those who offered to pay the government the most money. Granada Television had always been ITV's torchbearer of fine programmes. Under new management, the group ordered savage cuts in the running costs of its television division. John Cleese was so incensed by the mindless vandalism directed against a great television production house that he sent this message to Gerry Robinson, the new Group Chairman, formerly head of a food and beverage business: 'Fuck off out of it, you ignorant upstart caterer.'

It was a terrible shock for Michael and me to learn that our friends at TVS had failed to win back their franchise. Under the new legislation, franchises were now awarded to the highest bidding competitor, subject to a rather arbitrary 'quality threshold' hurdle. TVS passed the test but was then rejected by the ITC on the extraordinary grounds that its bid of £60 million was considered *too much*. The franchise was awarded instead to an untried newcomer, Meridian Broadcasting, the only other company to bid for the south of England region. Poor old TVS had no contingency plans for this disaster nor, as it turned out, had Griffin. The new ITV regime centralised the commissioning of programmes, partly to accommodate the independent producers it was now committed to employ. As a result, the ITV companies lost their guaranteed network slots and their ability to contribute generously to international co-productions. This, Michael and I feared, would turn out to be a mortal blow for Griffin.

Because of all these machinations on the home front Michael and I had rather neglected the internal politics at our head office in Paris so we decided that we would take our chairman, Sara Morrison, to the monthly Monday-morning meeting at our offices on the Champs-Elysées. There was a very strange atmosphere in the building. Michael and I were called in by the legal adviser and asked to shut the door. Michel Noll was 'leaving' the company, we were told. It was therefore imperative that we did not discuss meaningful programme plans at the meeting or pass round any papers that could be of use to the 'enemy'. Michel Noll's sin, in so far as we could judge it, was *lèse-majesté* towards Antoine. It crossed our minds that some of the financial deals that Revcom Australia had negotiated might, perhaps, have been a little questionable. On one occasion our colleagues in Sydney were incandescent with embarrassment when Revcom Paris couriered them a viewing cassette to be passed on to the ABC. It supposedly contained episodes of a series that needed to be delivered to the broadcaster before a large payment fell due. The ABC checked the tape and found it was blank. The production it purported to show had not even begun shooting – and never did.

Michael, Sara and I had no idea that the knives were out for Michel, although we did find it odd that he was allowed to operate in such a maverick way. He and Carol Drinkwater were restoring a modest villa, rather theatrically named 'Appassionata', on a derelict olive farm on the Côte d'Azur, a far cry from his office in Paris. In any case, Michel always seemed to be on an aeroplane to Australia via a long weekend stopover in Bora-Bora, Tahiti or Tonga. One day I picked up the telephone in the London office to find that I had the King of Tonga's private secretary on the line. Would I please graciously inform Mr Noll that His Majesty needed to know what date Mr Noll was planning to be in Tonga for his wedding? His Majesty was happy to officiate but he had many other engagements to be fitted in. We didn't complain about Michel Noll's visits to Australia. It was because of his good relations with the ABC that we had been able to make *Act of Betrayal* and *Secret Weapon*. He was a great sales and marketing man who spoke many languages and managed to make a good impression with broadcasters all over the world. He had a magnetic effect on women in powerful jobs. When he was on a charm offensive, paying calls on the commissioning editors of children's programmes in London, he would bring meticulously chosen presents, perhaps a *parfum du Midi*, a little clay pot filled with olives from his own farm or an irresistible box of Belgian chocolates. Candlelit dinners *à deux* lasted late into the night. It paid off. Revcom sold nearly all its Australian-made children's programmes in Britain and some of them were pretty rum. What Michael and I found exasperating was Michel's style of management – when we could find him.

This is how the relationship between Griffin and Revcom was supposed to work. Michael or I would interest a broadcaster in a good programme idea that Griffin could deliver substantially below cost because Revcom distribution would 'buy' from us the world rights to the programme outside the UK. We would then ask Revcom distribution in Paris for a sales estimate on that programme. If the figures were high enough, Michel was supposed to give us the go-ahead to start producing the programme. Revcom would fund the difference between the budget and the price for which we had pre-sold the programme in Britain. Revcom would then sell the programmes and recover its advance before sharing its profits with Griffin. That put Michel on the line both to meet the sales forecast and to recover the money that Revcom had advanced to Griffin. If the art of the smooth operator is never to get found out, our demands of Michel were doubly hazardous. As a result, decisions were seldom made and Michael and I became exasperated. We decided we had to confront Michel about the stalemate in Griffin's production plans. We presented him with an impressive list of all the programmes we had provisionally pre-sold to broadcasters in the UK yet we couldn't produce because no deficit finance was forthcoming from Revcom distribution. 'This is a very dangerous document,' glowered Michel. 'It could cause a lot of trouble.' It was and it did.

Because Sara was with us in Paris, Antoine decided to take us for lunch to the Jockey Club. If anywhere was smarter and more exclusive than our usual watering hole, Fouquet's, this was it. A perfectly manicured grass track, impeccably gleaming white rails and a restaurant fit for kings. Just as well, since there has not been a Jockey Club president of lower rank than a marquis since Napoleon Joseph-Ney, Prince of Moscow, in 1857. Poor old Michel wasn't sure if he was invited or not so he shuffled along rather uncertainly. Sara, Michael and I were not even entirely sure if Antoine had told him he was toast. Antoine always gave the impression that such distasteful duties should really be conducted by the family butler not the master of the house.

Michel had started out before dawn that Monday morning from Appassionata, his half-renovated villa nearly five hundred miles away. Not knowing that he would be lunching at the Jockey Club, he was dressed, as usual, in his *artiste assoiffé* outfit. He looked as if he needed vigorous ironing. The conversation over lunch was civilised tittle-tattle but no mention was made of the burning issue of Michel's departure. Indeed we wondered if Antoine had relented or chickened out. As three o'clock approached, Michel started looking at his watch. He had to leave if he was to reach Orly in time catch the flight back to Nice. He murmured something to Antoine. 'Where exactly do you live?' Antoine asked him. 'Cannes,' Michel replied. 'Isn't that rather a long way from the office?' Surely that was a question you should ask when you hire a fellow, not when you are giving him the boot.

CHAPTER 24

Intermezzo

Without an ITV partner, Griffin was no longer in front of the pack when it came to calling on our Los Angeles customers. Unless we could bring significant money to the table from our home market we had nothing to offer except good ideas, and our hungry American rivals put forward plenty of those. We had one distinct edge over our competitors if the films we proposed needed to be shot on our side of the Atlantic. Surprisingly few American producers were happy working abroad. The BBC and Channel 4 were now investing significant sums in films and Michael and I were on friendly terms with the people who made the decisions. The trouble was that both broadcasters wanted original and up-market films, not the high-ratings fare that satisfied most of the American cable stations. Our clients in America scoffed at such films as 'art-house movies', until of course some of them started making it big, like Channel 4's *Four Weddings and a Funeral*. The question the Americans always put to us, half-jokingly, was, 'Will it play in Peoria?' The catchphrase, made popular by Groucho Marx, goes back to the time of vaudeville theatre. If a comedy turn made the audience laugh in the desperately average Midwest town of Peoria, Illinois, it *had* to work anywhere. Similarly, with television now. What on earth use was it to an American customer if a TV movie of ours failed to pull in the punters? We had many irons in the fire but waiting for decisions was a frustrating affair while the overheads of the Griffin staff still had to be paid.

To keep everybody busy, Michael and I decided that we would initiate some really cheap factual productions that would be attractive to British broadcasters, faced with hours of air time to fill and pressure to employ independent producers. Michael had a stunningly simple idea that he sold to Alan Yentob, the BBC arts guru. He gave the series an evocative title, *Painting with Light*. Television graphics had recently been revolutionised by the British computer specialist, Quantel. It had invented the Paintbox, programmed with software specifically designed to produce instant television graphics like weather maps. All that the Paintbox appeared to be was a blank drawing board, of the kind you used to see in architects' offices, alongside a bulky personal computer activated by an electronic pen which worked like a mouse. By using the pen and a palette of electronic colours, an artist had almost unlimited scope. Now, of course such software is available on all computers. At that time, Michael discovered, most of the top artists had never even heard of the Paintbox, let alone realised its astonishing potential.

Michael knew David Hockney personally and was sure that he would be enthusiastic to try out the new technique. He was.* Michael soon managed to enrol five more internationally celebrated artists to experiment with the Paintbox and create original electronic paintings. Hockney, Sidney Nolan, Howard Hodgkin, Jennifer Bartlett, Larry Rivers and Richard Hamilton were all ferried to Quantel headquarters in Berkshire where the state-of-the-art equipment was tended by devoted boffins. They would patiently explain to our artists how they could use the Paintbox to create images of extraordinary luminosity, quite different in texture from anything that they could achieve on paper or canvas. Simultaneously, we recorded a soundtrack of the artists' reactions to the pictures they were creating. You learnt an awful lot about the techniques of painting just from watching these six renowned exponents trying something new. Not surprisingly Quantel allowed us the run of their facilities for free, much chuffed by the promotional possibilities of six such eminent artists working on their equipment. The only significant expenses of this unique *Painting with Light* series were the modest fees for the artists and a hefty editing bill. The BBC could describe the series in its Annual Report with its favourite cliché, 'innovative', and everyone was happy.

I persuaded the BBC to commission another cheap and cheerful concept. This time it was an anthology of popular verse, a series of six

---

* David Hockney: *Painting with Light* programme extract: http://www.nme. com/video/id/]vLJWVRJoqQM/search/David%20Hockney.

programmes. We called it *Unspeakable Verse*. Its format was incredibly simple: four well-loved actors and actresses reciting verse, in turn, from John Betjeman to Ogden Nash, Lewis Carroll to Dorothy Parker, and lyrics from such masters as Cole Porter and Irving Berlin. It was produced by Pat Houlihan, one of my *In at the Deep End* producers at the BBC. Our stars were Leo McKern, *Rumpole of the Bailey*, Hugh Laurie, now an icon as Dr Gregory House in the American series *House*, the great comic actress and fun person, Miriam Margolyes, and Louise Lombard, best known at that time for *The House of Elliott*. Although we provided each with a teleprompter none used it. Like the seasoned professionals they all are, they had learnt their lines. Miriam, as always, was magnificent. She loved Spike Milligan's 'Sardines'.

> A baby Sardine
> Saw her first submarine:
> She was scared and watched through a peephole.
>
> 'Oh, come, come, come,'
> Said the Sardine's mum,
> 'It's only a tin full of people.

By chance, and a little manipulation, three of our four *Unspeakable Verse* performers were soon to work with us again in two Griffin TV movies, Leo McKern in *Good King Wenceslas* and Hugh Laurie and Miriam Margolyes in *The Place of Lions*. Louise Lombard, meanwhile, set off to Hollywood to be elected one of the 'fifty most beautiful women in the world'.

We also launched into children's drama with the adaptation of a charming book by Anita Desai. Set in an impoverished fishing village in India, *The Village by the Sea* is the story of a young boy and his older sister struggling to help bring up their family while coping with their father who is always drunk. Anna Home, the BBC's Head of Children's Programmes, liked the project and so did her opposite number at Bayerischer Rundfunk in Munich. With the help of Revcom distribution, we managed to raise just enough money to make the six-part serial on a shoestring. We plumped to shoot it in Sri Lanka instead of

India, because it was even cheaper there, and because we had the support of the country's veteran film-maker, Lester James Peiris, and his wife Sumitra. We cast the production entirely with local actors, apart from a splendid cameo from Saeed Jaffrey who had just starred in *My Beautiful Laundrette*. We had hoped we were pioneering a way of making expensive-looking productions at a price that our clients would pay, so that the endless search for co-production partners would be over. Alas it was not to be. Now Michel Noll was gone we had lost our ambassador to the Paris court. Antoine wasn't interested in low-budget children's programmes. He wasn't interested in low-budget anything. He was a serial spender and the $25 million-plus loss on *La Révolution Française*, it was to turn out, was just for openers. It seems Griffin was too small for Antoine's grand vision. I do believe we were missing Michel Noll.

Antoine and the Shareholder astonishingly had now decided to break into Hollywood. The first part of their grand plan was to create Sovereign Pictures, a company specialising in the financing and distribution of international films, that is to say films that are made outside the United States. Antoine appointed two Hollywood veterans to run the business, Barbara Boyle and Ernst Goldschmidt, both established figures at Orion, best known for distributing Woody Allen films. Smart offices were acquired in Los Angeles and London. The spacious converted garment warehouse which was Griffin's home was on the 'wrong side of Oxford Street', we were all told. Sovereign settled for something far smarter, a full eight hundred yards away off Soho Square. The new company made a phenomenally successful start, achieving great critical acclaim. Guiseppe Tornatore's charming *Cinema Paradiso* won the Oscar for the Best Foreign Language Film and the Grand Prize of the Jury at Cannes. There was a double celebration in the Paris office because Les Films Ariane had co-financed this gem of a film. The same year Sovereign triumphed again. It had bought the American rights to *My Left Foot*, nominated for five Academy Awards. Daniel Day Lewis won the Oscar for Best Actor and Brenda Fricker for Best Supporting Actress. In *Sovereign*'s third year, Richard Harris was nominated for an Academy Award for his role in *The Field; Reversal of Fortune* won an Oscar for

Jeremy Irons; and Zeffirelli's *Hamlet*, starring Mel Gibson, Glenn Close, Helena Bonham Carter and Ian Holm, was nominated for two Oscars. In all Sovereign released twenty-five feature films of which fourteen were nominated for Academy Awards.

Antoine then launched another ambitious American operation, an international television distribution business called World International Network, WIN for short. The man whose idea it was, Larry Gershman, was so much larger than life – almost an absurd parody of the movie mogul – that you half expected him to explode into bubbles of hot air at any minute. So great was his mastery of bullshit that you couldn't help wondering whether he knew any other language. However, WIN was a canny idea. Larry had identified the twenty or so major buyers of TV movies throughout the world; together, they were responsible for over a hundred and thirty of the world's television stations. He first enthused them and then persuaded them to join a cartel, a club of buddies, that met regularly for reunion dinners at the countless international markets. Twice a year, for example, Larry hired the private house of André Surmain, the renowned chef of Le Relais at Mougins, one of France's most fabulous restaurants, conveniently close to the April and October sales conventions of MIPTV in Cannes.

Buyers are pretty low in the pecking order at TV stations. Their job is to acquire packages of old Hollywood movies and endless soaps and cartoons to fill the schedules of television stations that all have more transmission hours than good programmes to fill them. So producers think of buyers rather as others regard second-hand-car salesmen. Larry's WIN aimed to restore their self-esteem. The buyers were eager to show their appreciation, even gratitude, to Larry, and demonstrate their virility by bestowing patronage. Larry paid advances to American producers in exchange for the foreign rights to their TV movies. The deal was that the WIN club members would each guarantee to buy a minimum number of WIN's TV movies each year at premium prices. They could also sell their programmes to each other and, occasionally, Larry would pick up the US rights to a particularly good foreign movie offered by one of his club members. But Larry always made sure that a lot more money came in than ever went out. On top of that, WIN took a very fat sales commission before passing the balance on to the producer.

The Shareholder decided to recruit a financially experienced managing director for Revcom in London to supervise these two active volcanoes, Sovereign Pictures and World International Network, both British companies for tax reasons. In Paris, Antoine was well supported in legal matters by the personable and laid-back Michel Libermann. However, it had become glaringly apparent, especially during the production of *The French Revolution*, that there was no one in the group who had either the aptitude or the experience in financial matters to run a major media business. The Shareholder employed mysterious Swiss advisers to handle his tax affairs and it was to them he turned for recruitment advice. Michel Libermann was occasionally summoned to meetings in Geneva and the fetish for secrecy amazed him. Each visit he was reminded to keep the address and telephone number of his destination only on a scrap of paper, to memorise the details and destroy the evidence before entering Switzerland. One of these advisers, Michel told us, always took his six Dalmatians with him when he visited foreign clients and therefore only travelled by his own executive jet. Rather high-profile, you would have thought, for a professional mystery man. To recruit the right person to manage Sovereign and WIN, the invisible Swiss in turn employed the services of an extraordinarily resourceful tax adviser in London, Ali Sarikhani. He was so good at his job that he now features in those 'Richest in Britain' tables the newspapers are always publishing. The most recent one estimated Ali's personal worth at £300 million.

Ali recommended a friend and fellow Iranian for the managing-director post. Abteen Sai had been forced to leave his job as head of Grindlays Bank in Teheran when the Shah was overthrown. Educated at Trinity College, Dublin, and married to an Irish wife, Abteen was by this time a director at Grindlays merchant bank in London. Being something of a film buff, he jumped at the chance of working in show business. Michael and I took to him right away. He was softly spoken with the most elegant manners and he clearly enjoyed Michael's scurrilous briefings, caricaturing the foibles of our French colleagues. Abteen did not reciprocate with gossip from his frequent trips to

Geneva, but our sources in the Paris office compensated for that. Although Abteen was technically our boss, now that Michel Noll had departed, he sensed that we didn't really want anyone to come between us and Antoine, so he advised rather than commanded while helping us beyond measure, negotiating courteously but tenaciously on our behalf with the man-eating sharks that infest our business.

Abteen very swiftly pepped up the London operation. Ali Sarikhani introduced him to a multi-millionaire business client who was leading a hostile bid to buy British Pathé News. In no time, our offices were the battle zone, the boardroom taken over by clandestine comings and goings, raised voices and a portly New York lawyer, in shirt sleeves and red braces, working all night on his laptop to unscramble the American rights to the Pathé library that the previous cash-strapped management had unwisely sold. Television may have killed the newsreels but the Pathé name and the cockerel lingered on. No historical documentary is ever made without a good proportion of its archive film coming from Pathé. There was never a day when half a dozen film researchers didn't come knocking on our door to consult the encyclopaedic knowledge of Larry, the Pathé librarian. Abteen asked me to become a director of the company and I was presented with a box of visiting cards bearing my name, with the famous Pathé cockerel in the top-right-hand corner. As a child, I had watched Pathé newsreels in awe, probably for the first time when I was taken to see *The Wizard of Oz*. To be made a director of this symbol of my childhood wonder gave me a quite illogical feeling that I had now somehow arrived at the zenith of my profession. I was quickly brought down to earth when Abteen told me that I been made a director simply so that Revcom would have a majority on the board. Oh, well.

This was a great opportunity for Griffin to churn out more low-budget programmes, keep the staff gainfully employed and earn the company a little money. Equally, it was a free way of transferring a great mass of the Pathé film library on to tape. The library's oldest film in our vaults at Pinewood was highly inflammable nitrate stock that was deteriorating very quickly. Even some of the comparatively recent film was virtually impossible to access because it lay in rusting cans, unloved and uncatalogued. To help pay for sorting out the chaos we invented a

Griffin programme called *A Week to Remember*, the Pathé newsreel from exactly that week forty years earlier, with smart new opening and closing titles.* The BBC bought the series and ran it successfully in a daytime slot for over two years, an eccentric retro-favourite of British prejudice and clipped colonial commentary, an intriguing contrast to the monotonous contemporary news bulletins.

A ritual in the television business is the twice-yearly trade fair in Cannes, Le Marché International de Programmes de Télévision (MIPTV). There were so many such trade fairs around the world every year that some of the second-hand-programme sellers hardly needed an office back home. They could club-class it around the world, their hotels often paid for by the organisers, since a market without buyers is like a wedding without a bride. Over the years MIPTV had also become the meeting place for independent producers hoping to arrange co-productions or find a broadcaster willing to pay an advance for rights in their proposed films. It was hell. Held in the same Palais de Congrès as the Cannes Film Festival, it attracted tens of thousands of participants. The Croisette was crawling with every nationality, but the voices of the Americans and the Germans predominated because they spoke the loudest. There was no knowing whom you might run into as you made your way from a meeting at the Carlton Beach Restaurant to the Martinez Bar, from an appointment on a show-off yacht in the marina to a booth in the cavernous, cacophonous and claustrophobic basement of the Palais itself, a vast concrete monstrosity dumped by the city fathers in the middle of what used to be one of the Mediterranean's most beautiful fishing harbours. Each of thousands of companies rented a fearfully expensive plywood and plastic booth underground, from which TV monitors deafeningly blared meaningless excerpts of un-known, unwatched and unwanted programmes.

'Hi, darling!'

Who is she? Did I meet her last year? Has she mistaken me for somebody else? She's American. You surreptitiously fish for more.

---

* We chose to use Pathé archive from forty years earlier, rather than fifty, in order to avoid the over-exposed coverage of World War II.

'Can't stop now, darling, must dash.' She thrusts her card at you. 'Get your people to call my people and we'll do a quarter later in the week.'

'Doing a quarter' is MIP-speak for having a vapid meeting lasting no more than fifteen minutes. Every year you hate it more and vow never to go again. The fixed smile, the faked delight at seeing someone you hoped never to meet again; the rip-off restaurant prices and truculent, bloody rude waiters. But you do go again, ever hopeful that this time you really will land the deal of a lifetime; and because you need to prove you are still a player in this frightful game. Michael and I were convinced we spotted people cruising the Croisette who had been fired years before but couldn't lose face by staying away. Of all the thousands of participants at MIPTV probably fewer than a hundred people could make big decisions and write fat cheques. It was easier for a camel to pass through the eye of a needle than to track them down. And if you succeeded, how did you elbow and trample your way past all the other desperate supplicants? Not to put too fine a point on it, how did you get Mr Moneybags to sign the cheque?

Michael seized an unexpected opportunity and, goodness, how it paid off. We were both relaxing for a moment on the flamboyant and spacious Revcom stand when a five-foot-four grey-haired dynamo of a man dropped by with a project that needed co-production partners. He turned out to be Bob Cooper, once famous as the presenter of *Ombudsman* on Canadian television but now an independent producer like us. Michael greeted him. Cooper was at MIPTV seeking funding for *Murderers Among Us*, a TV movie to star Ben Kingsley as the Nazi hunter Simon Wiesenthal. Michael gladly offered to put in a good word for him and introduced him to our colleagues from Paris and Los Angeles. Cooper was impressed with Revcom's courtesy and professionalism. Michael and he took to each other instantly, two talented independent producers disgusted by the squalid awfulness of MIPTV and the humiliation of being treated like beggars by loud-mouthed and ignorant executives who only came to Cannes to been seen and to have a good time. Michael and Cooper gossiped wickedly about the ridiculous caricature characters they had encountered both in Cannes and Los Angeles. They became firm friends. This time MIPTV served its purpose. A few weeks after Michael and I had returned to London we heard that Bob Cooper had been appointed President of HBO Worldwide Pictures, the movie-making division of the top American cable network, Home Box Office. The trade press described it as the best job in Hollywood. Michael was among the first to phone Bob to congratulate him. Sycophants were showering his office with flowers, cards and champagne. The phones never stopped ringing. 'None of these ass-holes ever helped me when I needed it, Michael. You and I are going to do business together. Let's make your *Doomsday Gun.*'

CHAPTER 25

Doomsday Gun

Doomsday Gun in 1993 was by far the most expensive, fraught and long-drawn-out production that Griffin undertook. Three years in preparation, a budget big enough to fund a feature film and a *casus belli* with our clients, Home Box Office. But the end result was an outstanding TV movie that HBO ran again and again. It was packed with big names, visually stunning and up-to-the-minute topical because its subject was the supergun that Dr Gerald Bull had built for Saddam Hussein in Iraq. This was current-affairs fact as dramatic fiction, so well crafted that it was a gripping popular movie but as near to the truth as any drama documentary can be. Only when the motivation of our characters was unrecorded did we allow ourselves the luxury of speculation. When Gerald Bull was murdered at his flat in Belgium, nobody knew if his assassins were Israeli or American, Iraqi or British, Chinese or South African – he knew too many of all their secrets. We left the verdict open.

It all began with a small press cutting that Michael and I discussed in the office. It was cryptic to the point of meaningless but, with our antennae always alert for good stories that might work for the Americans, we decide to follow it up. Dr Gerald Bull, a top Canadian scientist, had been assassinated outside his Belgium flat. There had been many break-ins there during the previous months; spookily the furniture and crockery had been rearranged but nothing had been stolen. The burglaries had plainly been warnings. Dr Bull had a fascinating background. He was one of the world's top experts on the design and manufacture of heavy artillery. He had been a key scientist on Harp, the British-Canadian, high-altitude research programme. Harp had developed a huge, 36-metre gun that had broken all the records, firing a 185-pound projectile over a distance of more than a hundred and eleven miles. Yet, in a wave of public spending cuts Harp had been abruptly cancelled. Furious, Dr Bull went to work in the United States, developing powerful shells for American guns destined for the Israelis. Senator Barry Goldwater persuaded his government to reward Dr Bull with honorary citizenship in recognition of his outstanding achievements. Soon he was recruited by the CIA and Bull turned his hand to helping the South Africans modernise their artillery. When Jimmy Carter became President, US policy changed and the defeat of apartheid became the priority. The CIA abandoned Bull. He was charged and found guilty of aiding the white South African regime and sentenced to a year in prison. When he returned to his native Canada after his release, he was further humiliated by the imposition of a $55,000 fine for illegal arms dealing.

Betrayed by both governments and disillusioned, Gerald Bull left North America, he said for good, and set up a freelance arms business in Belgium. Customers soon came knocking on his door. As an artillery consultant to the Chinese and Iraqi governments he successfully updated their armouries. He dramatically extended the range of Iraq's American Scud missiles so that they could inflict real damage on Tel Aviv. As an incentive award, Saddam Hussein encouraged and paid for Gerald Bull to embark on his pet project, Operation Babylon, essentially the continuation of the Harp project. The supergun he planned was an artillery weapon so huge and so powerful that it could fire payloads into space for positioning in orbit. His inspiration was Big Bertha, the gigantic long-range cannon designed and built eight decades earlier by Krupp, the colossal German arms manufacturer. As the First World War ended Big Bertha was being readied to blitz Paris from over seventy miles away.

The intelligence services of many countries were watching the progress of Operation Babylon with alarm. Could the supergun be used to fire chemical or biological weapons at its neighbours Saudi Arabia and Kuwait or, even more likely, at Israel? In Iraq, Bull completed and successfully fired the forty-five-metre-long prototype, 'Baby Babylon'. The full-size weapon, by now dubbed 'the Doomsday Gun' in newspapers throughout the world, was never completed. Dr Bull was murdered five months before Saddam Hussein invaded Kuwait.

To this day Bull's killers have not been identified. His activities had made him the target of a whole host of governments. A month after Bull's assassination, British customs officials intercepted sections of the supergun's gigantic two-hundred-metre-long barrel as it was being secretly shipped by Sheffield Forgemasters to Iraq with the secret connivance of the British government.

Bob Cooper, the new President of HBO Pictures, was anxious to honour his pledge to Michael and commission *Doomsday Gun*. But the perennial question was nagging, 'Will it play it Peoria?' No one in California seemed to have heard of Saddam Hussein or Iraq. Then, suddenly, good fortune came our way – if no one else's. Saddam Hussein's lightning invasion of Kuwait was a total surprise to the world's intelligence services but it soon became apparent that this unprovoked act of war dangerously threatened the world's oil supplies. An invasion to recapture Kuwait seemed inevitable. Michael and I looked at the grim situation unfolding and realised that Saddam had cracked the Peoria problem for us. Michael sent a witty note to Cooper in Los Angeles: 'Have arranged small war to enhance American awareness of Iraq. Let's make *Doomsday Gun*.' It worked. We were under way.

It was agreed that Lionel Chetwynd would write the screenplay. A prolific British/Canadian writer, living in Los Angeles, he was, as it happened, the brother of Fleet Street's most celebrated agony aunt, the late Claire Rayner. Colin Callender, a British producer running HBO in New York, was put in charge. He later became a star, running the whole of the huge HBO production operation. Under his management, HBO has won fifty seven Emmy awards, eighteen Golden Globes and two Oscars. A clever fellow but very difficult to deal with. He wasn't happy with Lionel's screenplay and insisted that we bring in another writer to ginger it up, especially the dialogue. He proposed an icon in the movie business, seventy-three-year-old Walter Bernstein, blacklisted in 1947 by the House of Un-American Activities Committee and forced to work under a pseudonym. He wrote the new draft with the utmost good humour. Now we had a screenplay with which everyone was happy.

All this took an inordinate amount of time. Gerald Bull had been dead three years by the time we were given the green light to go into production and Michael had been working on it almost full-time, flying backwards and forwards from America, cajoling HBO, briefing Walter Bernstein and ensuring that he and the first writer, Lionel Chetwynd, didn't come to blows. HBO allocated a gentle but determined development executive who shared our enthusiasm for the project. Keri Putnam quietly pushed and lobbied on our behalf, and when the film was finally made, she was rightly given a lot of credit within HBO. Keri went on to run Miramax Films and is now director of Robert Redford's Sundance Institute – so obviously Michael and I were right to put our trust in her.

The scale of the production was stupendous. We were planning to shoot all the Iraq sequences in Tunisia. We would film all the interiors in England from our base at Twickenham Studios and travel to Brussels for the exterior shots of Dr Bull's offices and his flat. We also planned to shoot for a couple of days in Ankara, where we had discovered an international arms fair taking place that would look exactly like the arms fair in Baghdad where Bull had first shown off his wares. Now it all started becoming very expensive. We were signing up big names. Frank Langella was cast to play Gerald Bull. At that time he was a well-known Broadway actor, but it was the *Frost/Nixon* film, in which he was to play a truly convincing Richard Nixon, that first brought him international acclaim. Our Raymond Chandler-like CIA man was played by someone who was about to become a major star, Kevin Spacey. Then he was virtually unknown and he kept a very low profile, probably because he was very shy. Alan Arkin played the Mossad chief and Tony Goldwyn (as in Metro-Goldwyn-Mayer) the Defense Department heavy. The English artists were all a dream to work with: Michael Kitchen, Francesca Annis, James Fox, Rupert Graves and Clive Owen. Robert Young was chosen to direct the film. He was a thoroughly experienced, no-nonsense all-rounder. HBO had much admired his *Jeeves and Wooster*.

Cable television is utterly dependent on box-office names, but Michael and I realised that, with HBO's strong encouragement, we seemed to be hiring talent way outside our budget range. When Bob Cooper in Los Angeles had first expressed interest in *Doomsday Gun*, he had intended it to be a movie for the prestigious HBO Pictures, perhaps for cinema release, where budgets were in the $5 – $8 million range. However, for

reasons never explained to us, the project had been transferred to Colin
Callender's HBO Showcase in New York, the TV movie department,
where budgets were normally around $2 million. There was no way the
Doomsday quart would fit into a pint pot. Every day of pre-production
Doomsday Gun was becoming more like a major theatric movie than a
TV drama. HBO also wanted us to provide the best known British
technical staff. Inevitably they were more used to working on James
Bond or *Indiana Jones* at Pinewood than in television studios. Many
despised their television colleagues. Their roots went back to Ealing
and the great British films of the 1950s and 1960s. By now these crafts-
men and technicians had carved out a niche for themselves on major
international films. They had a reputation for providing outstanding
attention to detail, super-efficient delivery and that million-dollar-look
on the screen. The best known commanded huge fees and spent big
money, regardless of the budget's restraints. I once asked one of our
smartly suited-and-booted production managers why these people
showed such contempt for financial continence. He was blunt: 'The
reason we are hired again and again is because we can deliver and that
costs money. It's the producer's job to find extra money if it's needed,
not ours. We'll probably never work with you again so we don't care if
you scream and shout at us. If you don't get hired again, that's your
problem.' The legendary Hollywood producer, David O. Selznik, had
suffered from this sort of mentality too, as he wrote to a colleague over
seventy years ago:

> Perhaps the point of the Production Department in presenting this
> kind of an estimate is to play so safe that under no circumstances will
> they ever be in the position of having estimated the picture at less
> money than it winds up at – which is, of course, an untenable attitude,
> since it inevitably results in extravagances through the delusion that
> we are keeping within our budget . . . The reason that [it] maddens
> me so is that the department heads come back at me from time to
> time and tell me they are within budget, when the budget in the first
> place is something for which they should have been fired then and
> there.

HBO was fully commissioning *Doomsday Gun* so any overspend would be its responsibility. Griffin's fee was fixed so we had nothing to gain by artificially enhancing the budget. Bill Chase, a harassed account executive, had been sent over from New York to monitor the budget. He was horrified by what he found. He was probably the first of the HBO people properly to take on board that this was not a $2 million movie. It never had been and it could not possibly be made for the normal HBO Showcase budget. Since Michael and I were talking several times a day to the people at HBO in New York, seeking their approval for all the 'talent' we were hiring – and the rates at which they were to be paid – we assumed that all was well. We were also, of course, sending daily cost reports which specify not only the money spent but also the cost of the film to completion. Poor Bill was one of those money men who studied the minutiae, and he was quite unable to grasp the politics of the confrontation that he was about to trigger by his panic-stricken alarm call to New York claiming that the budget was out of control.

Meanwhile, I had taken the dramatic decision to pull the production out of Tunisia and move the filming of all the many Iraq sequences to Spain. Anti-American sentiment following the liberation of Kuwait and the rout of the Iraqi army were taking their toll on the loyalties of the Tunisian team constructing the supergun. Our English production manager there was becoming increasingly worried that essential work would be incomplete when the full crew arrived. He even suspected sabotage. Almeria, a hundred miles east of Malaga on the Spanish coast, had a first-rate film infrastructure because it was where so many spaghetti westerns like *The Good, the Bad and the Ugly* had been made, not to mention *The Magnificent Seven.* There was another important reason for choosing Almeria. We needed to replicate Saddam's palace and the exteriors of various military establishments in Baghdad. Just outside Almeria was the astounding tenth-century Alcazaba fort, one of the finest Moorish palaces in Spain and, unlike Grenada, off the tourist map. Colin Callender in New York agreed with me that the costs involved in this last-minute change of plan would be more than justified if we were now to have a trouble-free shoot.

We were therefore astonished to be told, a few days later, that the whole production was going to be taken over by HBO, a new producer flown in from Los Angeles and Griffin kicked out. This was Bill Chase's doing. Michael and I were flabbergasted and then angrily resentful that we should have to carry the can for the financial crisis which was not of our making and all this only a few days before we were due to start shooting on what was clearly going to be a very intricate and complicated production – and a really good film. It was snowing hard, late that night, when Michael and I finally managed to get away from the studios to our homes on the other side of London. Michael rode a powerful and flashy motorbike. As he struggled through the ice, the sleet and the traffic, he became more and more enraged with HBO. In the early hours, he telephoned me. 'I have an idea to fix those bastards,' he told me. 'Who owns the *Doomsday* screenplay, Griffin or HBO?' In a flash I realised that Michael had hit upon the one great flaw in HBO's plan to eliminate us – one that Bill Chase, their account executive, should have spotted but had totally missed. He was to pay a heavy price for the lapse. Because HBO was fully-commissioning *Doomsday Gun*, it had paid for the screenplays but it was Griffin that had contracted both of the writers. In an ideal world, from HBO's point of view, there should have been a document in place assigning the rights in the screenplays to HBO. However, that had been put on one side until the production contract between the two companies was finalised. Griffin owned the screenplay. Michael and I had HBO by the balls.

Keri Putnam, HBO's development executive, was in London by this time and she was as shocked as we were by the decision to sack Griffin. Nevertheless, she was the senior HBO person in London and it was in her lap that Michael and I dropped the bombshell. Michael spoke very quietly, very politely and rather fast. 'Keri, you should know that Griffin owns the *Doomsday Gun* screenplay, not HBO. We do not intend to assign the rights in it to HBO if Griffin is no longer the production company. We will help you close the production down as painlessly as possible but we will not allow it to go ahead.' Keri blanched. This was a career-shortening moment both for her and for Bill Chase. The transatlantic telephone line hummed all day between Twickenham and New York. By the end of it Griffin was back in charge and Bill Chase was on the plane back to New York. Until this incident Michael had always been the one with the jokes and the highly unlikely anecdotes that so enchanted American television executives. The nitty-gritty of contracts, lawyers and budgets he mostly left to me. It was simply not in his nature to worry about detail, the small print. Yet, in his anger, he had identified the one flaw that would transform HBO's bullying into so much hot air. Extraordinarily, there was no residual ill-feeling on either side. We just got on with it. There was too much to do to nurse grudges. Colin Callender must have persuaded his bosses that *Doomsday Gun* was something special and the bitching over the budget almost stopped. The replacement for Bill Chase very sensibly left money matters to our production accountant, preferring to be on location rather than hunched over a computer screen where the buck inexorably stopped.

As if to cock a snook at HBO's accountants, our production manager chartered an Airbus to fly us all to Spain, convincing me that it was the cheapest way of moving all our actors and props. Michael was thrilled to find that we had been allocated a Griffin check-in desk at Gatwick and I felt unreasonably chuffed when the captain asked my permission to take off. Our doomsday gun was mind-blowing. It had been built at a steep angle up the slope of a small mountain, its base in a quarry and the mouth of its three-metre-diameter barrel just visible nearly five hundred feet above. A specially-built wooden stairway climbed parallel to it, all the way up the mountain, just as Gerald Bull had constructed it in Iraq so that his men should have access to the real two-thousand-tonne doomsday gun. Frank Langella and I took one look at this stunning spectacle and hurried to climb the hundreds of steps alongside the gun to look out over the mountains and down at our production crew scurrying about like ants way below.

We needed scores of extras to play Bull's technicians and bring the mountain staircase to life. The nearby prison happily lent us its inmates. We also asked our local production manager to find us soldiers and military vehicles to play the Iraqi army. After she had done some frantic lobbying in Madrid, the Spanish army eventually provided a Dad's Army of troops, free of charge. I noticed that the very ancient and solitary army tank clinked rather noisily. It was full of bottles of beer. Passers-by stopped to gape at the extraordinary sight of a huge military operation, a colossal cannon and a film crew. They videoed us and took photographs, shrugged their shoulders and went on their way. Somehow, our production designer had managed to recruit the real scientist who had been Dr Bull's deputy, a standard-issue Englishman called Chris Cowley. In our film he was played by Michael Kitchen, but in real life, he busied himself ensuring that all our special effects looked convincing and that our Spanish soldiers were made to look as much like Saddam's republican guards as possible. We found ourselves in a surreal situation with the real Chris Cowley instructing Michael Kitchen on how to play Chris Cowley, while the real Chris's real son played his fictional self assisting Michael Kitchen who was playing his father. When the doomsday gun finally fired it was a truly incredible spectacle.

The finished film was a very classy and menacing thriller, the more so because it was a real, topical story. It finally cost $6 million, at the lower end of the price range for Bob Cooper's HBO Pictures but blowing a big hole in Colin Callender's HBO Showcase budget allocation. However, HBO was thrilled with the film and promoted it heavily, the budget crisis seemingly obliterated by the film's critical success. Colin Callender arranged a high-profile screening of the film for media bigwigs at the National Film Theatre in London. In his introductory speech, he went out of his way to pay tribute to Michael and me for finding the story, having the persistence to get it made and producing it so well. No one ever would have guessed that he had fired us both during the production and only reinstated us because Michael knew how to play Hollywood hardball – and now I did too. It was at this moment that Michael and I knew we had arrived where neither of us thought we would ever want to be – on the approved list of American TV movie producers.

Yet the omens at Griffin were unsettling. Antoine came to London for a routine meeting and ended it with a dignified speech saying that he had decided to leave the Cora-Revillon Group, relinquishing his job as head of Revcom, Editions Mondiales and Les Films Ariane to set up his own production company. Tell that to the Marines. Antoine had just been fired. The Shareholder had plainly had enough. Not only had he lost upwards of $25 million on *The French Revolution* fiasco, we were later to learn that Sovereign Pictures was haemorrhaging money too. Antoine's replacement was to be the French head of Benetton Cosmetics Worldwide in New York. Lesley Grunberg was motivated, animated and intoxicated with enthusiasm, but, sadly, he turned out to be no good at all. Not that he was given a fair chance. The time bomb was already ticking.

CHAPTER 26

The Cookie Crumbles

The Shareholder had become restless by Sovereign's third year when serious money was still not rolling in. Antoine had tried to raise his spirits with the news that Alan Parker's *The Commitments* was in the pipeline. Alan Parker, after all, had a golden track record with *Mississippi Burning, Midnight Express, Birdy* and *Bugsy Malone. The Commitments* was nominated for an Oscar and it won three BAFTA Awards but its performance at the box office was disappointing. Unusually, the Shareholder had called for a screening. He couldn't understand a word of the Irish-accented dialogue – and he spoke quite good English. As far as he was concerned this had been a disaster too far, more than enough to have cooked Antoine's goose.

Lesley Grunberg managed to hang on for nearly two years as Antoine's replacement. In Paris, Les Films Ariane was still reeling after the critical and financial catastrophe of *The French Revolution*. The Shareholder instructed Lesley to find a buyer for it. In London, Griffin and Pathé were performing satisfactorily, if modestly, but Revcom in Australia had never really recovered from the abolition of the government's 10BA tax break. In Los Angeles WIN, World International Network, brashly jogged along. The big problem was Sovereign. Sadly, it had no other films as promising as *The Commitments* in development, so there was no way it could protect itself. It had started so well with Oscars for *Cinema Paradiso, My Left Foot* and *Reversal of Fortune*. But artistic acclaim and making money are connected only by the most slender of gossamer threads.

An average-priced Hollywood film will cost about $65 million to make. Half as much again is required for P&A, prints and advertising. The rule of thumb in the industry is that for every ten films you make, three should do better than break even. Another formula in this inexact science is to assume that one good film in ten will cover the losses on the other nine and, if you are lucky, reward you with a profit as well. So the prudent investor needs to set aside half a billion dollars or so, just to start playing the Hollywood game. He can shorten the odds by hiring good people and poaching expertise from the major studios, but unless he has money to burn, he's likely to go the way of so many before him – bankrupt. In the 1990s, Credit Lyonnais lent the fraudster Giancarlo Paretti $1.3 billion to buy the Metro-Goldwyn-Mayer studios. Within five months, MGM was bleeding $1 million a day. Ultimately, Credit Lyonnais was forced to sell the studio back to its original owner at a staggering loss. This was only one of many disastrous investments that the bank made in Hollywood. By the time the French government had secretly rescued it the wags had renamed it 'Debit Lyonnais'.

We all knew that some sort of pruning was on the cards but the news that it was to be *la guillotine* was quite shattering. The Shareholder had decided to close down his whole media empire, even selling the profitable magazine business Editions Mondiales. His adventures in the media world had cost the family business, Cora-Revillon, around $50 million. Later, his relatives were to take their revenge, secretly selling off their forty-two-per-cent share to Cora's most bitter rival, Carrefour. Michael and I were surprised when the Shareholder made a personal appearance in the London office for the very first time. We had assumed that he would send one of his henchmen to perform the unsavoury task of shutting us down. Not a bit of it. You probably don't get to run a $1 billion family business if you can't do the dirty work yourself. Later we heard that his Swiss advisers had been unanimous in advising him to close the whole business down. They had seen the sense in employing Ernst Goldschmidt, Larry Gershman and Lesley Grunberg to head up Cora-Revillon's media interests because they were convinced that the media business was controlled by a Jewish mafia. Now one of them joked cynically, 'If Goldschmidt, Gershman and Grunberg can't make a go of it, who can?'

It was a bitter time. Les Films Ariane, one of France's intellectual treasures, was sold to the down-market commercial television station TF1 in which the crook, Robert Maxwell, owned a substantial holding.

Les Films Ariane had been approaching its fiftieth anniversary when it was thrown to the wolves. Not very much later the great Alexandre Mnouchkine died at the age of eighty-five. His family was convinced that the cause of death was a broken heart. His daughter, Ariane, after whom the company had been named, articulated her fury with Revcom by publicly ejecting Lesley Grunberg from her father's funeral, an event attended by *tout* Paris. Ignominiously, the rest of the Shareholder's media empire just withered and died. Revcom was closed in France, England and Australia. Sovereign Pictures just faded quietly away. World International Network still had life in it, thanks to the irrepressible Larry Gershman, and it was sold for a million-dollar profit to a German broadcaster. Pathé was bought by Associated Newspapers and Griffin was shut down but given a brief stay of execution until we had delivered *Doomsday Gun* to HBO. All that remained for Michael and me was the Griffin name. We were now joint shareholders in Griffin Productions Limited, a £3 off-the-shelf company. However, fortune smiled on us unexpectedly. Suddenly we were given the green light by a new American customer for another of our projects, this time a TV movie called *Good King Wenceslas.*

Since there was only a handful of customers for our films in the United States it was necessary to pursue them all. While we preferred to be seen as bespoke tailors, fashioning fine films to our own design, Michael and I were realistic enough to accept that sometimes our films had to submit to the requirements of less discerning patrons. Near the bottom of the market was the Family Channel. It had begun life as the Christian Broadcasting Network, owned by Pat Robertson, one of those frightful TV evangelists. Twice daily it broadcast his religious ravings. This is what he thought of feminism: 'A socialist, anti-family political movement that encourages women to leave their husbands, kill their children, practise witchcraft, destroy capitalism and become lesbians.' Not surprisingly, the Family Channel mostly attracted little old ladies in tennis shoes, while advertisers wanted to target children and teenagers who had more to spend than the blue-rinse brigade. So the Family Channel started commissioning wholesome family films. That's where *Good King Wenceslas* fitted in.

When Michael visited the Family Channel's grim headquarters in downmarket Virginia Beach, joining the staff in a mind-shatteringly banal prayer session before a frugal monastic lunch, the idea of *Good King Wenceslas* was met with enthusiasm. Extraordinarily, a film of the good king had never been made. I had already been to Prague several times to talk to the studios there. The problem was that everything was so tatty. The technical equipment was mostly Russian cast-offs, the telephones in the production offices didn't work and the thousands of costumes stored at the film studios were infested with fleas. Our Prince Wenceslas was played by Jonathan Brandis, a blond, blue-eyed, all-American seventeen-year-old who was in the middle of making fifty-seven episodes of *SeaQuest*. His wicked mother was played by *Hart to Hart* star Stefanie Powers and the legendary Joan Fontaine was enticed out of retirement to play Ludmilla, the good Queen Mother. A quite unremarkable American soap star called Perry King was cast as a duke or a prince, or perhaps both, simply so that the Family Channel could put his name on the posters. Rather endearingly for one who was paid so well, Perry used to wash his clothes in the hotel bath and pocket the daily laundry allowance. There was a succulent cameo part for the much-loved Leo McKern, as Duke Philip, the father of Prince Wenceslas's bride to be. Leo had the most extraordinary repertoire of dirty stories, bad limericks and tales from his long acting career that helped to while away the endless waiting time that consumes most of any filming day.

Our main location was the stunning, mediaeval Pernstein Castle, set in the heart of the Bohemian countryside. We had horses and stuntmen, moats and drawbridges, swordsmen and jugglers – and magnificent flea-free costumes from the celebrated British theatrical costumiers Angels. In a magnificent scene, Leo McKern as Prince Philip, dressed in purple cloak and plumed hat, drove his horse-drawn sleigh through the glistening snow to the gates of Pernstein Castle. His beautiful daughter Johanna, who is to marry Prince Wenceslas, followed on horseback accompanied by a mounted column of soldiers. I watched as this astonishing, epic scene was being shot and I began to understand the buzz that motivated the likes of Cecil B. De Mille. At the same time

I recognised, with sinking heart, that our *Good King Wenceslas* would soon be just another of those swashbuckling movies that serve no purpose but to fill the gaps on Saturday-afternoon television.

The one thing we lacked was snow. We had sold the project to the Family Channel on the premise that Good King Wenceslas is a perennial Christmas story and therefore our film could go on making money for them indefinitely. Indeed ITV ran it for years every Christmas morning. Christmas means snow, however, and snow is crucial to the story, but there wasn't any due for another eight months. We checked the snow-making equipment at the studios in Prague. It looked rather like those pumps firemen use to drain water out of flooded basements, but rustier. Our production designer was unhappy. He was the archetypal play-safe and damn-the-cost man. 'We'll have to bring the snow from London,' he announced. I argued, I pleaded, I practically went down on my knees. But in the end I reluctantly conceded that he was right. Two large trucks, towing generators and pumps, lumbered on to the M25 to begin their eight-hundred-mile trek from Pinewood to Pernstein. Each of the vehicles was emblazoned with the name of the company, 'It's Snow Business'.

Joan Fontaine really was legendary. The best remembered of her Hollywood films is *Rebecca*, directed by Alfred Hitchcock. Joan was nominated for an Oscar as Best Actress. The next year she won the Oscar for her performance in *Suspicion*, again directed by Hitchcock. Joan appeared in fifty Hollywood movies throughout the 1940s, '50s and '60s, in deadly competition with her sister, Olivia de Havilland. By the time we were making *Good King Wenceslas*, Joan was seventy-seven years old and she had not acted for many years. When she arrived at the hotel in Pernstein she was quite aggressive, brandishing her contract at me. 'I never sign these until I have met the producer,' she announced. What would she have done had I not been to her taste? It's a long way back to Hollywood from Pernstein Castle. Luckily Michael was at hand to help massage her undimmed ego and soon she warmed to us. However, when Michael later introduced Joan to Stefanie Powers, her response was pointed. 'I think I might have seen you on The Television,' she remarked rather crisply. To which Stefanie replied, as quick as lightning,

'And I think I might have seen you on The Television too, Miss Fontaine, but only very late at night.' Later, when filming started, Miss Fontaine and I were to spend many happy hours chatting together on the set. Even then I knew that I was probably the last producer that she would ever work with.

Michael had come out to join us in Pernstein with great news: Griffin had been offered a home by Yorkshire Television. His old friend Ward Thomas, YTV's erstwhile Chairman, had been recalled from retirement to pull the company through a financial crisis. While Michael and Ward couldn't be more different in character they had always got on famously. Michael had also produced many award-winning programmes for YTV. After Ward had retired to the South of France, Michael had kept in touch with him, entertainingly dispensing the latest television gossip. Now Ward was happy to grant Michael a favour. He was employing every trick in the book to enhance YTV's share price, fattening it up for what had become its inevitable sale to Granada. He immediately recognised that the diversification into TV movies that Griffin would represent could be spun to YTV's advantage. Ward saw Griffin as a weapon in his arsenal. We saw him as a knight in shining armour.

Our first film at YTV was a family adventure movie called *The Place of Lions*. Based on a first-rate children's book of the same name, it was about a boy going to visit his father in South Africa. The light plane that is flying him crashes in the middle of nowhere and a lion, of course, guides the boy to safety. YTV had identified a reliable co-production partner in Johannesburg, the commercial broadcaster, M-NET. To our great delight YTV also introduced us to a tax-investment consortium that was happy to pick up the budget deficit. We cast two of our actors from *Unspeakable Verse*, Miriam Margolyes and Hugh Laurie. At that time Hugh was no longer working regularly with Stephen Fry and *House* was yet to make him into an international star. Miriam said she would take any part in any film if it allowed her to travel to a place she had never seen before. The boy was played by thirteen-year-old Guy Edwards, a surprisingly mature actor, who went on to star in David Mamet's re-make of *The Winslow Boy* the very next year. I spent most of my time on location engaging Guy's doting mother-cum-chaperone in earnest conversation. My purpose was to prevent her from fretting as her beloved son spent hours each day in the company of our lion behind a robust fence, while an armed trainer kept a wary eye. The director and the film crew very prudently remained on the other side of the barrier. I couldn't help thinking of Albert. His mother, Mrs Ramsbottom, I remember, had been most put out when Albert was eaten by a lion, as I imagine young Guy's mother would have been too.

> The Magistrate gave his opinion
> That no one was really to blame,
> And he said that he hoped the Ramsbottoms
> Would have further sons to their name.
>
> At that Mother got proper blazing,
> 'And thank you, sir, kindly,' said she.
> 'What, waste all our lives raising children
> To feed ruddy lions? Not me!'*

Back in London we faced an urgent problem. Much sooner than anyone had thought possible Granada completed its purchase of YTV and suddenly it was gone as if it had never existed. Granada had already bought London Weekend Television and was itself to become history when it merged with Carlton Television to become just plain ITV. Ward Thomas retired from YTV for the second time and Griffin was once again looking for a place to call home. Out of the blue, we were summoned to lunch by two of the TVS executives who had helped us make *Act of Betrayal* and *Secret Weapon*. Both were by then working for Chrysalis, a major player in commercial radio with Heart FM and Galaxy. It was expanding into television by setting up joint ventures with a handful of successful independent producers like Clive James's Watchmaker and Bentley Productions (*Midsomer Murders*). Our former colleagues had heard that Griffin was looking for a home and they invited us to join them.

A year or two earlier, at the much-dreaded MIPTV in Cannes, Michael and I had made a very valuable new contact. Jerry Offsay was

* from 'The Lion and Albert' by George Marriot Edgar, 1932

the head of Showtime, a TV-movie channel that commissioned a substantial number of new films every year. We had arranged a breakfast meeting with him in his suite at one of the many over-priced five-star hotels on the Croisette. As we arrived, we found him leaving the hotel, clutching a blood-soaked towel to his face. He had cut himself very badly shaving and he was looking for a pharmacy. He spoke not one word of French so he was overjoyed that Michael and I had shown up in time to do the talking. Jerry always gratefully remembered our angels-of-mercy routine and he had subsequently co-produced one of the films we made at YTV. Now we had another proposal that was exactly right for Showtime.

Michael had spotted a magazine article about a young American called Varian Fry who had gone to Marseilles during the Second World War to rescue Jewish writers and artists fleeing the Nazis. Varian Fry helped them to cross the Pyrenees into Spain and then to Lisbon from where they could fly to safety in New York. We called the film *Varian's War* and commissioned a screenplay from our *Doomsday Gun* writer, Lionel Chetwynd. It was clearly going to cost a lot more than Showtime would pay, so we teamed up with Kevin Tierny, a Canadian producer. By shooting the whole film in French Canada, Kevin managed to pre-sell it to a broadcaster there and, more importantly, to trigger the Anglo-Canadian co-production treaty which brought us substantial extra funds. So Montreal pretended to be 1940s Marseilles. It all looked surprisingly convincing.

Cable channels only survive if they can make their programmes stand out from the hundreds of others from which zap-happy viewers can choose. The tried and trusted method is still the best – heavily promoting the names of the stars, the 'marquee names', as they are still called, from the days when the circus came to town. Showtime decided that *Varian's War* even needed a marquee name to attract the right marquee name to star in the show. They told us that they wanted Barbra Streisand's Barwood Films to co-produce our movie with us and, of course, to embellish the ever-growing list of credits. Michael was surprisingly nervous about his meeting with Barbra and her formidable executive producer, Cis Corman, but Barbra behaved like a pussy cat and Cis turned out to be an ace casting director. It was she who found us our star. Everyone agreed that William Hurt was the perfect actor to play Varian Fry. He had been nominated for Oscars for his roles in *Kiss of the Spider Woman, Children of a Lesser God* and *Broadcast News.* Since then his career had slowed down a bit but for Showtime he was a full-blooded marquee name and if he agreed to play Varian Fry the film would be given the green light. 'But William Hurt doesn't do television,' his agent told us. This was always the conundrum. We needed big names if our TV movies were to be given the go-ahead but actors regarded TV movies as a signal to Hollywood that they were on the slippery slope.

To break the deadlock, Showtime negotiated an extraordinary deal that infuriated Michael and me. We could have William Hurt, we were told, if we agreed to credit Prince Edward – who? – alongside Barbra Streisand and Cis Corman as an executive producer. We would also have to credit his production company. This was a bolt out of the blue. Showtime had never mentioned the prince to us before. He had in no way been involved with the production and we were just weeks from beginning the shoot. It turned out that the prince had hired a Hollywood agent to help him and his company break into the TV-movie business. There had been a trade-off. Showtime would tell us no more but insisted, rather apologetically, that we must agree the deal or lose our principal actor and, probably, the film as well. Neither Michael nor I had ever met 'Edward Wessex', as he was credited on our film, nor even talked to him on the phone. He probably never even read the screenplay or bothered to watch the finished film. Fortunately his credit on our film did him no good at all. 'Edward Wessex' was soon to enrage his brother, Prince Charles, by allowing one of his company's film crews to film Prince William at his university when the media had given an undertaking to leave him alone. Their mother regally adjudicated the matter and ordered her youngest son to abandon his thoroughly un-distinguished film career.

Michael and I were old and wise enough not to lose any sleep about sharing credits. It was the sharing of fees that was the problem. Our Canadian co-producer Kevin Tierney deserved his. Michael and he were both credited as the producers because Kevin had managed the whole

of the film shoot in Montreal and raised some of the money for it too. Barbra Streisand's company of course expected a handsome reward and now Prince Edward we were told was on the books too. Griffin's modest production fee had been negotiated before the bandwagon had begun to roll. Now that *Varian's War* was successfully completed, there was nothing left in the kitty to redress the disparity of rewards.

Sometimes it is easy to forget that the *raison d'être* of commercial television is not to make good programmes but to make good money. The programmes serve only as a means to that end, attracting punters to watch the commercials. Some countries are lucky enough to have powerful public-service broadcasters or high-quality subscription services, like HBO, that originate much of the output and control its quality. But the trend is towards countless lookalike movie channels, competing for the same audience. So the big money is no longer spent on the content but on the wrapping. Look at any listing of what's on the telly and the choice is seemingly overwhelming. Yet all that distinguishes one channel's movies from the next are the marquee names. There's simply no space to tell you what if anything the film is all about.

Every year that Griffin produced TV movies the money available for production declined as additional movie channels came on stream. It doesn't take a genius to work out that the more there are to share the cake the thinner the slices will be. We had many more estimable projects waiting in the wings. Would they turn out to be loss leaders too? Michael and I had been in the business long enough, we both decided. There were better things to do with our lives than wait for the diminishing rewards of the ever less frequent green light.

CHAPTER 27

A Place in the Sun

Retirement offers many freedoms apart from the obvious one of no more work. In my case, I most wanted to escape the British winter. It is not so much the cold. When the weather is crisp and the sun is shining you can be in the best of spirits; when it rains you wait for a better day. The killer is the lack of light in the shortened days between November and March. In tropical countries you can come in from work, bath, change and start a whole new day, out and about with your friends. After struggling home through the rush hour in Britain, you shut the front door against the winter night and hope you won't have to venture out again till morning. It's dark when you go to work, dark when you fight your way home on public transport or in the nose-to-tail traffic. Winter for me is a prison sentence. Sensible animals like hedgehogs and tortoises hibernate, sleeping through this suicide-inducing time.

Over the years I have spent a great deal of time in India and I have come to love it. So my hunt for a new home was at least focused. I planned to spend at least six months of the year there. India is a vast country so the question I faced was, where? The easiest way to answer that question was first to decide where not. I knew I wanted a sea or river view away from the winter cold. That eliminated the north-east, the Himalayan hill stations and those in the south, where winters call for hot-water bottles and log fires. Because the east coast is blessed with both the north-east and the south-west monsoons it is too wet and humid; and Mumbai which I love is prohibitively expensive and, in my view, a much nicer place to visit than to live. The sheer struggle of competing for existence with twelve million other people is the antithesis of retired tranquillity. So, by a very simple process of elimination, I knew that I should be looking for my new home on the west coast of

274

India. Gujarat it is too hot and too cold and too full of hate. The coast of Maharashtra is pretty inaccessible because it takes so long to get out of Mumbai; only the fishing villages on the Alibaug peninsular are easy to reach because they are served directly by ferries from the Gateway of India. Alibaug has become the millionaires' hideaway, far beyond my budget. So my choice whittled down to Goa, Kerala and Karnataka.

I wanted to live near a sizeable town where I could make friends and near an airport so that I could travel. I crossed Goa off my wish list without a second thought. I know it well and I have many friends who live there permanently or who make it their winter home. It is breathtakingly beautiful. The Portuguese influence ensures wonderful seafood and the booze is cheap. But it is not proper India. Centuries of Jesuits converting its people to Christianity have tarnished its *joie de vivre* with the concept of sin. And the affluent British community has imported an ambience of the retirement colonies in Malta, Cyprus and Spain. There are too few new faces at the endless parties, too much regurgitating of the tittle-tattle of yesteryear. You can of course escape the party life and drop out with the ancient hippy beachcombers or drop in with the string-vested pot-bellied lager louts. Not for me. I thrive in real India. That is where I wanted to be.

Fort Kochi was top of my shortlist for Kerala. It is a town of fine Portuguese merchant houses, shaded by gigantic trees, with superb views of the sea and the surrounding islands. There's a fabulous sixteenth-century synagogue and the classically simple church of St Francis is the first Christian church in India. Here you can watch vast ships swing past the Malabar Hotel as they enter the harbour from the sea. Sinister grey Indian navy vessels slide watchfully and silently by. The backwaters begin here. After the Kashmir Valley they say this is most beautiful place in India. You can meander by rice boat for days through the rivers and canals feeding Vembanad Lake, ending your voyage in the enchanting and colourful fishing port of Alapuzzha. Kochi's waterbuses ply the vast estuary that separates the fort from its commercial centre at Ernakulam just like the *vaporetti* in Venice. You have to travel by ferry since the roads are in permanent gridlock, an all too familiar symptom of India's growth. Recently I visited Kochi for the first time during the monsoon.

For days on end you are marooned. Nothing moves except the ferries. There is no limit to the number of their passengers, no life jackets and no one can swim. Drenched to the skin, packed like sardines, transported like cattle and dumped in the mud. No one would choose to live half the year like this.

The state of Karnataka is almost the size of Great Britain and its population much the same size as ours. I naïvely chose to explore its coastline by bus from Goa. All right, people have to bring their chickens with them; and there's no point in travelling and leaving the market produce behind. I understand all that. But the seat in front of mine was only nine inches away and I measure twenty inches from knee to bum. The driver seemed hell-bent on an imminent rendezvous with his maker – daring the oncoming traffic with his flashing headlights and blaring, shrieking horn. Superimposed over all of this, Hindi music to deafen the dead. The bus stopped to draw breath at Karwar and I leapt off. I have never travelled by bus in Karnataka since. Luckily, you no longer need to, thanks to the Konkan Railway. Tunnels, bridges, cuttings and embankments – a glorious feat of engineering that the British claimed could never be accomplished – a new railway line that runs the seven hundred miles from Mumbai to Mangalore. Over the river at Karwar, the trains traverse a spectacular pencil-thin viaduct that seems almost to skim the surface of the water. In a country renowned for the ugliness of its Soviet-style ferro-concrete edifices, it is a design with extraordinary flair.

Karwar is a small port on a big river surrounded by mountains that fall into the sea. It is a sublimely beautiful place, reminiscent of the Côte d'Azur or the Amalfi Coast. There was a serious possibility that I could build my home here. A plot of land or, to be accurate, a part of the river was for sale. The boundary was marked out in the water by granite posts perhaps twenty metres out from the riverbank. Of course, the whole lot would have to be filled in with stones and ballast, but what a spectacular place! My dream house would look north across the river, west as far as the Arabian Sea and east across the rice paddy to the smokey-blue mountains beyond. A Walter Mitty dream? The district surveyor said not. He wanted me to buy. This was an urban-renewal project close to his heart. An architect suggested that I built my own jetty so that I could go by water to shop in the town. In fact, it would be much easier to use the back door that would open directly on to the main street. The agent told me that this was a respectable part of town. My next-door neighbour, he said, was a member of parliament. Later I learned that the politician had been murdered there by hired gunmen from Mumbai.

The plot of land – that is to say, the designated piece of river – belonged to an extended Brahmin family. Their spokesman was a distinguished eye surgeon in Mumbai. It was a tough negotiation spread wide across the world. Aunts in New Zealand had to be consulted, cousins in Australia, brothers in Canada, even sisters in England. But, in the end, it was not the price that broke the deal. The government had sensibly brought in tough new regulations to control building on river-banks and near the seashore. Permission, I was told, *might* be given if the case had merit or, I suppose, if the *baksheesh* were right. But I would have to buy the land, that is to say the water, and turn it into land before I could apply for permission to build. Permission refused would mean money down the drain – lots of it. I could not take the risk. Nor of, course, would the owners. I realised, too, that I had travelled an awfully long way from the airport in Goa. How on earth would my guests and I get to Karwar and away again? There was a final, more important, worry that clinched it. A nuclear power station had recently been commissioned at Kaiga, only twenty miles inland from Karwar. A second reactor was under construction. Pressurised heavy water reactors need cooling and the Kalinadi River provides it before flowing past my dream plot to the sea. Great for India, no doubt, but not for me.

To explore the rest of the coast I splashed out on a taxi, an ancient white Ambassador. That way I could stop where I liked and explore off the beaten track. In Karnataka the main road does not run beside the sea as it does elsewhere. The estuaries are so wide that the highway has been built some distance inland where the river is narrow enough for bridges to be built. Unlike in Europe and America, where dual carriage-ways and even motorways often hug the seashore, destroying it, here you find unspoilt fishing hamlets at the water's edge. The coast of

Karnataka runs from Karwar, in the north, for two hundred miles, just beyond Mangalore, to the Kerala coast. Extraordinarily the beach that runs its full length is quite unspoilt by tourism. There are only two decent hotels, no beach restaurants, no water sports and no swimming pools.

I hoped to find a place to build my home within easy reach of the airport at Mangalore. But I planned to keep my eye open for possibilities along the way. What an extraordinarily beautiful drive south it was. Mountains to the left, occasional glimpses of the Arabian Sea to the right. First, Om Beach, refuge of the sophisticated hippies wearied by the Goan scene. Then vastly wide rivers spanned now by bridges where once only ferries plied. The toll bridge at Honavar seems a mile long, reaching out over the anchored fishing trawlers, their brightly coloured flags sparkling jauntily in the sunlight. The bridge is a rickety, make-do-and-mend affair that twists and groans under a constant burden of lorries and buses. It's hard to credit that this is the main road from Mumbai to Cape Comorin, the southernmost tip of India. At Maravanthe the road runs along the crown of a two-mile causeway separating the Arabian Sea from a great river estuary on the landward side. This is the halfway point between Goa and Mangalore. Everyone stops to admire the scene where waves break noisily across the beach on one side, in contrast to the tranquillity of still, green water on the other. Now we were in the home strait, passing the temple town of Udupi, a major pilgrim centre and the home of south-Indian vegetarian cooking. And, at last, Mangalore itself, a chaotic city. It's a hotchpotch of elegant but decaying *Gone with the Wind* bungalows, overshadowed by ungainly blocks of flats, built with Gulf money for investment and retirement. Mangalore is a civic planner's nightmare of country lanes and potholed streets, a cacophony of horns from the pestilence of motor rickshaws, motorbikes, buses and trucks, driven like bumper cars at a funfair. Forming a triangle with the sea, two great rivers envelop the town, converging at the old port, their banks cluttered with dilapidated tile factories. Mangalore once exported terracotta tiles to the world. Now it exports brains and skills and is internationally renowned for its medical colleges that pump out new doctors and nurses almost incontinently. Its young people are also brilliant at IT. Now there are many international flights from Mangalore to speed the export of this talent. However, the reservoir seems inexhaustible because the mantra of Mangalore is education, education, education.

In India, real-estate agents are hard to find. They have no high street shops and they hardly advertise. Property dealing is almost a furtive affair – often with good reason. I badly needed help, someone in Mangalore who knew his way around this labyrinthine world. When I was deepest in the dumps, because I could not find the place of my dreams, I was pointed in the direction of a man who several people advised might help me. He was Avil Mathias, a great bear of a man, a jack of all trades, a wheeler dealer *par excellence.* He owned buses and trucks, built flats, rented houses – anything that would turn a tidy profit. There was not a seaside plot we didn't visit together, nor a building site on the river we ignored. We were not always welcome. Often fishermen converged on us like angry wasps, hotly to deny that any land was up for sale. Why should they move their boats and their nets? Who was this bloody foreigner anyway? Without comparing notes, Avil and I had come to the same conclusion. Maybe I should first be looking for a rental property rather than immediately planning to build one. Permissions take for ever. The monsoon is long and fierce, badly disrupting construction schedules. It could take two years before I was properly installed in a finished house of my own. Avil made a few telephone calls and disappeared.

The next day he showed up at my hotel looking excessively pleased with himself. 'I have found what you want,' he boasted. 'In fact, I am so sure you will like it that I have agreed we will sign the lease this afternoon. Come, let's go and see.' We drove ten miles north of the city, past the port and then turned towards the sea. After little more than half a mile we turned right into a seaside lane, beside a five-mile virgin beach of golden sand. And there was Sharath Villa. It is a large, ugly, modern house with a huge first-floor balcony overlooking the sea. It was love at first sight. Within a week I was installed – and I find it suits me very well. Soon Avil arranged for a cook and a driver. Already a married couple lived in a small house at the end of the garden. They both work at the nearby cashew-nut factory and, in the evenings, they clean the house, tend the garden and wash the clothes. They all help look after my three beloved canine friends: Mr Bruno is a feckless and extrovert Alsatian, Laura a dotty yellow Labrador puppy and Mrs Dog is, well, just a beach dog. Every day there are fresh fish and prawns from the fishermen. In the garden there are coconut trees, mango, banana and papaya. As companions I have frogs, a passing mongoose or two, green parrots, black bulbuls and, occasionally, a majestic cobra. I sit in my rocking chair on the veranda watching the ships entering and leaving Mangalore port. Some early mornings, when the sky is clear and the air cool, a shoal of dolphins will dive playfully among the country boats as they return from their night's fishing. On the horizon I can sometimes spot an Arab dhow, bound perhaps for Cochin or Colombo, routes that they have sailed for a thousand years.

I had hoped that I would never need to stir myself from here. However, as time has gone by, I have sensed a change in the rhythm of my world. India is undergoing such an extraordinarily rapid transformation that it has become impossible to ignore, even in this idyllic setting. There are twenty-six manufacturers selling cars in India. Maruti Suzuki, the largest, will sell a million cars this year. Bangalore, the capital of Karnataka, registers a thousand new vehicles a week. A mile away from my home, centuries-old Banyan trees are being felled to make way for the new four-lane dual carriageway. And while it used to be quite difficult to visit my village because the lanes were so narrow, now it is too easily accessible, demonstrably desirable commuter territory. At night I notice that the stars have dimmed. An amber glow now illuminates the sky behind my house. The port, just five miles away, has attracted polluters like the Pied Piper attracted rats. There are thousands of overloaded open lorries illegally delivering India's precious iron ore for export to China. The oil refinery now provides much of south India's petrol and diesel. Its turnover grew to $8 billion this year, and the nearby chemical-fertiliser factory looks pretty evil too. Round the clock, smoke and God knows what else, billows poisonously into the sky. Now the government is constructing a vast, free-trade zone right next to the refinery. Half of it will be used to manufacture petroleum products. Mangalore, it has recently been reported, has become the most polluted district in Karnataka, one of the top fifty in India.

With great reluctance I decided I would have to move before I was overwhelmed by the march of progress. I was lucky, really lucky. A friend has found me a spot of such beauty that I simply can't believe my good fortune. I'm building a house there, on the bank of the River Udyavara, just twenty-five miles away from my present home. All along the river's bank are coconut groves that give it shade. The river has formed a sharp U-bend loop round the dazzling green rice paddy fields before flowing four miles into the Arabian Sea. Migratory birds in their thousands have decided that this particular sanctuary is a winter heaven on earth. I very much hope to prove them right.

Acknowledgements

On the rare occasions that the BBC reluctantly agreed to screen a programme in advance of transmission, in my time, it pedantically explained that the only comments that would be entertained were those on the programme's factual accuracy. That way the Corporation believed it preserved its virginity. On the same basis, but for a different reason, I have asked a few friends and colleagues to comment on the accuracy of those contentious parts of the book in which they feature. It is not that I am uninterested in their opinions; rather that I want to absolve them from the responsibility of endorsing mine. They are Ted Childs, Brian Elliott, Sir Denis Forman, Dick Gilling, Mick Jackson, Christopher Jeans, Edward Mirzoeff, the Hon. Sara Morrison, Abteen Sai, Tim Slessor and, of course, Michael Deakin, who first introduced me to Griffin Productions when it was no more than a gleam in anyone's eye. Michael later jumped on board himself for what turned out to be fifteen entertaining years of professional partnership.

My thanks to Random House for permission to quote from *Blacklist: The Inside Story of Political Vetting* by Mark Hollingsworth and Richard Norton-Taylor and the BBC for *Man Alive*, *Americans* and *Let's Go Naked*. The owners of other copyright material whose permission I have sought are: Selznick Properties for *Memo from David O. Selznick*; HarperCollins for *The Last Days of the Beeb* by Michael Leapman; Aurum Press for *The Fun Factory* by Will Wyatt; Peters, Fraser and Dunlop for *DG: The Memoirs of a British Broadcaster* by Alasdair Milne; Francis Day and Hunter for 'The Lion and Albert' by George Marriot Edgar; and Spike Milligan Productions for 'Sardines'.

I would particularly like to thank my brother Marcus for convincing his fellow publisher David Elliott that *Blood on the Carpet* should be published by Quartet Books. And I thank my lucky stars that its illustrious chairman, Naim Attallah, enthusiastically agreed with them.

Bibliography

Andrew, Christopher, *The Defence of the Realm: The Authorised History of MI5*, Penguin (2nd edition), 2010

Barnett, Steven and Curry, Andrew, *The Battle for the BBC*, Aurum Press, 1994

Cameron, James, *Indian Summer*, Macmillan, 1974

Clapham, Adam, *As Nature Intended: A Pictorial History of the Nudists*, Heinemann/Quixote Press, 1982

—— Beware Falling Coconuts, Rupa, India, 2007

Darlow, Michael, *Independents Struggle*, Quartet Books, 2004

Drinkwater, Carol, *The Olive Farm*, Time Warner, 2001

—— *The Olive Harvest*, Weidenfeld & Nicolson, 2004

Dyke, Greg, *Inside Story*, HarperCollins, 2004

Foster, Buddy, *Jodie Foster: An intimate biography*, Heinemann, 1997

Greene, Hugh, *The Third Floor Front*, Bodley Head, 1969

Hennessy, Peter, *The Secret State: Whitehall and the Cold War*, Allen Lane, 2002

—— *Having It So Good: Britain in the Fifties*, Penguin, 2007

Hollingsworth, Mark and Norton-Taylor, Richard, *Blacklist: The Inside Story of Political Vetting*, Hogarth Press, 1988

Houlihan, Patricia, *Unspeakable Verse*, Boxtree, 1996

James, Clive, *The Blaze of Obscurity*, Picador, Pan Macmillan, 2009

Lacey, Robert, *Aristocrats*, Hutchinson, 1983

Leapman, Michael, *Treachery? The Power Struggle at TV-AM*, George Allen & Unwin, 1984

—— *The Last Days of the Beeb*, George Allen & Unwin, 1986

MacGregor, Sue, *Woman of Today*, Headline, 2002

Mansfield, Michael, *Memoirs of a Radical Lawyer*, Bloomsbury, 2009

Marr, Andrew, *A History of Modern Britain*, Macmillan, 2007

Milne, Alasdair, *DG: The Memoirs of a British Broadcaster*, Hodder & Stoughton, 1988

Selznick, David, *Memo from David O. Selznick*, Samuel French, Hollywood, 1989

Slessor, Tim, *Lying in State*, Aurum Press, 2002

Tracey, Michael, *A Variety of Lives: A Biography of Sir Hugh Greene*, Bodley Head, 1983

Trethowan, Ian, *Split Screen*, Hamish Hamilton, 1984

Whicker, Alan, *Inside Whicker's World*, Hamish Hamilton, 1982

Wilcox, Desmond, *Explorers*, BBC Publications, 1975

——— *Americans*, Hutchinson, 1978

Wyatt, Will, *The Fun Factory*, Aurum Press, 2003

Index

Index

Negev Nuclear Research Center,
  Israel, 237, 238
Negro Next Door, The (This Week),
  32
Neill, Sam, 237
Network 7, 222
Never Say Never Again, 221
New Musical Express, 222
New York, New York, 137
Newman, Sydney, 14–16
Nixon, President Richard M., 45,
  157, 159, 257
No Trams to Lime Street, 14
Nolan, Sidney, 245
Noll, Michel, 217, 218, 228–32, 241,
  242, 243, 247, 250
Norddeutscher Rundfunk, 26
Noriega, Manuel, 233
Norman, Jessye, 237
Normanbrook, Lord, 108–11, 117
Northern Ireland, 98–105, 117, 230
Norton, Graham, 207
Norton-Taylor, Richard, 124
Norwich Union, 9, 10
*Not a Penny More, Not a Penny
  Less*, 219, 220, 226, 227, 233
Nudists, 163
Nuestra Señora de la Concepción, 28

O'Reilly, Sean, 68, 74
Observer, 22, 118, 119
Odyssey, 218
Official Secrets Act, 101, 121, 193
Offsay, Jerry, 270
O'Hara, Scarlett, 7, 51, 52
Old Bailey, 193, 212
Old Grey Whistle Test, 180
Old Vic, 3
Omen III – The Final Conflict, 232

Omnibus, 122, 123
On the Braden Beat, 64, 66
One Pair of Eyes, 37, 112
OPEC, 73, 143
Operation Babylon, 255
Operation Desert Storm, 60
Operation Nifty Package, 234
Opinions, 203, 204
Oriental Club, 166–168
Orion, 247
Orwell, George, 120
Oscars, 39, 139, 248, 256, 264, 272
Oval Office, 154, 155
Owen, Alun, 14
Owen, Clive, 257

Packer, Kerry, 216
Paintbox, 245
Painting with Light, 244, 245
Pakenham, Kevin, 184
Pakistan, 78–81, 202
Panama, 233
Panorama, 231, 79, 99, 101
Papal Nuncio, Panama, 233
Paramount, 219, 220, 221, 226, 227,
  238
Parapluies de Cherbourg, Les, 221
Paretti, Giancarlo, 265
Parfums Caron, 218
Parker, Alan, 44, 137, 264
Parker, Dorothy, 246
Parkinson, Michael, 178, 191, 215,
Parsons, Charlie, 222
Paskin, Barbra, 136, 164
Pathé, 250, 252, 264, 266, 289
Pather Panchali, 196
Paxman, Jeremy, 99
Peacock, Michael, 31, 91, 216
Peck, Gregory, 136